Rube Larsen

Nov 2014

Mark —
Thank you
for your friendship!
You'll enjoy
this —
Amy

GOLF IS MY GAME

In New York, January 1960

Robert Tyre (Bobby) Jones, Jr.

GOLF
Is My Game

Illustrated with photographs and drawings

DOUBLEDAY & COMPANY, INC.

Garden City, New York ∘ 1960

Library of Congress Catalog Card Number 60-13386

Printed in the United States of America
First Edition

To my father,
to whom I owe all this—
and a lot more

ACKNOWLEDGMENT

The publishers wish to express their thanks to the following for permission to use photographs reproduced in this volume:

Atlanta *Journal*, page 99 (lower); Dundee (Scotland) *Courier*, page 247; *Golf Monthly*, page 117; Edwin Levick, page 177; Bill Mark, Frontispiece and page 187; New York *Daily News*, pages 97, 150, 152, 159; George Pietzcker, pages 86, 87, 95; A. G. Spalding & Bros., pages 51, 56, 57; Jay Leviton for *Sports Illustrated*, page 254; Mark Kauffman for *Sports Illustrated*, page 200; Underwood & Underwood, pages 44, 124, 167; United Press International, pages 57, 149, 151; Warner Brothers, page 174; Washington *Post*, page 10; Wide World Photos, Inc., pages 72, 144, 169, 191.

The publishers have made every effort to acknowledge all photographs. If any errors or omissions have inadvertently occurred, they will be corrected in subsequent editions, provided notification is sent to the publishers.

CONTENTS

ILLUSTRATIONS

A surprise appearance to President Eisenhower at a birthday dinner tendered to him by the White House correspondents, October 1959, at which I made the presentation to him of a silver-plated copy of "Calamity Jane," my old putter.

INTRODUCTION

I have written this book because I thought I could help golfers of all classes to play better and to get more enjoyment from their play. I have never tried to teach golf, having always been on the receiving end of any such exchange, but I have spent many years trying to learn something about the game. At times I have thought that I had learned pretty well, but I always found more to learn.

Teaching anything requires a great deal more than knowledge of the subject. It is one thing to possess knowledge or the ability to perform—quite another to be able to impart that knowledge or skill. I am sure that I do not even know all the qualities needed by a teacher, although I have read several treatises on the subject. It is enough for me to know that I have no right to pretend to be one.

On the other hand, in golf at least, I can claim to have been a fairly successful learner, and I more than half suspect that any golfer may rightfully attribute more of whatever skill he may possess to his own ability to learn than to the ability of someone else to teach. At any rate, I have written my book as a learner, rather than as a teacher. I am not ambitious to teach teachers to teach, but if I can help learners to learn, I shall consider my reward sufficient.

It is a popularly accepted notion that golf is a difficult game to teach and a difficult game to learn. It doesn't have to be either. It is all a question of the level of skill to which the learner aspires, or upon which the teacher intends to insist. Considered objectively, it is quite obviously a very simple matter to propel a ball with a stick across some specially prepared ground and into a hole which is of sufficient size to accommodate it by a good margin. Simple, that is, provided there is no limit upon the time or the number of strokes required. The matter is further simplified by reason of the fact that many earnest people have spent a lot of time, thought, and money upon the development of clubs and balls ideally suited to the process, and of greenkeeping methods which assure that the field of play will be more than reasonably well conditioned.

I must insist, therefore, that one who sets out with the object of learning to play golf well enough to get both pleasure and benefit from the pursuit of the game has a very good, if not one hundred per cent, chance of success, provided he sets for himself exactly this goal, and no other.

It seems to me that there are two quite reasonable ways in which a person may take his golf. If he has the time and the inclination to do so, he may set out to give the game a proper amount of serious study and practice with a view toward elevating himself considerably beyond the average-golfer class; or if he has only a very limited amount of free time, as many have, he may be content to knock around with his regular foursome, who play about as he does, in search of a little fun. But it will not do to mix the two, especially to hang the ambitions of the first man upon the labors of the latter.

Just now, I do not intend to try to produce a guide for a real study of the game. I may attempt such a thing later on, but even if I do, I shall be ever mindful that this sort of development takes a lot of time and is best done under the supervision of a competent instructor.

What I have attempted in this book, although less ambitious, I believe will appeal to the vast majority of people who play golf. I have suggested ways of making a mental approach to the game, of thinking through the playing of shots and of managing one's resources so as more often to enable the player to approximate the highest level of performance to which he has a right to aspire.

The virtues of golf as a pastime and a means of recreation have been appropriately extolled, but no one with more than the barest outside chance of being believed is going to tell me or any other golfer that he gets any fun out of hacking around the golf course in ten or more strokes above his normal game. The ninety player does not expect to break eighty. He ought to be, and usually is, satisfied to play a game that is reasonably good for him. But when he plays a really bad round and drags himself into the locker room, it is easy to see that he is tired and disgusted and has done anything but enjoy himself.

Long ago I described form in golf as a measure of efficiency. I can think of no better way to say it today. When one has good form, he is able to make the maximum employment of his physical resources in producing a powerful, accurate contact between clubhead and ball. Good form also affects the regularity with which the player may be able to repeat the process. To become a really fine golfer, a person must have a knowledge of the basic requirements of the proper golf swing and work hard to drill his muscles in the performance of this exacting ritual, but he still does not need to do this in order to play enjoyable, often very good, golf.

Never should I knowingly discourage any man from trying to learn to swing a golf club correctly, for I think that the game is well worth whatever effort one may make toward this end. But if one is not willing to take lessons and practice, he will do better to make up his mind to worry along with what he has, rather than mess up all his rounds with misguided tinkering. It is my very definite conviction that any player will consistently perform closer to his usual standards if he will refuse to tinker and experiment during a round and will play the game, instead of practicing it.

I have also written of my experiences in tournaments and especially of the Grand Slam year. I have hoped that these accounts may have some interest, even for nongolfers, because it has become obvious to me that many of the ingredients of success in strenuous accomplishments are the same, no matter what the field of effort may be. Also, from the particular viewpoint of the golfer, every round is a competition, and his success will be measured on the basis of his worth as a competitor. I should hope, therefore, that it may help him in his own golf to have a more intimate view of championship play.

There are many sides to the golfing picture—truly something in the game for everyone. I have not written of all these things just now, but I could not help expressing my thoughts about some of them, mainly golf-course architecture and the perennial controversy concerning the modern game against that of my time. I hope I have not wandered too far afield.

R.T.J., Jr.

PART ONE

Improving Your Golf

CHAPTER *1*

Learn by Playing

O I began playing golf a few months after I became six years old. I began life as a sickly child, and at the age of forty-six was stricken by a crippling ailment. Even so, to this day, golf has been the major interest of my life.

No one could possibly owe a greater debt to the game than do I. With all the odds on the health side against me from the beginning, I know that I can thank golf for having given me forty years of active life filled with exciting experiences and warm human contacts. I know that my physical affliction was not derived in any sense from playing the game, and I doubt that without this playing I should ever have lived to see a full maturity. I am convinced, too, that golf has taught me much about life and provided for me a philosophy, a treasure of memories, and an appreciation of human attachments which have immeasurably enhanced both the reality of the past and the prospect of the future. The game for me will always be, as it has been in the past, a consuming interest.

Throughout the period when my physical faculties were unimpaired, I was always an ardent player of the game. I was somewhat of a student or analyst, I suppose, but mainly I liked to play. And whatever thoughts I had about the game were directed toward enjoyment of competition. This did not have to be formal competition, because I could throw myself as enthusiastically into a four-ball match for a dollar Nassau as into a tournament for a national championship. I admit the strain was not so great, nor the prize of such importance, as to inspire the intense concentration of tournament play. Nevertheless, the zest was still there. The proposition is thus very clear to me that golf is a game meant to be played, and played as a contest worthy of the best effort of any man alive.

Golf has a very great and sometimes mystifying appeal to busy men. Some of its most ardent devotees are men of affairs whose lives are filled with responsibilities for making important decisions. To those who know little of golf, it is difficult to explain how a game so apparently frivolous could interest men such as these.

To those who know something of the game, there is no mystery at all. Golfers know, and have known for a long time, that when playing golf, it is almost impossible to think of anything else. The most complete rest for the mind, and the most effective renewal of mental keenness and vigor, come not from thinking of nothing, but from putting one's mind completely upon fresh and stimulating activities. It is, therefore, the all-absorbing challenge of golf which makes it such an effective agent of mental therapy.

In this view then, it seems to me that we are defeating or detracting from the effectiveness of the game as recreation when we urge people to relax, take it easy, or be casual and carefree on the golf course. I think we should urge them to do just the opposite—to put themselves wholeheartedly into their play. What they want and need most from the game can be had only when the intense concentration upon the play helps to sweep away the problems, worries, and even troubles of everyday life.

Since I have not been able to play for more than ten years, I have had that much more time to think. Much of my thinking has been of golf and how best to teach or to learn the game. It seems obvious to me that writing about the golf swing has become too technical and complicated, and even the most earnest teaching professional presents the game to his pupil as a far more difficult thing than it really is. It is equally obvious that what the game needs most if it is to continue to grow in popularity is a simplification of teaching routines which will present a less formidable aspect to the beginner, and offer to the average player a rosier prospect of improvement.

The trouble could be, and I think it is, that golf is not taught as it is learned. It is taught more as a science or as a prescribed set of calisthenic exercises, whereas, it is learned as a game.

Most of our successful tournament players have come up as caddy boys, like Sarazen, Hogan, and Nelson, or, like myself, as sons of members of golf clubs, turned out to pasture with a club or two and a few balls. They have learned to play golf, just as others have learned to play baseball, by playing and playing and playing because they liked the game. In most cases it has been only after gaining considerable proficiency that thoughts of method have been of much concern. My own experience, I think, is fairly typical.

A month or so before I reached my sixth birthday my mother and father began a procedure which was to become a habit. They took boarding quarters in a small summer colony near the East Lake Golf Club.

East Lake is only six miles from the center of downtown Atlanta. Yet in 1908 it was, in truth, out in the country. Simultaneously, my parents began to play golf.

One evening that summer a golfing friend of my father's made to me a most significant present. He gave me from his golf bag an old iron club, called in those days a "cleek," which he had cut down to a length suitable to my size. Although the need for doing so seems a bit strange, perhaps I should explain to golfers of this modern era that a cleek was an iron club with a blade only a little more that a half-inch wide, with a loft approximating that of the present day number two iron. My benefactor also provided a couple of old balls.

My first golf strokes were very short ones, even for a six-year-old. Along with another boy in the colony I scooped some holes in the common lawn, which incidentally boasted very little grass, and began to chip or putt the ball around this decidedly miniature course.

In a short while, a few weeks perhaps, my friend and I enlarged our activities by moving to the dirt road in front of our domicile and began to plunk back and forth along the hundred yards or so of clay thoroughfare between our house and the ditch alongside the East Lake Golf Course.

The next step was to tag along when my mother and father played. And from this, logically, slowly, but inevitably, I began to play golf. When I actually started to play, and when I was provided with a complete set of clubs, I do not know. There was nothing very conscious or contrived about the whole procedure. The game was there, I liked it, and I kept on playing.

I do recall that as I became a little more aware of the general object of the game, I began also to be aware that some people played better than others, and I began to swing my clubs as nearly as possible as the club professional, Stewart Maiden, swung his. I was fortunate, I suppose, that Stewart was a good model. His method was simple. It seemed that he merely stepped up to the ball and hit it, which to the end of my playing days was always a characteristic of my play.

Although Stewart Maiden has quite properly been known as my first instructor and the man from whom I learned the game, it is yet true that I never had a formal lesson from him while I was in active competitive play. In fact, it was not until he had returned to Atlanta, only two years before he died, that I ever went onto a practice tee with him.

Although neither Maiden nor I ever saw much point in spending laborious hours on a practice tee, there were many times when I required a few words from him to put my game back in the right groove. I suppose we didn't wear out the practice tee because it was never necessary, and Stewart never liked to waste his own time. There was, however, one lesson which was memorable, and at the same time typical.

I had been having a most trying time with my long irons, and some sort of tournament was in the offing. I had tried to work the thing out for myself, but could not do so. There didn't seem to be any pattern to work on. I would hook a few and then hit one a mile out to the right. In desperation at last, I told Stewart of my troubles while he was at his bench planing down a hickory shaft.

At first he said nothing, which I had long before learned was a normal response for him. After a while, though, he took the club out of the vise, squeezed the grip end as no one else could ever do, so that a barely perceptible tremor agitated the whole club, appeared not wholly displeased, and set it aside for further attention later on.

"Let's go," he said. With no more conversation my caddy, with my clubs, and I followed Stewart down the first fairway to a spot some two hundred yards from the green. "Hit a few," he said. I hit two. As I stepped up to the next, he said, "Wait." With the grip end of a club he was holding in his hands, he rapped quite sharply on my left arm just below the shoulder. I moved back. Again he rapped. "Move back," he said. I moved back some more, then looked up to see where I was aiming. "Stewart," I said, "I'll knock this ball straight into that left-hand bunker." "Never mind," he said, "back some more. Now, that's good." "What do I do now?" I asked, trying to be bitterly sarcastic. "Knock hell out of it," said Stewart. I did. The ball almost landed in the hole. I hit another and another straight at the flag. I looked up for Stewart, but he was on his way back to his shop to finish that club.

All this may seem a pointless discussion, but it does have a purpose. By this means, I am trying to show how I think instruction in golf can be most useful. A good instructor can be helpful at all stages of a player's development, but it is most important that the doses of instruction should be simple, direct, and practical. It is folly for either teacher or

With Stewart Maiden at the 1923 Open. Stewart's method of instructing was entirely simple and direct—and successful.

pupil to expect that any swing can be made over in an afternoon, a week, or even a season. It is significant that Stewart did not try to fill my head with theories. He merely put me in position to hit the ball and then told me to go on and hit it.

Stewart Maiden was a successful instructor because his eye went always to the point of basic disturbance. He seemed always to be able to pick out the one point in a swing at which the making of a small change would work an improvement in the performance of the whole. I am sure he never once thought of trying to remake a swing or to create one from scratch precisely along copybook lines. Throughout all the years I knew Stewart he never once allowed himself to be drawn into a discussion of the golf swing. To him, the game of golf consisted entirely of knocking the ball toward the hole, or into it, and that in the simplest manner possible.

One time a little later, when I was in high school, I became a bit excited over an article I read in the *American Golfer*, purported to have been written by Harry Vardon, describing the "push shot" and how to play it. I read the article several times, tore the page out of the magazine, and tucked it into my pocket. I could scarcely wait next day to get out to East Lake to try it. On the trolley returning from school I pored over the article until I thought I had it firmly in my mind.

As Vardon described the shot, it was to be played with a minimum of hand action, striking the ball a sharply descending blow and sending it on a low trajectory toward the green. It was described as the ideal manner of playing an iron shot into the wind, so that it would be little affected by the wind and would stop quickly at the end of its flight.

I had no notion whatever of discussing this experiment with Stewart. I knew that whatever discussion might take place would be all on my side. I even almost gave up the idea when I found Stewart giving a lesson on the same practice tee I had to use. I knew he would give me a good razzing, no matter what the result of my effort might be. But I was just stubborn enough to go through with it anyway. Maybe I could show Stewart something.

I know I hit over a hundred shots from the tee, following as closely as I could the procedure described in the article. I know I hit not one effective shot. When I finally decided to give it up, I turned to find Stewart had finished his lesson and was sitting on a bench watching me. He was shaking wth silent laughter, as nearly hysterical as a Scot can ever get.

Never again did I try to learn a shot or stroke from a written description, and ever after, I have been careful in writing or talking about the golf swing. Certainly, there are ways of translating from one person to another ideas which can be helpful in playing golf, but it is not feasible for the learner to follow a prescription for the entire performance. No matter how clear the complete picture may be, the mind cannot possibly think through the process from beginning to end within the time required for the accomplishment.

CHAPTER 2

Striking the Ball

o When I was playing competitive golf, I had, with some golf writers at least, a reputation for being a regular player. When I scored sixty-six in the third round of the Southern Open at East Lake in 1927, Kerr Petrie wrote for the New York *Herald Tribune:*

> They wound up the Mechanical Man of Golf yesterday and sent him clicking around the East Lake course.

I remember the round quite well, and it was as nearly perfect as any I ever played; the only real mistake being a tee shot pulled into some woods on the fourteenth hole. That "Mechanical Man" stuff, though, did make me laugh. How I wished it could have been made to fit!

I have always said that I won golf tournaments because I tried harder than anyone else and was willing to take more punishment than the others. More immodestly, I will say now that I think a large factor in my winning was a greater resourcefulness in coping with unusual situations and in recovering from or retrieving mistakes.

Jim Barnes said to me once, when as a youngster I was in the midst of my lean years as a golfer:

"Bob, you can't always be playing well when it counts. You'll never win golf tournaments until you learn to score well when you're playing badly."

I think this is what I learned to do best of all. The most acute, and yet the most satisfying recollections I have are of the tournaments won by triumphs over my own mistakes and by crucial strokes played with imagination and precision when anything ordinary would not have sufficed. And I think I was able to do this because I had learned so well what a golf ball could be made to do and how it had to be struck to make it perform as I wanted it to.

Of course, I learned these things by playing. I kept on hammering at that pesky ball until I found a way to make it behave. When I hit it one way and it didn't do right, I'd try hitting it another way. I didn't try different swings. I probably didn't know there were such things, or even a swing at all for that matter.

I watched other players, too, and when one of them made a shot that I especially admired, I would begin to try to produce the same result. But I didn't observe how they took the club back or measure the "body-turn" they used. I watched that clubhead strike the ball and saw how the ball responded. Then I tried to make my ball do the same thing.

A kid growing up without a teacher but with a golf club in his hands may be under a handicap, but he has some advantages, too. No one is trying to teach him to play. If someone should try to explain the golf swing to him, he would be completely baffled. Even more bewildered would he be by even the most elemental discussion of why a golf ball acts as it does. But he has plenty of time to learn these things for himself.

Those players we see today who have the appearance of naturalness and ease in their play are immediately identified as having begun to play as youngsters. I think they have this appearance because they first thought of the game in terms of striking the ball. So they set about doing this with no more self-consciousness than we would associate with chopping wood, throwing stones, or beating rugs.

I am confident that the adult golfer can and should approach the game in the same way. He may not have the time available to the youngster, but he has the advantage of adult understanding. In a few minutes' study of the material in this chapter, he can learn as much about the possible means of controlling a golf ball as a boy could learn in years of play.

I am not one who enjoys heaping ridicule upon the average golfer. It seems to me that those grotesque characters we see in the cartoons are rare in real life. The unskilled golfer often looks uncomfortable, strained, unsure, sometimes even unhappy, but he hardly ever presents a ludicrous aspect. And I think that a great measure of his discomfiture is derived from his conscious efforts to follow prescribed routine, to look and move like someone else, or as he has been told. I think he would present a more natural appearance if he should put his mind upon striking the ball, rather than upon swinging the club.

This will be the most important chapter of this book. It will describe the most useful learning you will ever acquire as a golfer. You may gain knowledge from the mere reading of this chapter that will help you in the playing of every golf shot you make for the rest of your life. This knowledge can make you a better golfer overnight.

If you are a beginner, this chapter will start you off on the road to a correct understanding of the nature of golf. If you are an average golfer, it will give you the means of deciding upon the club to use and the shot to play on the basis of reasoned judgment, rather than guesswork. If you are a better than average golfer, it will broaden your perception of the possibilities in the game so that you may become a player of imagination and resourcefulness. If you are weary of being told to concentrate without having knowledge of what you should concentrate on, this is it.

Golf is played by striking the ball with the head of the club. The objective of the player is not to swing the club in a specified manner, nor to execute a series of complicated movements in a prescribed sequence, nor to look pretty while he is doing it, but primarily and essentially to strike the ball with the head of the club so that the ball will perform according to his wishes.

No one can play golf until he knows the many ways in which a golf ball can be expected to respond when it is struck in different ways. If you think that all this should be obvious, please believe me when I assure you that I have seen many really good players attempt shots they should have known were impossible.

The first diagram (figure 1) is intended to represent a ball being struck by a clubhead moving precisely along the intended line of flight with its face square to the objective. In the absence of wind, of course, the only possible result is a straight shot directly on target. This is the ideal for most golfing situations.

If you have ever been told that the clubhead should strike the ball while traveling from inside the line of flight to the outside, forget it. This advice may have been of temporary helpfulness on occasion when the player, in attempting to follow it, has corrected a natural tendency to hit across the ball from the outside. But the player who actually succeeds in hitting from inside-to-out more often finds himself plagued by a ducking hook.

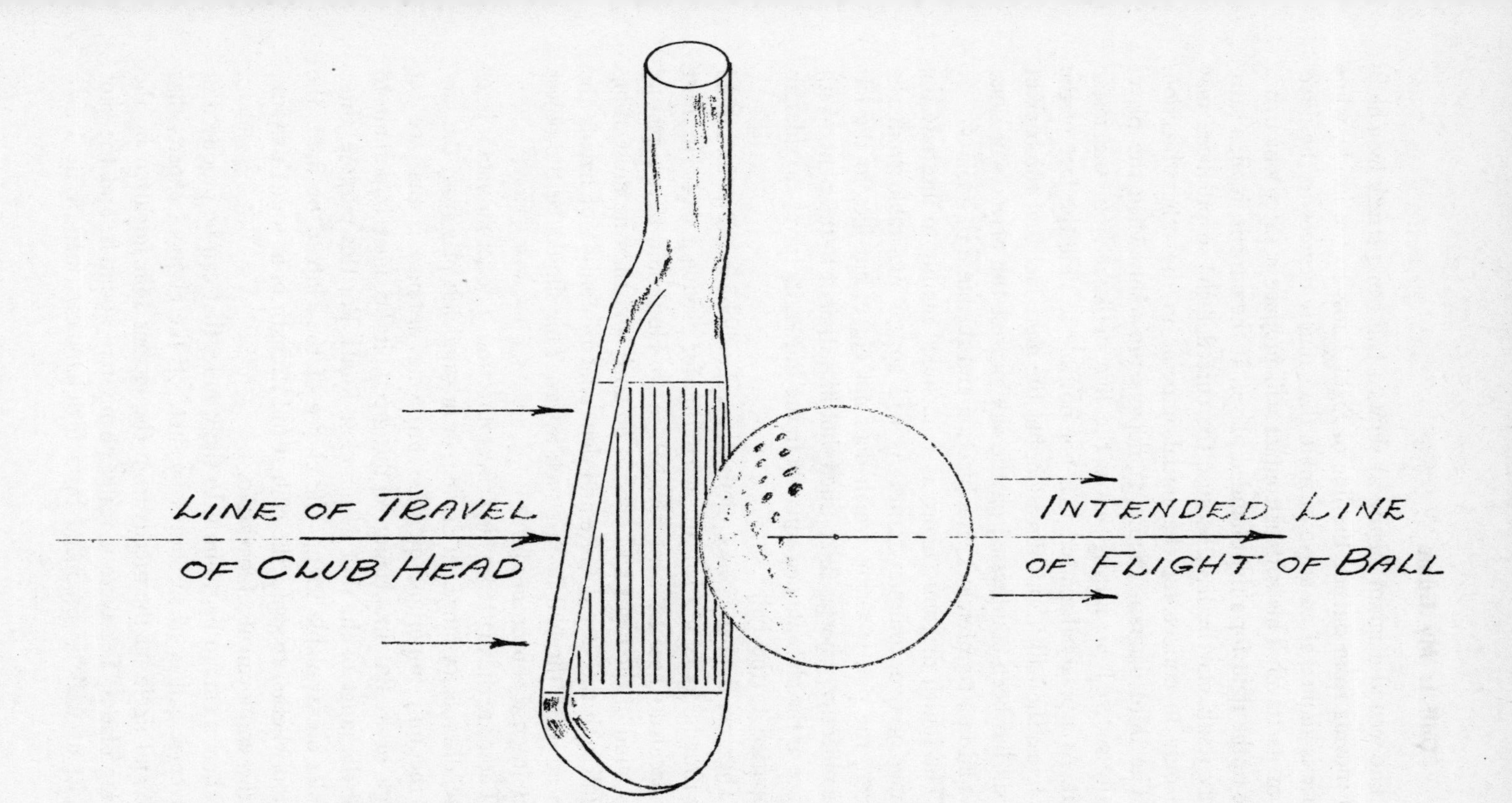

Figure 1. Plan view

The second diagram (figure 2) shows a ball being struck by a clubhead moving from outside the line of flight across to the inside, while its face is aligned at an angle of more than ninety degrees to the direction of its travel. This sort of contact will produce a slice, which is a curve to the right for a right-handed player. If the error is small, a satisfactory result may be had, because the curved flight so produced may serve only to correct for the initial impetus in the other direction.

The third diagram (figure 3) depicts the result when the player actually succeeds in hitting across the line of flight from the inside to out. As a practical matter, it is not possible to slide the face of the club across the ball in this direction, but the mere fact that the back of the ball has been compressed on the side nearest the player will cause it to spin in a counterclockwise direction and therefore to hook.

The fourth diagram (figure 4) is included mainly to illustrate the meaning of two common terms. As will appear inevitable from the diagram, the pull is a shot which does not curve, but flies to the left of the objective, whereas the pushed shot flies straight to the right. With the face of the club aligned squarely to the line of its travel, no sidespin is imparted to the ball.

These are the basic conceptions which should be in the golfer's mind every time he looks at a ball in preparation for playing a shot. He must have decided where he wants the ball to go. He should have a picture in his mind of the flight he hopes to produce, and then he must swing his club with the very definite and determined intention of having the clubhead meet the ball in just such a way. This should be the object of his intense concentration.

These are the matters which effect direction. The second factor is, of course, distance or range. In driving, or in woodclub play from the fairway, the only important question involving distance is that we get enough of it. But in playing to the green, it becomes important to adjust the range of the shot within close limits. For this purpose, three variables are available to us—the choice of the club to be used, the decision whether to swing the club at full strength or at something less, and the employment of backspin.

There seems to be no limit to the wonder that can be produced in the average gallery of spectators by shots off the clubs of experts that dance and jiggle on the greens from the vicious spin imparted by the pitching blades. Yet there is really no mystery about it, and the shot can just as well be produced by a high-handicap man if he knows

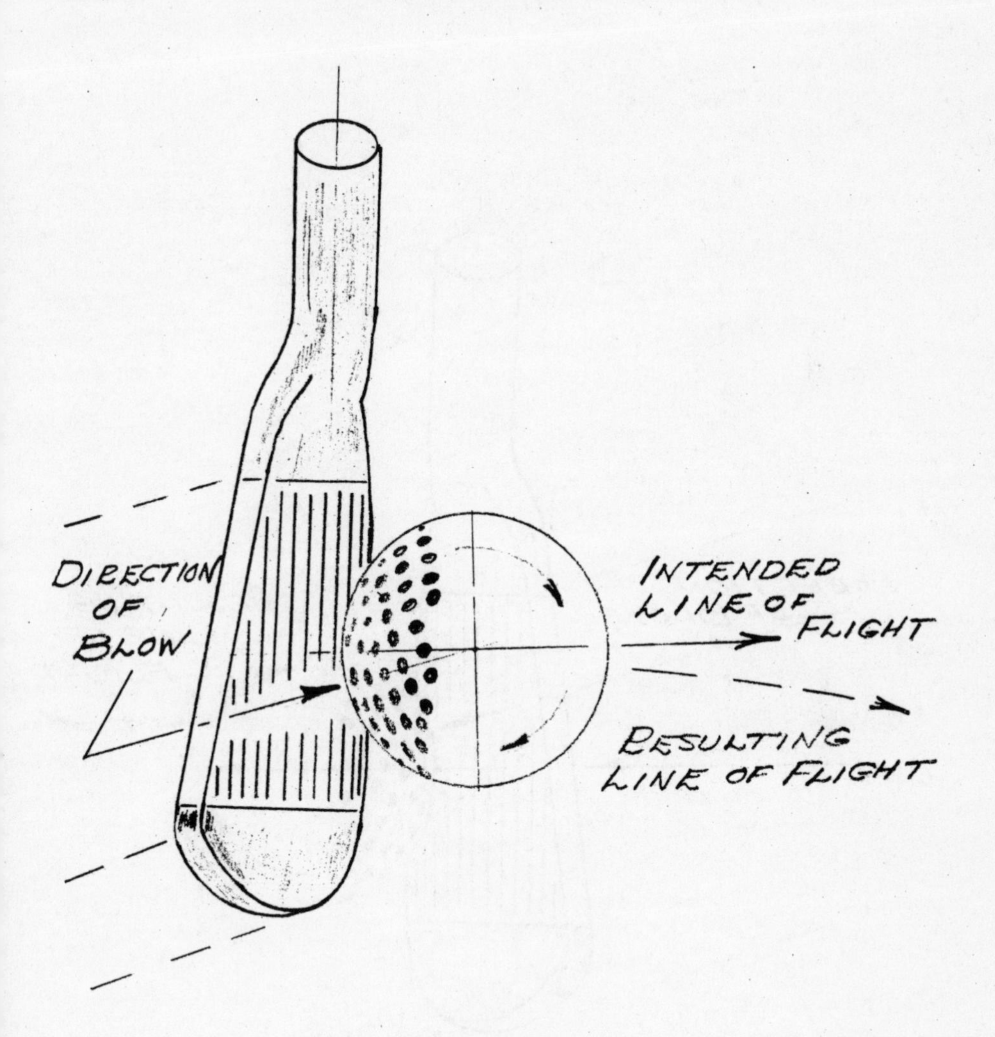

Figure 2. Slicing contact

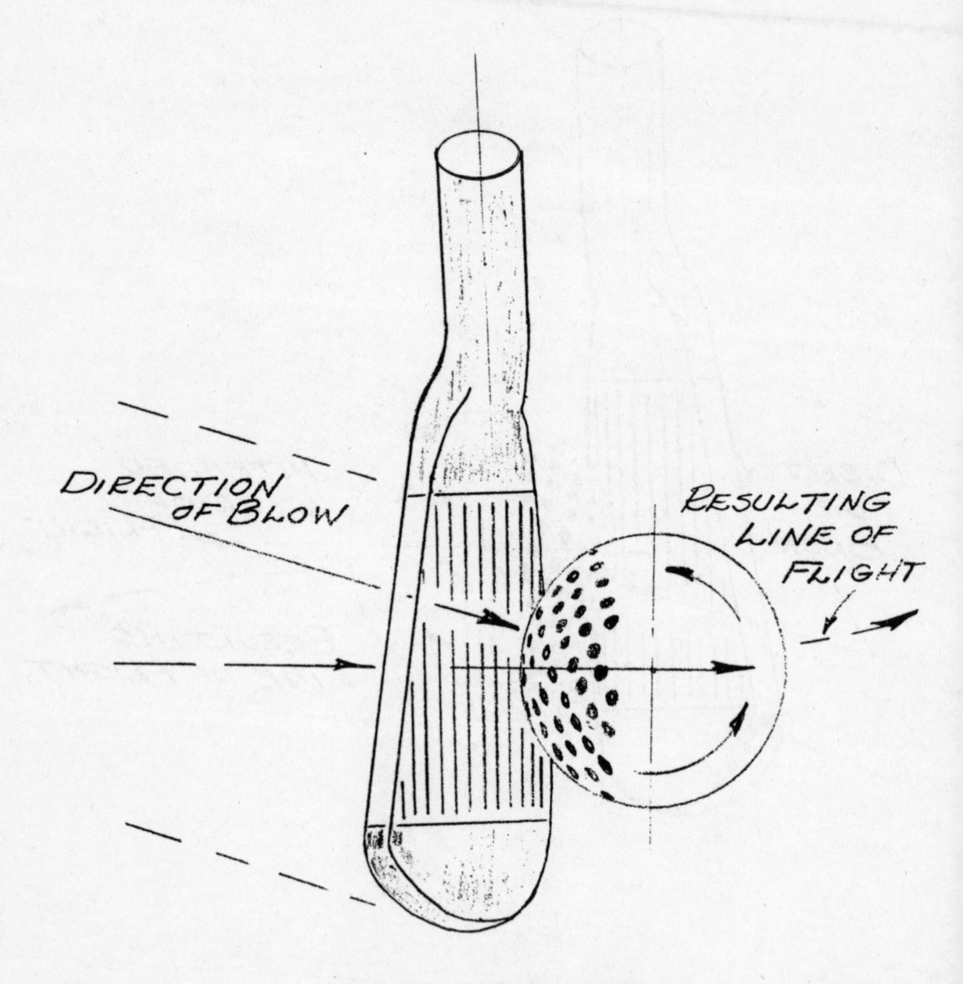

Figure 3. Hooking contact

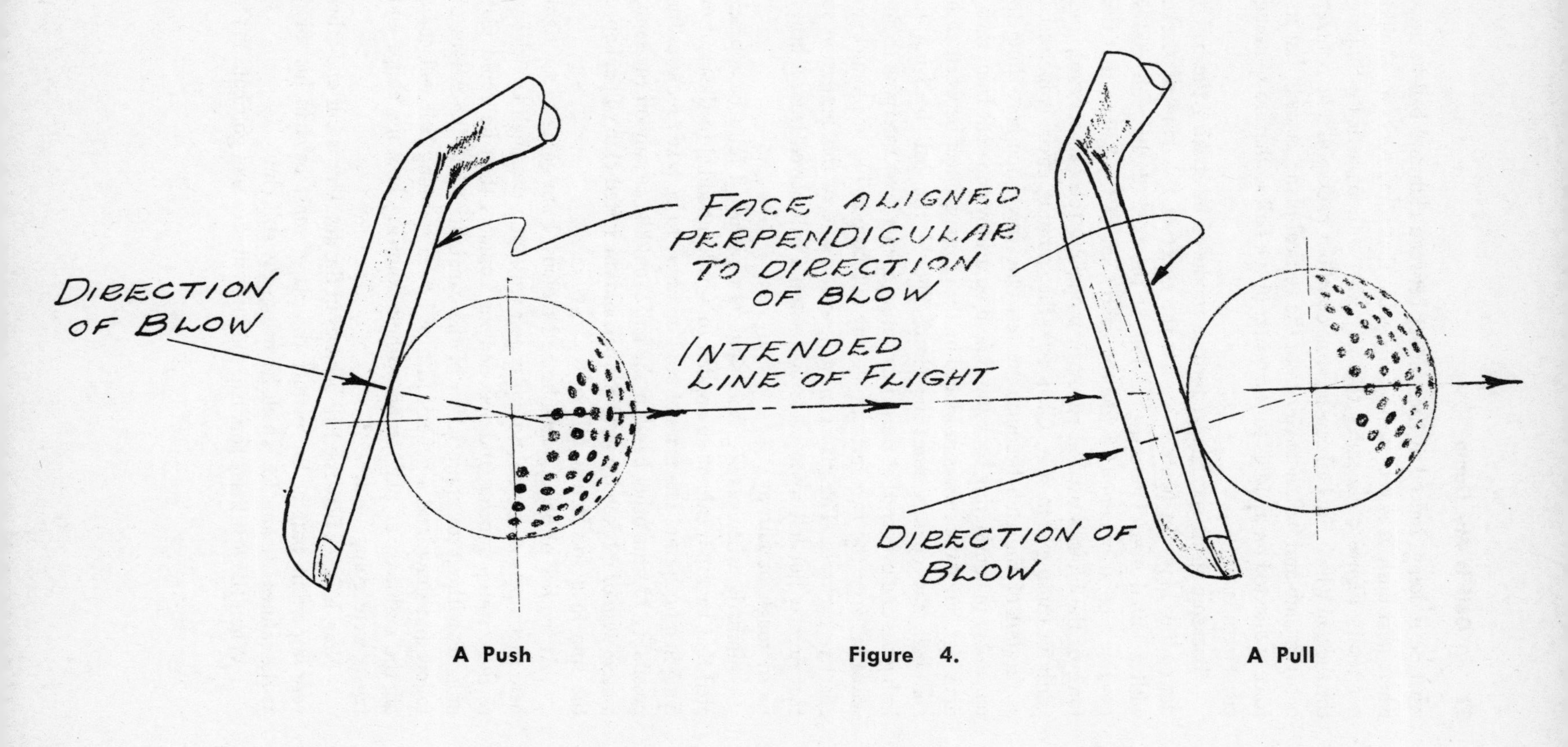
DIRECTION
OF BLOW
FACE ALIGNED
PERPENDICULAR
TO DIRECTION
OF BLOW
INTENDED
LINE OF FLIGHT
DIRECTION OF
BLOW
A Push
A Pull

Figure 4.

what he is doing. Indeed, if the contact between club and ball be anywhere near flush, it is very nearly impossible that some backspin should not result. Figure 5 illustrates the only way, without actually topping the shot, in which the ball can be struck without backspin. The contact between club and ball, now shown in the vertical plane, is such that its force is directed on a radius to the center of the ball so that no spinning effect results.

Backspin in its spectacular form is produced by striking the ball a descending blow. In figure 6 we see the effect of this kind of stroke with a lofted iron. The angle of loft of the face of the club makes possible a point of contact below the center line of the ball so that the force of the blow is exerted partly in propelling the ball forward, and partly in causing it to spin. Obviously, the spinning effect is increased as the loft of the club becomes greater. One very important thing to remember in considering backspin should be readily apparent from these drawings. Since the spin is produced by the gripping effect between club and ball, the contact must be clean. Should the ball be lying in lush grass or clover so that these lubricating agents must interpose themselves between the two surfaces, it may not be possible to produce an effective backspin. The player must be ever aware of this limitation so that he may not rely upon backspin to stop a ball played from a heavy lie in rough or fairway.

Similarly, when playing from sand in a bunker, it must be appreciated that backspin cannot be applied to a ball imbedded in the sand or lying in a heelprint. The mass of sand necessary to be taken removes the possibility. On the other hand, if the ball should lie cleanly on the sand, a mere wisp of it taken between the ball and the lofted club will enhance the spin in a spectacular fashion.

At the risk of being dogmatic and tedious, I am going to say right here that a person can no more play golf without a thorough knowledge of these spin-producing and spin-denying contacts than he could play billiards without an appreciation of the capabilities and limitations of follow and draw, and a general idea of how a spinning ball will come off the cushions, or play tennis without knowing how his chops and twists were going to act.

Now, let's see how the ball behaves in the air. This is but one other very important part of the picture the player must have in his mind as the immediate aim for which he swings the golf club.

When the first brave soul had the brilliant idea that golf balls made

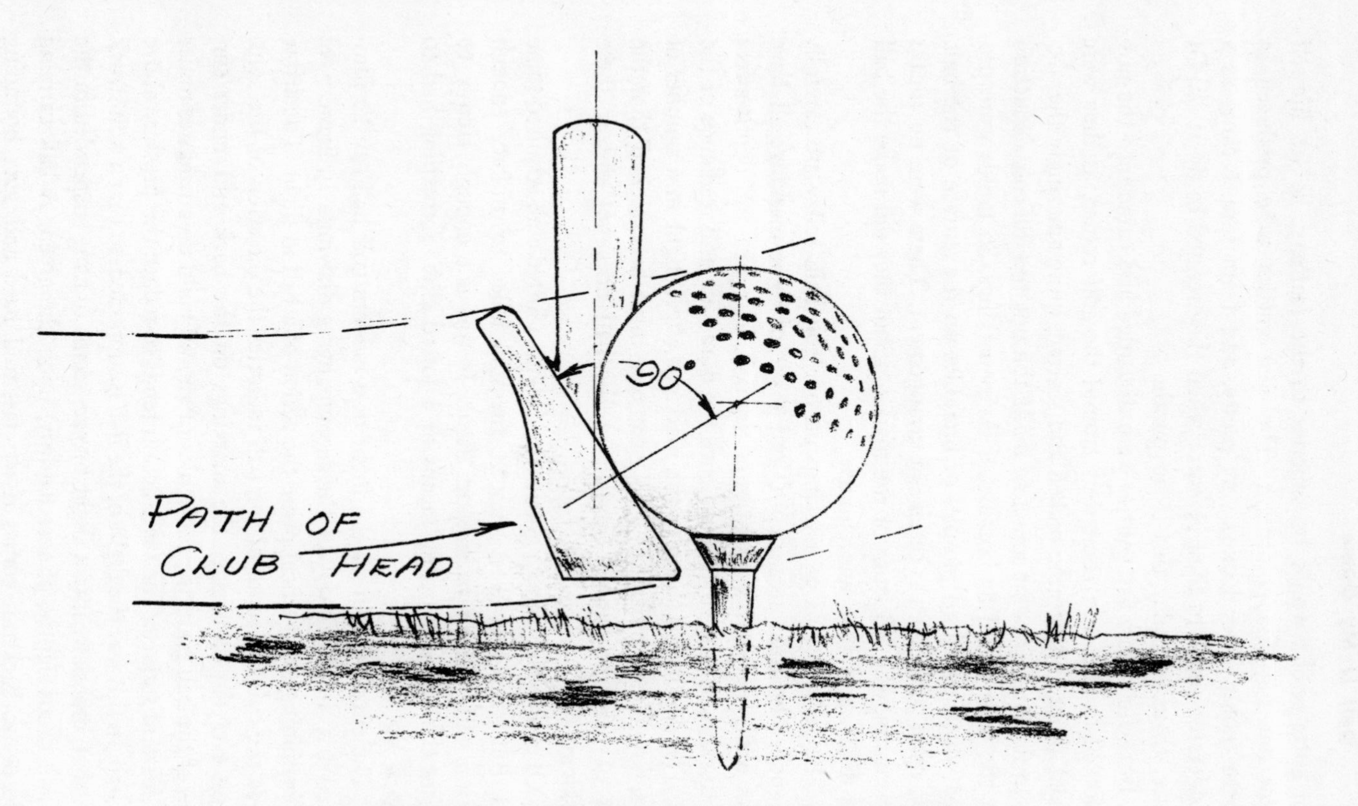

Figure 5. Striking the ball without producing backspin.

from gutta-percha would be superior to the feathery, he let himself in for one big disappointment. The first gutties were produced in smooth molds. They looked very pretty, and I am sure it came as a considerable shock to their inventor when they refused to fly at all. Of course, to us of today this is no puzzle.

But when these first gutties were discarded and came into the possession of caddies and youngsters around the golf course, as they were hacked about and became nicked and scarred, quite amazingly they began to fly. At this point someone made the not too difficult deduction that the balls would fly because of their markings. So molds were prepared which produced pimples or brambles on the surface of the ball. It was sort of a catch-as-catch-can arrangement. There were no means of measuring the efficiency of the markings, but they did make the ball take flight, and that was enough.

The indentations or markings on our golf balls today are carefully designed. The total area, depth, and shape of these markings all have effect upon the playing qualities of the ball. The area and depth affect the thickness of the cover and hence the durability and resilience of the ball. The depth and shape of the markings affect flight in a number of ways, notably in trajectory, and great care must be exercised that the coat of paint or enamel applied to the ball does not distort these markings.

Of course, the smooth gutties struck with a lofted club acquired some spin. But since they were smooth, the spin failed to produce enough friction with the air to support flight. It was not enough simply to project the ball upward by means of a lofted club. Something had to keep it up.

The effect of spin on the flight of a modern golf ball can be illustrated in a simplified way by the accompanying drawings. In figure 7 we are examining in a vertical plane the action of a ball in flight. The arrow inside the circumference of the ball indicates the direction of the spin. Using everyday language, the markings on the back and under surfaces of the ball grasp the molecules of air and build up air masses under the forward surface. The same action tends to reduce the pressure above the ball. In this way the flight of the ball is supported, so that a well-struck iron shot, especially into a slight breeze, seems to hang suspended in the air and drops lightly, almost daintily, upon the green. A ball carrying little or no backspin comes down fast and hard and goes bounding merrily away.

Figure 6. Producing backspin with a lofted iron.

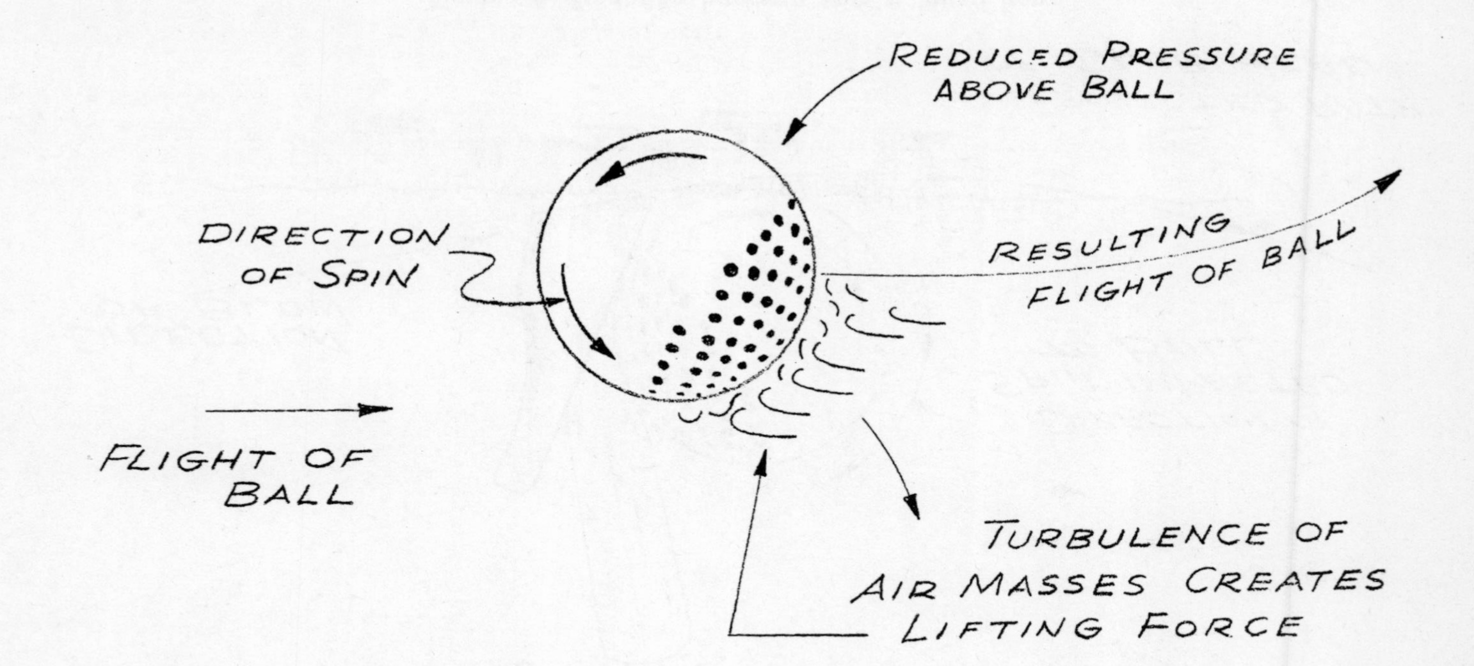

Figure 7. Side view of ball in flight, showing effect of backspin.

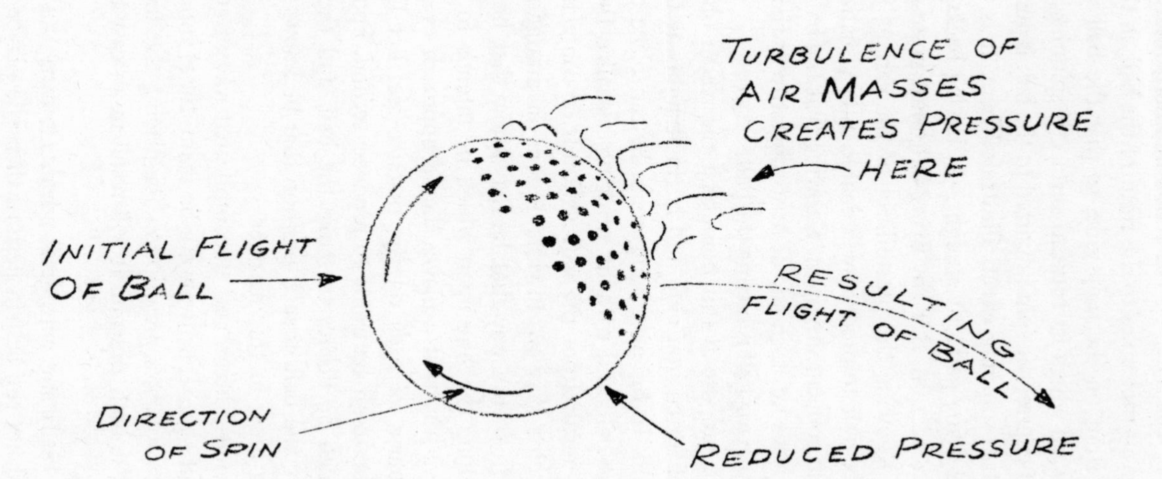

Figure 8. Looking down on ball in flight showing effect of slicing spin.

In similar fashion sidespin tends to build up air masses in the manner illustrated in figure 8, which depicts the action in a horizontal plane. The clockwise spin drags air molecules to the front of the ball on the left side and away from its front on the right side, so that the ball must curve in the direction toward which its forward surface is spinning.

In actuality, of course, the spin imparted to the ball is almost always a resultant of the two spinning effects illustrated here. It is possible to conceive that a ball flying perfectly straight, yet having backspin, would be totally lacking in sidespin. But any flying ball must possess some element of backspin. Knowing the possibilities of the various flight characteristics we may be able to produce will enable us to visualize the kind of contact we should concentrate upon. Knowing that the ball will fly as we hit it, and only as we hit it, should at least suggest to us that the most important thing in playing golf is hitting the ball.

I should like to propose at this point that the reader obtain a golf ball and any sort of lofted iron club and begin straightway to fix these concepts in his mind. In his own living room he can place the face of the club behind the ball, and without swinging, visualize the spinning effects which must result from the various kinds of contacts. He may also give himself some very worthwhile lessons in arranging his feet and body position in such a way that he may know that he is able to strike at the ball along the line upon which he intends to project it.

It is in this very way that a player should approach every shot he hits on the golf course, or even on the practice tee. Let him always decide first upon the result he wants to produce; second, upon the precise manner in which he desires to strike the ball; and then let him place himself before the ball in such position that he knows he will be able to deliver the blow in this manner.

This is the obvious, direct, and uncomplicated way of going about the playing of a golf shot. It will always be many times more effective than any attempt to follow a prescription for placing the feet and adjusting the rest of the body posture. It will result in an easy fluidity because it is natural.

One may very easily and with great advantage carry this thing one step further. Indeed, for the best in performance, the player must keep in the forefront of his mind throughout the entire stroke this very clear picture of the precise manner in which he intends to strike the ball.

Years ago I described the mental attitude I tried to attain in a

Figure 9. Wrong Way: improper upward stroke, improper spin.

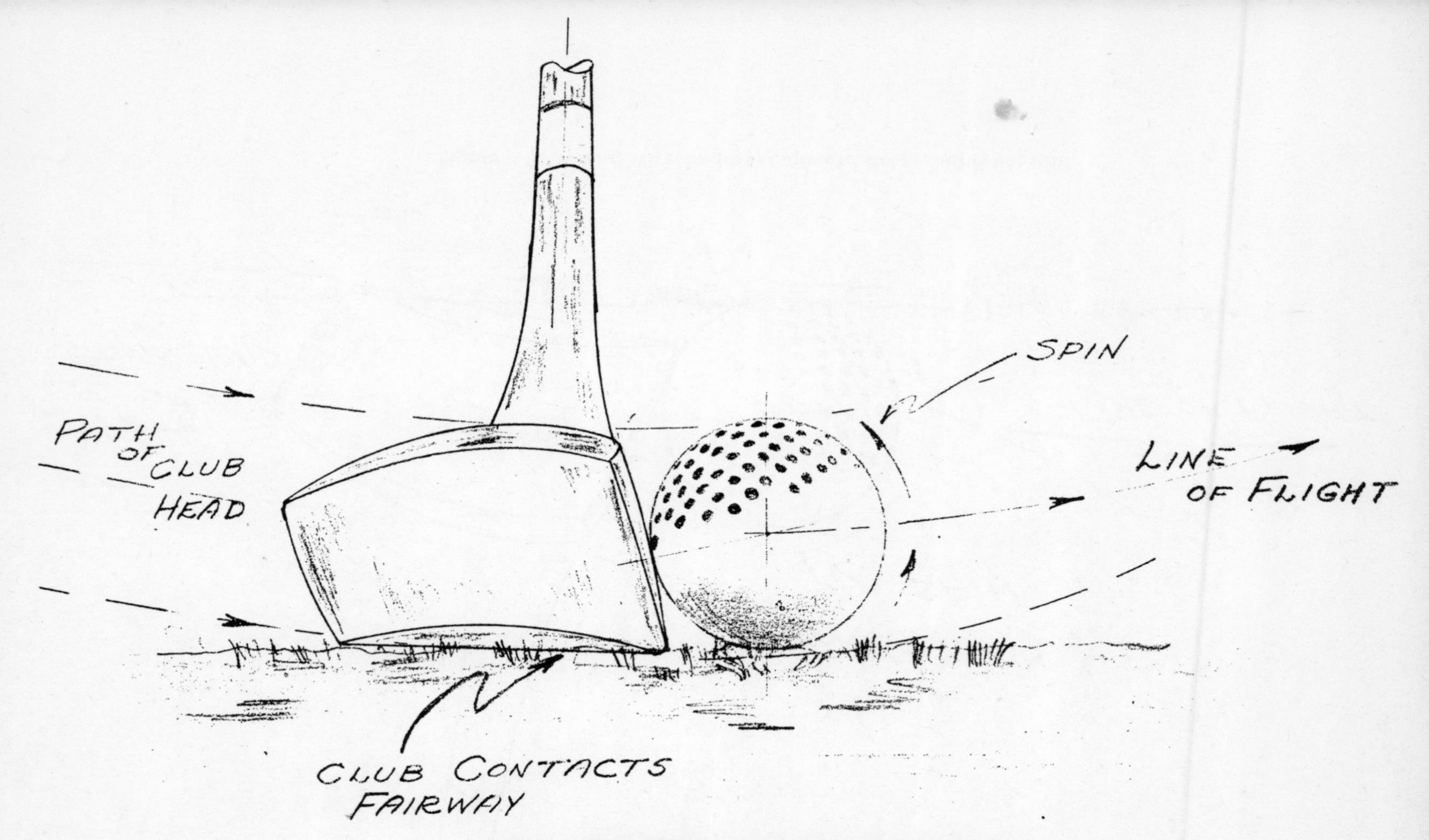

Figure 10. Right Way: proper club loft, proper spin.

tournament round as a concentration upon producing a desired result so intense as to preclude any possibility of concern with the manner of swinging. I liked to think of erecting a wall or other vertical plane containing the ball and my left eye, and then focus my entire concentration upon producing the desired result in front of the wall. I wanted to leave my swing to take care of itself. I was confident that the movement behind the ball would adjust itself to the proper striking.

I am very certain that whenever I could achieve this detachment, my swing would slow down to its proper rhythm and its effectiveness would be restored. As so often happened, a game which had caused me concern in practice would be pulled together by the strain of competition, whereby anxiety was proved to be a more powerful force than the will.

If one has not learned enough of golf by the time he steps onto the first tee, he has run out of time. He must realize that he has to play the game or the match with the equipment he has. Only results count from this point on.

I cannot see how one may avoid the conclusion that any player must swing and play better when he makes every move of his stroke with the aim of getting himself into position to strike in a clearly defined way, and delivering the blow in this way.

Before leaving this subject of spin, I should like to use it to point the way to help for the average golfer in playing one of the shots he needs most in the game—the wood club from the fairway. The chances are that he will never think of it as a backspin shot, but that's what it is, and it should be played as one.

Figure 9 shows what happens when the inexpert player goes after a ball in a close fairway lie. With a lofted iron he can see some hope that the loft of the club will get the ball up. But he does not have this confidence with the wood. So he tries to get under the ball and lift it into the air. Result: he either catches his club in the ground behind the ball, or, if he misses the ground, he commits a half or full top on the ball.

The proper method of playing this shot is illustrated in figure 10. The direction of the stroke is descending—not sharply so as to take a divot, but enough to skin the grass from the surface of the ground. Even the meager loft of the wood club is enough to produce spin to aid in getting the ball up. If the average player will merely trust his club and strike the ball in this way, he need have no fear of his fairway woods.

CHAPTER 3

Gripping the Club

o Even if a person may not have begun to play golf at an early age, I believe that he may gain much by emphasizing naturalness in his learning processes. I think he has the right to convince himself that an effective golf swing can be made without rigid adherence to a prescribed routine and that there is room for differences in physical structure and capabilities. No matter how nearly equal in performance the top-rank players may be, they are yet as recognizable by their swings as by their faces.

What the average golfer needs more than finespun theories is something that will give him a clearer conception of what he should try to do with the clubhead. The golf swing is a set or series of movements which must be correlated. The minutest change in any makes a difference in one or more of the others; and while for consistent first-class performance there can be only a very small deviation in any particular, it is still a fact and always will be so, that there are more ways than one to swing a golf club correctly.

When we speak of a sound method or good form, we mean nothing more than that the possessor of either has simplified his swing to the point where errors are less likely to creep in and he is able consistently to bring his club against the ball in the correct hitting position. We think, talk, and write so much about the details of the stroke that we sometimes lose sight of the thing which is all-important—hitting the ball. It is conceivable that a person could perform all sorts of contortions and yet bring the club into correct relation to the ball at impact, in which case a good shot must result. The only purpose of discussing style and form at all is to make it easier for the player to maintain this correct relation. In a crude way, he may do it only occasionally. In a finished, sound, stylish way, he will be able to do it consistently and with assurance.

Let's say that what we know now is merely what a golf club looks like and what effect it will have on a ball when the two come together in certain ways. Since the head of the club is mounted at one end of a shaft, and it must be actuated by a human being operating at the other end, the connection between that human being and the grip end of the club must be important.

Many things, of course, can be said about the placing of the hands upon the club. But just now, I am thinking only about the over-all conception of swinging, and to that end I am only concerned that the club be held so that the action of the hands and wrists may be free, so that the club may be retained in the hands against the centrifugal force generated by the swinging of it, and so that the head of the club may be placed in comfort behind the ball.

Since a golfer must play the ball from the ground while he himself is more or less erect, a couple of angles are introduced into the mechanism. One of course, is the angle between the shaft of the club and the face, or striking, surface. The manufacturer or club maker takes care of this one.

The other angle or angles between the shaft and the arms of the player are to be accommodated by the grip. These angles vary as the player is tall or short and as his hands are large or small, lean or fat. The precise placement of the club in the hands cannot be prescribed. The obvious requirement that the two hands work together should be a sufficient guide on this point. The grip end of the club should lie to some extent diagonally across the palms, but it must be controlled and felt mainly in the fingers.

I like to think of a golf club as a mass attached to my hands by a weightless but rigid connector, and I like to feel that I am throwing the clubhead at the ball with much the same motion I should use in cracking a whip. By this simile I mean to convey the idea of a supple, lightning-quick action of the hands.

Stiff or wooden wrists shorten the backswing and otherwise destroy the feel of the clubhead. Without the supple connection of relaxed and active wrist joints and a delicate, sensitive grip, the golf club, which has been so carefully weighted and balanced, might just as well be a broom handle with nothing on the end. The clubhead cannot be swung unless it can be felt on the end of the shaft.

I have seen numbers of players who take hold of the club as though it were a venomous snake and they were in instant peril of being bitten. A tight grip necessarily tenses all the muscles and tendons of the wrists and forearm so that any degree of flexibility is impossible.

The only way I know of achieving a relaxed grip which will at the same time retain adequate control of the club is to actuate the club and hold it mainly by the three smaller fingers of the left hand. If the control is at this point, the club can be restrained against considerable force, and yet the wrist joints may retain complete flexibility.

The great fault in the average golfer's conception of his stroke is that he considers the shaft of the club a means of transmitting actual physical force to the ball, whereas, it is in reality merely the means of imparting velocity to the clubhead. We would all do better could we only realize that the length of a drive depends not upon the brute force applied, but upon the speed of the clubhead. It is a matter of well-timed acceleration rather than of physical effort of the kind that bends crowbars and lifts heavy weights.

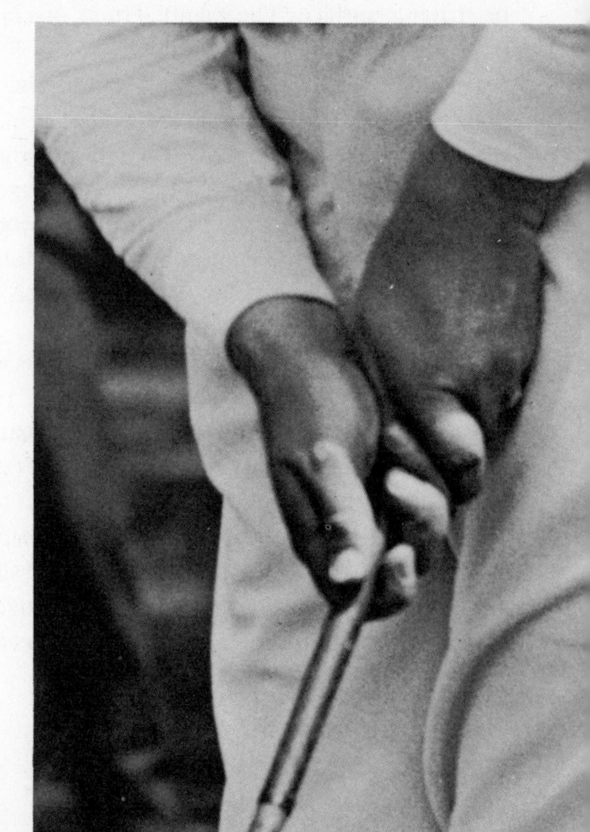

The reverse overlapping grip used only for putting. For the other strokes, the little finger of the right hand overlaps the index finger of the left hand.

My prescription is, therefore, only that the club should b
mainly by the three smaller fingers of the left hand, and that the s
should be laid across the middle joint of the index finger of this han
The remainder of the gripping should be done as lightly as possible, exerting pressure upon the shaft only as this becomes necessary in order to move or restrain the club.

Let it be known right here that many acceptable golf shots and drives of good length can be produced by players who have nothing more than active hands and a good sense of timing. These players will never achieve the consistency nor the extremes in length attainable by the expert with good form, but they will, nevertheless, be able to get a lot of fun out of playing golf.

4

Addressing the Ball

The act of beginning to play a golf shot is called addressing the ball. We already know that at this point there must be in the player's mind a very clear picture of the manner and the direction in which he intends to hit. As he approaches the ball and places himself before it preparing to strike, he must, of course, arrange his posture so that he feels capable of delivering a blow along the desired path. He must become aware of this capability before the swinging of the club can have any purpose. But the striving for this awareness of proper positioning can be far more effective than any effort to fit the stance to a prescribed diagram.

The keynote of the address position should be ease, comfort, and relaxation. Above all else, the first posture must be one from which the movement of the swing may be started smoothly without having to break down successive barriers of tension set up by taut or strained muscles. To go a bit further, the player should feel himself alert, sensitive to impulses, and ready to move in either direction.

It is always better at this point to be one's own natural self than to make an effort to look like someone else. Any posture that feels uncomfortable is certain to produce a strain somewhere that will cause the ensuing movement to be jerky. It is well to remember that there are no forces outside the player's own body that have to be resisted or balanced. There is no need for him to set or brace himself, for there is nothing to brace against. If one can conceive that he is standing naturally with a golf club in his hands, and that he then bends over enough to ground the club behind a ball not too far distant, the resulting posture will be quite good.

Abe Mitchell, the famous English professional of my era, made himself even more famous with me by coining a picturesque golfing phrase. Abe said, "A golfer must always move freely beneath himself." If this conception should appeal to others as it does to me, it should be a fine thing for the player to have in his mind as he addresses a ball.

Naturally, the balance of the golfer should be as perfect as possible throughout his entire stroke. But the balance desired is that of the ballet dancer rather than of the flagpole sitter; dynamic rather than static; balance in motion as opposed to a steadfast immobility. The player's connection with the ground must be positive and secure, but this requirement should not imply that his feet must take root in the turf.

I suppose Mitchell's phrase seems so useful to me because I have observed that it is difficult to persuade beginners and inexpert golfers to make sufficient use of their legs and hips. My reason for stressing alertness in the address position was to prepare a learner for this conception of using the ground. His inclination will be to swing the club wth his arms alone. It is not enough in most cases to expect the turning of the body to be a natural response to the act of swinging the clubhead. Few players find the body movement to be the natural consequence of anything. In nine cases out of ten the player will never move his legs and body as he should unless he deliberately sets out to do so.

My conception of the correct golf swing is built entirely around the one thought of assuring a full backward turn or windup of the trunk during the backswing. This must be accomplished by the legs; and since the trunk must be turned around the spine as an axis under a motionless head, I think the player must truly "move freely beneath himself."

This much is about enough for the beginner, but for others, and for him after he has played a bit, I want to make the suggestion of a further preliminary which I have found to be very helpful. It is essentially to standardize the approach to every shot, beginning even before taking the address position.

It is far easier to maintain a complete relaxation if one keeps continually in motion, never becoming still and set. It sounds far-fetched, I know, but I have had a few players tell me that after taking great pains in addressing the ball, they have reached the point where they simply could not take the club back. It is a manner of freezing and is well known to tournament players as a form of the "yips."

Long ago, and with no remembered intention, I standardized my approach in the following way:

Having decided upon the club to use and the shot to play, I could see no reason for taking any more time in the address than was necessary to measure my distance from the ball and to line up the shot. The more I fiddled around arranging the position, the more I was beset by doubts which produced tension and strain.

I began then to approach every shot from behind the ball looking toward the hole. It was easier to get a picture of the shot and to line it up properly from this angle than from any other. Ordinarily, coming up from behind, I would stop a little short of what my final position would be, just near enough to the ball to be able to reach it comfortably. From there, the club was grounded, and I took one look toward the objective. The club gave me a sense of my distance from the ball; looking down the fairway gave me the line, while my left foot swung into position. One waggle was begun while the right foot moved back to its place. When the club returned to the ground behind the ball, there was a little forward twist of the hips and the backswing began. I felt most comfortable and played better golf when the entire movement was continuous. Whenever I hesitated or took a second waggle, I could look for trouble.

The little twist of the hips I have mentioned is a valuable aid in starting the swing smoothly, because it assists in breaking up any tension which may have crept in. Often referred to as the "forward press," it has been regarded by many as the result of a movement of the hands. In actual fact, the hands have nothing to do with it. The movement is in the legs, and its chief function is to assure a smooth start of the swing by setting the hip turn in motion. Without it, the inclination is strong to pick the club up with the hands and arms without bringing the trunk into use.

I do not think it wise to prescribe any definite number of waggles. This depends too much upon how long is required for the player to settle into a comfortable position and obtain a proper alignment. But it is important to make the movement easy, smooth, and comfortable and to form the habit of getting the thing done without too much fussing and worrying.

CHAPTER 5

Backswing

o Some thirty odd years ago I discovered that an effective position at the top of the swing could be reached from a normal address position by making just three separate consecutive movements—first, from the position of address, by employing only the hands and arms, to lift the club directly over the right shoulder (as though to bash the ball into the ground), assuring a full cocking of the wrists; second, to execute a full rotation of the trunk to the right, keeping the head immovable and using the spine as an axis; third, to lift the hands and arms straight up to the normal top-of-swing position.

Upon the execution of these three movements, the player will find himself in perfect position to begin his hitting effort, lacking only the sense of rhythm that he can have only by passing through this position in a complete swing. The sources of power represented by the windup of the trunk, the cocking of the wrists, and the swinging of the arms are all there. The player's performance will be determined by the efficiency with which he employs these sources.

The primary aim in teaching golf must be to communicate to the learner as much as possible of the feel of making a proper golf stroke. I believe the particular photographs I am using in this book are especially well suited to this purpose because they emphasize the action of the golf club and of the player's hands without being confused by showing the successive positions of the rest of the player's body. All the exposures were made upon one film by intermittent flashes of light, all precisely timed as to duration and interval. The process was developed for A. G. Spalding by the Arthur D. Little Laboratories of the Massachusetts

Institute of Technology. These pictures of my swing were made in July of 1940.

Photograph A shows that the three simple movements I have described are all present in a proper backswing. It is very plain that the hands and club are started back by the rotation of the player's trunk and the movement of the arms. During the early stages there is no visible independent action of the hands and wrists and therefore no alteration in the relationship between the left arm and the shaft of the club. However, in starting the club back, the player should produce a little firming of the left-hand grip, preparing for the pickup to come later. At the third position the hands and arms begin perceptibly to lift the club up to the top of the swing. At about this point of the backswing the pickup with the hands is to be definitely applied.

As the hands approach the topmost position, the weight of the clubhead and its momentum will exert a mild tug on the hands and so encourage a full cocking of the wrists. If the player's grip is as light as mine at this point, he will feel the fingers of his left hand open a little; but he will not lose control if he is gripping with the three smaller fingers of this hand.

I ask that special attention be directed to the hands in the two or three topmost positions in this photograph. It will be seen that the wrist joints have been flexed or cocked so that the hands are sprung back over the forearm, and so that there is an inward set to the wrists. If the reader will try flexing his wrists in this manner, he will find that it is in this way that the hands can accomplish the widest range of movement.

The obsession with single-position photographs had led to one very obvious absurdity often heard in modern teaching or theorizing. Because a few players of ability appear to arrive at the top of the swing without achieving a full cocking of the wrists, some authorities have been induced to say that in the modern swing the wrists must operate so that the back of the hand and the top of the forearm are in the same plane. A simple trial will convince anyone that so long as such a relationship is maintained, no hand or wrist action is at all possible. The fact is that those players who fail to cock the wrists during the backswing do so as the very first movement of the downswing.

If one should care to demonstrate the absurdity of this idea that the wrists can be flexed to any appreciable degree while the back of the hand and the outside or back of the forearm are in the same plane, he

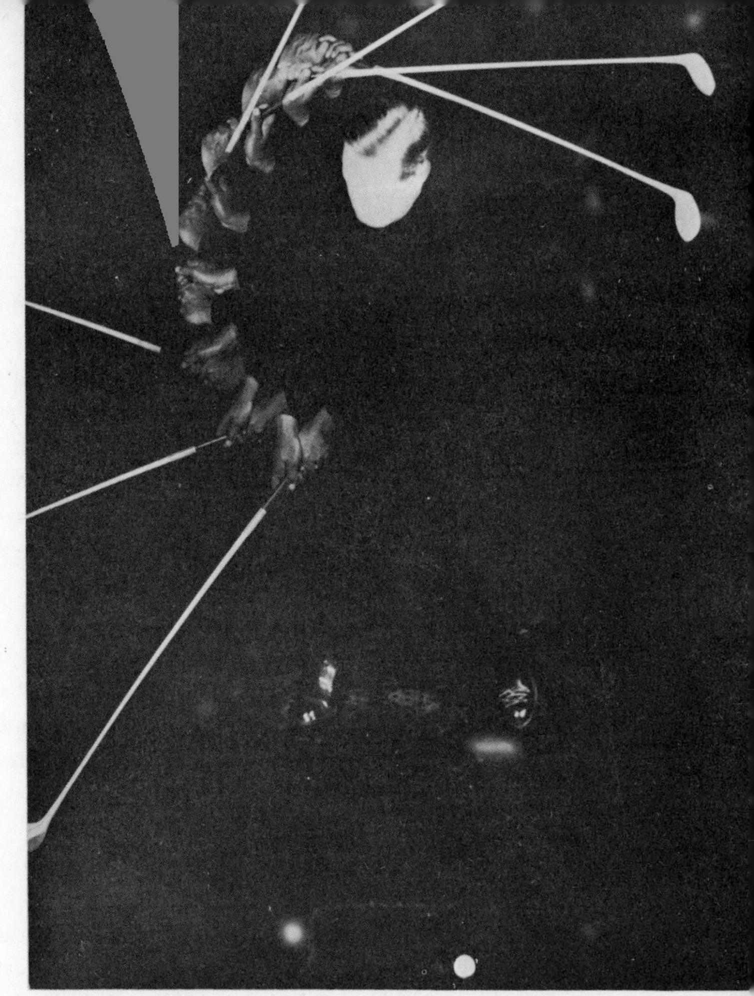
A. The backswing.

can do so by means of a very simple test. He has only to seat himself before a table and rest his elbows upon it with the palms of both hands flat upon the table in what is known as a "prone" position. Then let him try to produce a flexion of either wrist joint which will move his hands over the table top. It simply can't be done.

The maximum angle of cocking of the wrists can be achieved only by the pickup I have described. The same movement can be produced at the table with either hand by lifting to the lips a glass of water from the table top. It is that simple and that natural. At the top of the swing, the combined movement of the two hands holding the club seals their union by setting both wrists under the shaft with both elbows down.

In almost any discussion of the mechanics of the golf swing one is likely to hear frequent use of the word "pronation." Generally the controversy concerns whether or not the wrists should be pronated during the backswing. I have heard this sort of thing since I was a small boy. The most obvious fact revealed by recalling these discussions is that the participants had very little idea of the true meaning of the word "pronation" and merely confounded confusion by trying to apply to golf a word carrying a special meaning in another field.

I have before me a copy of a book called *Applied Anatomy and Kinesiology* published by Lea and Febiger of Philadelphia in 1949. In this book it is explained that when either hand is extended in an approximately horizontal plane with the palm downward, the hand is said to be in a "prone" position and when by any means the hand is rotated toward this prone position, it is "pronated." The position of the hand with palm upward is called the "supine" position, and rotation toward this position is called "supination."

Thus when we speak of "pronation of the wrists," we are talking about something that does not exist. Since the golf club is held in both hands, both hands cannot pronate at the same time while holding the club. Should either hand be pronated, the other must supinate.

The actual fact is that in the correct golf swing there is very little pronation of the left hand or rotation of the left forearm during the backswing, and the effort to introduce either is about as harmful as anything the player can do.

Reasons for the contrary impression are not difficult to find. It is certainly true that any position close to the halfway mark, either going up or coming down, exhibits the left hand, presenting its back approximately square to the front of the player, or very nearly at right angles to its position at address. It is not unnatural to assume (incorrectly) that this is in great measure the result of pronation of the left hand, and that it is in itself mainly responsible for opening and closing the face of the club.

So we not uncommonly observe the average golfer beginning his backswing by a sudden pronation of the left hand, turning the palm downward and directing the club in a very flat arc around his knees. In this manner he conceives himself to be opening the face of the club, when in actual fact he is doing nothing more than removing all possibility of correct body movement. In a great majority of cases this sort of action is accompanied by a left shoulder that comes around too high and a movement of weight toward the left foot during the backswing.

In the downswing, too, this misconception leads to trouble. For conceiving that in order to reclose the face in the act of hitting, the left hand must be turned back over, the player forces his left arm into his ribs in such a tight place that it must collapse. There used to be a lot of talk about the right hand climbing over the left in the act of hitting, but it must be understood that this takes place only after impact when everything has relaxed after the hitting effort.

There is one other reason why this pronation idea is so appealing. Any golfer will have been cautioned many times about the danger of yielding to the natural inclination to pick his club up abruptly from the ball. Pronation seems to be the opposite, so that it must be right.

In truth, no independent action of the hands at the beginning of the backswing is correct, or at least likely to be correct, simply because if the swing should be started by the hands, the proper winding up of the trunk will never be undertaken.

Any person who expects to get anywhere with his golf game must resolve to go beyond the flat-footed swing which all are inclined to favor until they grow more sure of themselves. One of the most important necessities is to get the hips and legs moving at the beginning of the backswing, for in their movement lies the essential difference between a true swing and a hacking stroke.

It is desirable that both upswing and downswing should originate in the trunk. If the clubhead has been picked up from the ball or thrown from the top of the swing with the hands, it is then too late for the hip turn to catch up. In the one case the backswing must proceed outside its proper path, and in the other the wrist-cocking is used up before the unwinding of the hips can have its effect upon the speed of the clubhead.

The opening and closing of the face of the club are amply cared for by the correct winding and unwinding of the trunk. When the player addresses the ball, he squares his club to the hole, and in his grip he determines the relationship of his left hand to the face of the club, the striking area. This relation, of course, remains the same throughout the swing, so that in order to bring the face back squarely to the ball, the left hand must come back to the same position, and in the correct swing the body movement will see that it does so without a great deal of manipulation.

CHAPTER *6*

Downswing

O The swinging of the golf club back from the ball is undertaken for the sole purpose of getting the player to a proper position for striking. So the one influence most likely to assure the satisfactory progression of the swing is the clearly visualized contact between club and ball still at the forefront of the player's mind. Just as the backswing should not begin until this picture is adequately established, so the movement should continue until there results an awareness that the player has become capable of striking in the intended manner.

I stress this point, and intend to continue to do so, because I know that the unrelenting effort to play golf in this way can do more for a player than anything else he can possibly do. When every move of the swing is dominated by the determination to strike the ball in a definite fashion, the complicated sequence of movements must acquire purpose and unity attainable in no other way.

I have already said that the backswing and downswing as nearly as possible should be blended together so as to compose one movement. This sounds like a tall order when the two are necessarily in opposite directions. Yet the expert player actually accomplishes just this. In the swing of the expert there is no single stage at which all backward or upward movement comes to a halt and a fixed position is attained from which the downswing begins. This transition from upswing to downswing is a truly crucial point, and it is here that ninety-nine out of a hundred bad golf shots are incubated. Just let the player's hands move a few inches toward his front, or let him turn his head a few degrees toward the objective and the shot will be spoiled beyond any recovery.

Even in the most competent golfing company this is the real danger point of the swing.

Photograph B illustrates the plane of the downswing in a properly executed golf stroke. The series of pictures was begun at about the point where the motion of the club changed direction. The clubheads facing toward the player's front and with toes pointing upwards are those of the downstroke. Those faced to the rear with toes pointing downward are positions of the follow-through. It is obvious that the clubhead could not be made to follow this path unless the full cocking of the wrists should be preserved during the early stages of the downstroke, the swing having been brought through these early stages entirely by the unwinding of the trunk and the movement of the arms. The all-important feel which I experience as the swing changes direction is one of leaving the clubhead at the top of the swing. To whatever degree this feeling is present, the result is that the cocking of the wrists is completed as the unwinding of the trunk begins.

Consider the club with its head nearest the camera. It is obvious that at this point the angle between the player's left arm and the shaft of the club is very nearly ninety degrees. It is from this position to the point of contact with the ball that the straightening of the wrists and the final violent completion of the unwinding of the trunk produce the maximum striking effort. The clubhead is shown striking the ball squarely in the back while moving on a line straight to the objective.

It is my feeling that this is a wholly natural performance which will be accomplished in this way, provided only that the player have in his mind striking the ball in this direction and with this sort of timing.

In photograph C we may examine the hitting stroke and follow-through where the interval between exposures is considerably wider. The important point to observe here is that the face of the club is brought up squarely against the ball, not by rolling the right hand over the left, but rather by the completion of the unwinding of the trunk, which in turn pulls the hands in and causes the entire left arm to roll over.

Far better, I think, than could be done by separate pictures of the successive positions, these photographs A and C depict the movement of the head, or the lack of it, in a very impressive fashion.

In photograph A the stark whiteness of the head was brought about by being held substantially immovable throughout the sequence of eight exposures. The outline of the face and the part of the hair are almost as

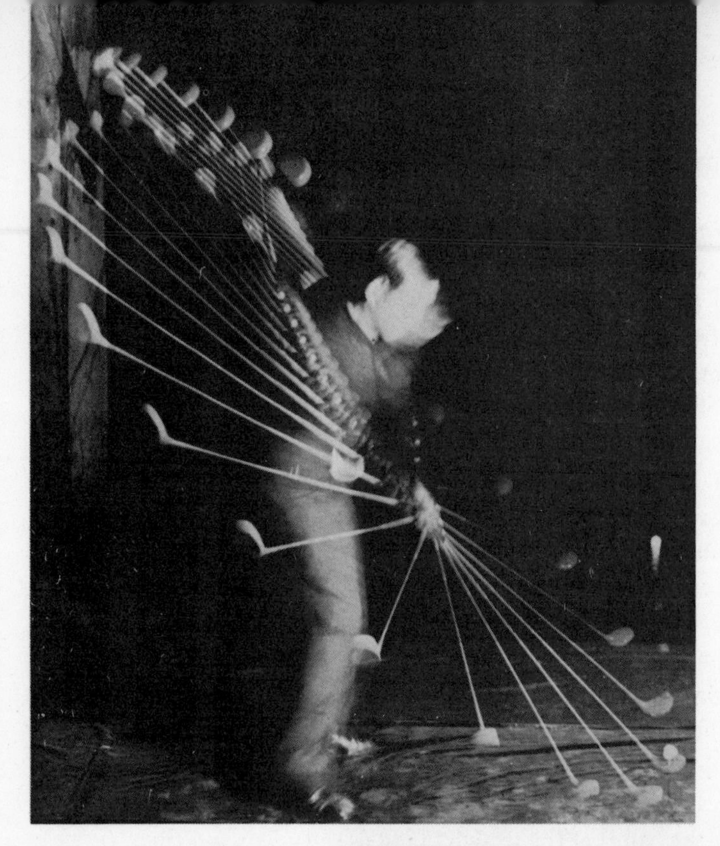

B. The downswing.

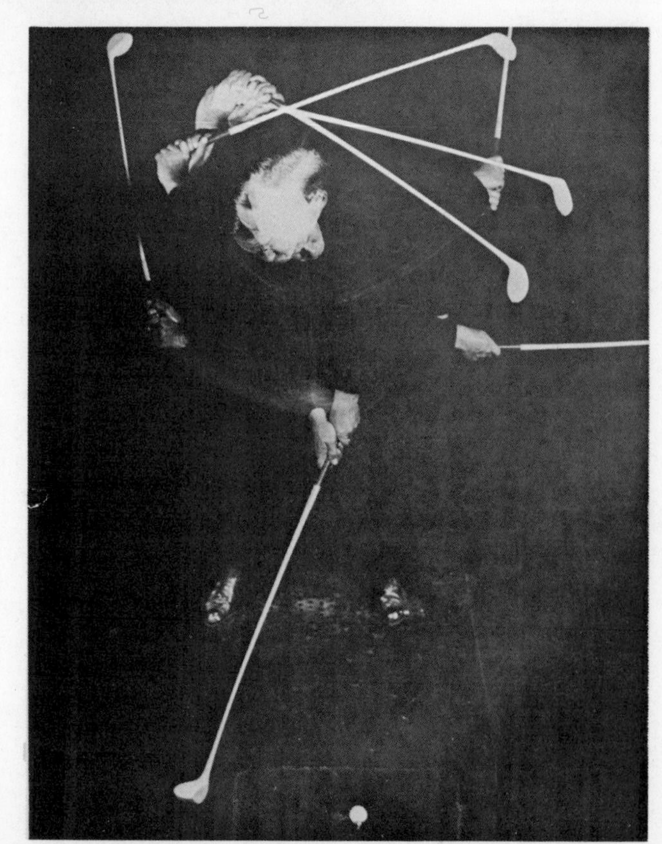

C. Striking the ball.

D. Hitting hard.

A brief instant after the start down. Note that the unwinding of the trunk has produced a tension up the left side which pulls on the grip end of the club through an extended left arm.

they were in the beginning, a very striking illustration of Abe Mitchell's conception of the player moving freely beneath himself.

In photograph C five outlines of the head may be distinguished. Obviously then, there was no perceptible movement of the head between the topmost position and the next in order. For hand positions three and four from the top, the head moved slightly backward and then definitely down as the ball was struck. When the hands had reached a position ninety degrees past the ball, the head was still farther down, but being pulled up and rotated forward by the turn of the trunk and the momentum of the swing.

It is often very helpful for the player to determine that he will never see less of the back of the ball during the swing than he sees at address. I have many times been able to help my playing companions by asking them to try to peer up underneath the back of the ball as they hit it.

There is nothing more important in this whole procedure than holding the head back, or even moving it backward, in the act of striking. The golfer speaks of "head-lifting" and "looking up." Actually, he does not lift his head because of any overeagerness to observe the result of the stroke. When trying to strike the ball, the most natural thing in the world is to look at it. In almost every case the head comes up because the wrists have been uncocked too soon, and with the angle between the left arm and the shaft of the club being less acute, the head and shoulders simply must come up in order to afford room for the completion of the swing.

If ever anyone should hold the notion that a golf ball may be propelled great distances by some magic of form without the need for physical exertion by the player, I ask him to observe the facial contortions in the photograph on page 57. In answer to this proposition and to the claim that golf is a left-handed game, let it be said that the only way to make a golf ball travel is to strike it mightily and with both hands. The expert hits long drives with such apparent ease and effortless grace because he makes efficient use of all sources of power, and mainly because he builds up a considerable rate of speed in the clubhead by the unwinding of his trunk before the hands unleash their explosive force at impact.

The golfer must strike strongly with his right hand, but he must first put his hands, both of them, in position to strike in the desired direction. This is done as the swing changes direction at the top. Initiating the downswing with the unwinding of the trunk provides space and time for the hands to drop down along the proper plane whence they may strike toward the objective. Once this move is made, there is no need to hold anything back.

The point at which the swing changes direction from up to down is one of those spots where the motion slows down enough so that a bit of conscious control may be applied. A very useful trick at this point is to make certain of returning the elbow of the right arm directly to the ribs as the downswing commences, at the same time relaxing the right wrist and thereby increasing its inward set. This has the effect of dropping the club a bit toward the player's rear and thus enhancing the opportunity of hitting straight through the ball on the line of play.

I have nearly always written of the golf swing as subjected to left-hand and left-side control. I have done so because it is obvious that the width and arc of the swing is limited by the extension of the left arm. Since the left hand is above the right on the club, the left arm may be extended throughout all of the movement taking place back of the ball, or before impact. So in order to get the club away from the player to the greatest possible extent, this left arm must be straight, or nearly so. It is, therefore, helpful to think of pushing the club back with the left side and arm.

In the same way, since the downstroke is led by the unwinding of the trunk, the left side again becomes a convenient focal point. If complete use is to be made of the power latent in the player's legs and back muscles, there must be a sense of pulling or stretching up the left side and arm to the grip end of the club. If ever the hands and arms get ahead of the unwinding of the hips so that this feeling of tension should be lost, the power in these big muscles must likewise be lost. Such a thing would result in the interruption of an important line of communication so that the effect would be like pushing on the end of a string.

As nearly as I can describe the sensation of striking a golf ball, it is a combination of a pull through with the left side, combined with a slapping action of the right hand and forearm, the left being responsible for keeping the swing on track, or in a groove, and the right being the agent responsible for bringing the movement to a well-timed climax as the ball is struck.

An ample cocking of the wrists and the retention of the greater part of the angle for use in the hitting area is not only important for good timing and increasing the speed of the clubhead, it is absolutely necessary in order to enable the player to strike downward and so produce backspin. When the angle between the left arm and the shaft of the club becomes straight too early in the downstroke, the clubhead at that point will be too low, and the subsequent arc will be too flat. I found a very valuable application of this principle in the spring of 1930 when I played several rounds of golf with Horton Smith.

For many years I had been a very poor mashie-niblick player simply because I was inclined to be a bit wooden in my wrists when playing the shorter strokes. The backswing ample for the lesser distances was still not long enough to free me of this restraint.

Watching Smith's play, I took note that at the top of his swing for a short or medium pitch the angle between his left arm and the club was quite open. He was gripping the club quite firmly and allowing very little cocking at this point. But in making his first move downward, his wrists relaxed, so that while his arms moved perceptibly, the angle of his club to the ground or a vertical plane changed scarcely at all. In other words the wrist cock, which is usually completed at the top of the swing, was being completed by him at the beginning of the downstroke.

For me, this proved a most valuable lesson. It gave me something to think about when the pitches were not behaving, and I think it can very well be passed on to any others who may have trouble getting their hands and wrists to working. It will not matter so much where the cocking takes place, so long as it is there when it comes time to hit.

CHAPTER 7

Timing and Rhythm

o Apart from the intention to deliver the blow in a proper way, there is nothing more important to the golf swing than that it have the qualities of smoothness and rhythm, and I can conceive of no reason why it should not possess both these qualities so long as it is not interfered with by the conscious effort to pass by rote through a series of prescribed positions.

Now, let us talk about rhythm. It is not easy to provide an impression of rhythm by means of the written word. Yet I believe it can be done.

In playing a full shot in the tempo of my swing, the club requires about one second going back and one-half second to come down. A very good approximation of the timing can be had by counting during the backswing, one, two, and on the downstroke, one, two, with the downward one taken at the same cadence as the backward counting and a staccato two as the ball is struck.

Helen Hicks, one of our really good lady champions of the past, at one time had stamped on the top of her driver—oom-pah. Helen said that this was an important aid to the attainment of the proper rhythm.

The main thing is that the backswing should be long enough so that there may be no need for hurry in the downstroke. The aim should be to blend the backswing and the early part of the downstroke into one smoothly flowing movement culminating in a maximum effort and a maximum clubhead speed when the face of the club contacts the ball.

The use of the word "culminating" immediately above may not have been the result of an entirely happy choice. I am a bit fearful that it might have in it a suggestion of too much finality, for it is an integral part of this conception of smoothness that the motion of the clubhead should not be stopped, or even impeded, as or after it strikes the ball. Indeed, the player must always be aware that he must hit through the ball and not merely at it. He should strive for the feeling that throughout the downstroke he is continuously building up momentum until his clubhead reaches the maximum possible speed, at which point he should turn the whole thing loose and allow the weight of the club and the effort of swinging to carry him along to a proper finish. A graceful, poised position at the finish of the stroke is not an end in itself, but it is nevertheless a very good indication of what has gone before.

Since the immediate purpose is to provide a broad, general appreciation of the golf swing as a whole, I think it may be helpful and perhaps add conviction if I quote impressions from other writers, going back to the very beginning of the century, and to add a very emphatic declaration on my own part that nothing in modern-day golf has operated, or can operate, in any manner to affect the validity of these descriptions.

Beginning in the middle, I shall quote first a description of my own method, written in 1927 by a writer who signed himself "A Roving Player," that appeared in a British magazine called *The Tatler*. Parenthetically, I might add that it was in this year that, having made the worst showing of my life in the U. S. Open, I had made a hurried trip to St. Andrews to defend my British Open title. I record the fact that I won at St. Andrews, with a record score, only in order to indicate that I was playing quite well at the time. I must admit, too, a bit sheepishly perhaps, that I like the quote also because it reports the first blossoming of what Herb Wind, thirty-one years later, called "the love affair between an athlete and the people of a town." Quite seriously, though, I present it as a very good description, if not of my own swing, certainly of that for which I strove, and one which I recommend without qualification.

> St. Andrews' people, who have golf in their very blood, are shrewd judges of players, and in Mr. Jones they see one who is a purist as regards style and method. They are elusive because no other player has been able to copy them. I have met golfers from all parts of the world, but none, for example, stands with feet so close together or quite so near the ball. The effectiveness of the method is perhaps due to the fact that it is essentially

natural. Mr. Jones stands to the ball just as if he were engaged in ordinary conversation. There is no straddling of legs, no tying of muscles into a knot, no extravagant poses, nothing to suggest that he is thinking of or doing anything in particular. The clubhead is placed at the back of the ball, and the swing commences, so slowly in fact as to suggest that it is indolent. Of the millions of golfers in the world, I do not suppose there is another who swings a club back so smoothly or so sweetly. It is the very poetry of motion.

But there is nothing indolent about the downswing. The suggestion it gives of power, speed and momentum is majestic, while the quality of the blow itself suggests the force of an explosion. It is not a blow in the sense that immediately it takes place it is over and done with. There is the glorious follow-through, with the clubhead finishing 'round the neck and the hands high up. These are the things that denote the master golfer and in giving expression to them in a way that reveals the touch of genius, Mr. Jones has become the idol of St. Andrews. . . .

The other quote I mentioned, written in 1903, was quoted in an article I myself wrote in July 1932. In order to reveal my thinking on the subject at the time, I am going to set down here the quote from my own article. It was as follows:

I have chanced upon a thing written by Harold Hilton in 1903 which so closely parallels what I myself have written and said so many times that the similarity is startling. A comparison of this and present day utterances on the subject shows that the rhythm of the well-timed swing has not been altered much through the change of implements and balls.

Mr. Hilton wrote of S. Mure Ferguson, one of the long drivers of that era:

"On the upward swing, Mr. Ferguson always appears to take the club up in a most leisurely and deliberate fashion, and maintains this leisurely method at the beginning of the downward swing; in fact, he always appears to be swinging slowly and well within himself, and this probably accounts for the fine, free action of the body when following through; but by the length of ball he drives, it is manifest that the clubhead must be traveling fast when it reaches the ball."

Of this passage, the most important part is to be found in the statement that Mr. Ferguson "maintains this leisurely method at the beginning of the downward swing." We hear "slow back" on every side, but "slow back" is not enough. There are numbers of players who are able to restrain their impulses to this extent, but who, once back, literally pounce upon the ball with uncontrolled fury. It is the leisurely start downward which provides for a gradual increase of speed without disturbing the balance and the timing of the swing.

The steel shaft has made it possible to produce a golf club that is better balanced and hence more easily manipulated. It is, therefore, possible that in the hands of a competent player it can be swung somewhat more rapidly without sacrifice of control. Nevertheless, the inexpert player or average golfer will still do well to take to heart the descriptions quoted above. Let him always strive for rhythm and make certain that both the backswing and the start downward are made at a leisurely pace. And let the player always swing the club back far enough so that there will be plenty of space and time for the clubhead to gain speed between the top of the swing and contact with the ball.

I like to think of the head of a golf club as acting in the manner of a free projectile as it strikes the ball. During the backswing, the player winds up his hips, raises his arms, cocks his wrists, and swings himself into position to deliver that projectile upon the ball.

In the downswing, by calling successively upon these resources of energy, he manages to build up the speed of his swing until it attains a maximum just before it reaches the ball.

At this point, there occurs a very definite feeling of releasing the projectile, of a complete cessation of effort. It is as though the final flailing action of the hands effected a launching and a complete surrender of control. I have always considered this release to be important because any attempt to continue the hitting effort longer seemed always to detract from the force of the blow.

I cannot write this today without remembering with some amusement what I wrote on the same subject some thirty-five years ago, when my engineering degree from Georgia Tech was still fresh. Quite smugly, I recall, I admonished my readers to remember Newton's Law of Motion to the effect that a body in motion would continue that motion in a straight line until acted upon by some outside force. I suppose the principle is applicable all right, but today I am thankful that I got my college credits is physics and chemistry while the atom was still indivisible.

CHAPTER *8*

Management

Adjust Your Mental Attitude In Advance

O When I was forced to give up golf some ten or a dozen years ago, I began to find my recreation in fishing and bridge. I have had a fishing companion, Charlie Elliott, Field Editor of *Outdoor Life,* who knows well enough where and how to catch fish. But I had to play my own bridge. So my bridge teacher, Margaret Wagar, has given me more lessons than Stewart Maiden ever did, and I have read more of the writings of Charlie Goren than I have those of Harry Vardon and the other golfing masters.

It seems to me that the bridge teacher or writer has a considerable advantage over his counterpart in the golfing field. As Margaret Wagar put it one day, "I am only trying to teach you things you could figure out for yourself if you had the time and inclination." Although I can't claim to have been one of Margaret's prize pupils, at least I recognize that the project as she defines it is not wholly without hope, granted a reasonably intelligent response on my part. I know it is much simpler than trying to teach a person to execute every move of the correct golf swing. At least we don't have to bother with grip, stance, backswing, and downswing with a deck of cards. The question is not how to play each card, but which card to play.

All this experience has led me to determine to devote one section of my book to a discussion of the use of judgment in the playing of golf. Having played the game for over forty years, always with the utmost in thought and attention, I think I can tell a golfer a few things about the management of his ability which will enable him to get better results without the painful necessity of hours of practice improving his technique.

The businessman golfer takes lessons and reads books; he imitates good players; he buys new clubs; he does everything he can to improve his swing, his shot-making ability. But he overlooks one important feature—he doesn't ask himself often enough if he is scoring as well as he ought with his present ability.

In every club there is always at least one man who has the reputation of making a poor game go a long way, the man who seems always to beat a player a bit better than himself. He doesn't do it by any divine inspiration, nor yet by any trick of fate. He simply uses his head, analyzing each situation as it confronts him, always keeping in view his own limitations and power. That is what we call judgment, and it is a lot easier to use good judgment than it is to learn to swing a club like Harry Vardon.

"No man has mastered golf until he has realized that his good shots are accidents and his bad shots good exercise."

These words brought a round of sympathetic applause from a golfing audience of the mid-Twenties at the East Lake Country Club. The speaker was Eugene R. Black (later governor of the Federal Reserve Bank), father of Gene Black, currently famous as President of the International Bank for Reconstruction and Development or "World Bank."

Although I joined in the laughter and merriment produced by these words, they have been long remembered and oft recalled; and the more I ponder them, the more convinced I am of the accuracy of the old saying that many a truth is spoken in jest.

Like most amusing quips, there is an element of exaggeration here. But also a great measure of merit as an appreciation of the game of golf; for not only does it reflect the one unavoidable certainty that very few of any golfer's strokes will, except by accident, fulfill the hopes he had for them, but also recognizes the salutary and sobering effect of the humorous self-examination the game forces upon us.

The challenge of golf is well known. But I feel that the average player sees the wide superiority of the expert and concludes that this is perfection. Is it not better for him to realize that there is no such thing as perfection, and that no one has ever produced, or will ever produce, except because of the intervention of some chance, a shot in which no improvement could be made?

Golf, in my book, is the most rewarding of all games because it possesses a very definite value as a molder or developer of character. The golfer very soon is made to realize that his most immediate, and, perhaps, his most potent, adversary is himself. Even when confronting a human opponent, the most crucial factor is not the performance of the opposition, but the effect of this performance upon the player himself.

The play of the game at times exerts enormous pressure urging frantic efforts exceeding reasonable limits; at other times it offers a beguiling invitation to complacency and overconfidence, which can be equally deadly. The only effective defense in either case is a rigid discipline of self which will at one time shut out panic and at another maintain an appropriate vigilance. The main idea in golf, as in life, I suppose, is to learn to accept what cannot be altered, and to keep on doing one's own reasoned and resolute best whether the prospect be bleak or rosy.

I have often found help in remembering that few things turn out to be as bad as promised, or as good; and that neither championships, nor even matches for that matter, are won by giving up when you are down or by becoming too happy during periods of prosperity.

In my early years I think I must have been completely intolerant of anything less than absolute perfection in the playing of any shot. I often heard Grantland Rice tell of seeing me break a club after hitting a pitch that stopped two feet from the hole, simply because I had not played the shot as I had intended.

I don't remember this incident, but I know that I habitually played every shot for its ultimate possibilities, regardless of risk. This lack of discretion must have been fairly obvious, for Bill Fownes, the resourceful Pittsburgh amateur, once said to me, "Bob, you've got to learn that the best shot possible is not always the best shot to play."

J. H. Taylor, of the famous "triumvirate" of Vardon, Taylor, and Braid, once described the ideal attitude of the golfer as one of "courageous timidity," with courage to bear adversity coupled with enough caution to cause him to be aware of a limit to his powers.

It took some doing, I'll admit, but it is a fact that I never did any real amount of winning until I learned to adjust my ambitions to more reasonable prospects shot by shot, and to strive for a rate of performance that was consistently good and reliable, rather than placing my hopes upon the accomplishment of a series of brilliant sallies.

My resolution along these lines was immensely fortified by a bit of objective analyzing of my own play, which came up with a rather surprising result. I began by reviewing in my mind each round of golf as I played it in order to determine how many strokes in the round, exclusive of putts, had resulted precisely according to the conception I had in my mind as I played them. Since my scores around my home course at East Lake were rarely ever as high as the par of seventy-two and had a normal range of sixty-six to seventy, I expected that a fair number of shots in each round would have been completely satisfactory. I was amazed to find that in some rounds, fairly good from a scoring standpoint, I could find only one or two shots which had not been mis-hit to some degree. Many, of course, had finished on the green or near the hole, but most had been hit a little too high or too low on the club; some had faded or drawn when the action had not been intended; some drives of good length had barely missed the sweet spot.

I finally arrived at a sort of measure of expectancy that in a season's play I could perform at my best rate for not over a half-dozen rounds, and that in any one of these best rounds, I would not strike more than six shots, other than putts, exactly as intended.

If one should have confidence in such an appraisal, which I had, the following conclusions were inescapable:

1 I must be prepared for the making of mistakes.
2 I must try always to select the shot to be played and the manner of playing it so as to provide the widest possible margin for error.
3 I must expect to have to do some scrambling and not be discouraged if the amount of it happens to be more than normal.

The main point of all this for the play-for-fun golfer is to emphasize the importance even for him of adjusting his attitude toward the game before he goes out on the course. Let him first divest himself of any thought that it may be unsportsmanlike or unworthy to prepare himself for the play as best he can. There is no point in going out to play a game unless one has the desire to play well, and golf was not meant to be played impetuously; nor is one likely to exercise the needed restraint and self-discipline unless he has prepared himself in advance. You don't need to go into any ostentatious seclusion, but only quietly and within yourself, to get your mind on the game before you step on the first tee.

Respect the Rules and Etiquette of the Game

It is of the very essence of golf that it should be played in a completely sociable atmosphere conducive to the utmost in courtesy and consideration of one player for the others, and upon the very highest level in matters of sportsmanship, observance of the rules, and fair play. There is no place at all for gamesmanship in golf.

The game was certainly not devised in order to make possible much-advertised professional tournaments for large sums of prize money, nor are tournaments of any kind a part of the fundamental requirements. Contests such as these are merely the natural outgrowth of the steadily increasing numbers of people who enjoy the game, indulge in controversies with respect to the relative abilities of various players, and take pleasure in watching exhibitions of the highest order of skill. The people who really support the game and those to whom all golfers owe an immeasurable debt are the so-called average golfers. Actually, these people are golfers, no more, no less. Those of us who write on the game merely tend to describe them as average, because we can think of no better term to indicate that we are not presuming to speak to the more expert players who, no doubt, would know as much about the game as we do.

No one knows exactly what an average golfer is. Some wag once could not resist the temptation to quip that according to his observation, the average intellect was far below the average. On the contrary side, I believe that most golfers who regard themselves as average are far above the average. Nevertheless, to me, anyone who plays golf regularly and with a wholesome respect for the rules and etiquette of the game is a golfer.

Since we want to enjoy our golf, one of the most important necessities for this enjoyment is that we make of ourselves agreeable companions on the links. We want other people to enjoy playing with us just as much as we enjoy playing with them. There is nothing at all inconsistent in being competitive and at the same time companionable.

So one of the most important things for the beginning golfer to acquire as soon as possible is an adequate understanding of the rules and etiquette of the game. The rules of golf, considered in their entirety, provide material for almost a lifetime of study. The diversity of situations arising in the course of play make necessary many very nice decisions with respect to the application of the rules. It is not possible to expect that a merely cursory reading of a rule book can provide this kind of knowledge.

On the other hand, there are two basic conceptions upon which the game of golf has been developed which most effectively point the way to the proper solution of any question that may arise.

The first, with respect to the rules, is that the player must start and finish each hole with the same ball, playing each stroke as it lies, or accept some penalty for failure to do so. The second, with respect to etiquette, is that the player must in no way interfere with the play of his opponent or anyone else in the game. This right of the player to play his own game unmolested by other players or agencies outside his own game is fundamental to golf. So it is quite enough in the beginning, I think, if the player should understand that he is to play every shot with the ball as it lies, or accept a penalty, and that he must so conduct himself as to interfere with his opponent or partner in no way, shape, or form.

Most books of rules of golf include a chapter or two on etiquette. The beginning golfer should keep such a book handy and make frequent references to it as he progresses in the game.

Let me emphasize right here that no one should set out to learn the rules of golf with the idea that they will be useful in calling penalties upon other players. Throughout the forty years of my golfing experience, I never once found it necessary to call a rule against an adversary or a playing partner in a stroke-play competition. The reason for being well up on the rules is to avoid yourself making a mistake which might prove embarrassing. A player must be vigilant to see that he does not unwittingly violate some of the rules of the game. It must be admitted that golf is a very easy game in which to cheat if one should be so minded. Yet the occurrence of this sort of thing is so rare as to be almost nonexistent in competition. Players whose skill is great enough to encourage them to play in important tournaments have learned such a respect for the traditions of the game that any sort of unfair play never crosses their minds.

On the side of etiquette, I think the golfer could well be guided by the rules of simple courtesy. He knows well enough not to take practice swings while his companions are trying to play shots, or to talk or make distracting noises while the same process is going on. Golf requires a considerable concentration which is not possible in this sort of atmosphere.

Always play to win. You don't have to be a doormat to be a good sport. You owe it to your opponent to let him know that he only wins from you when he overcomes the best you can do.

It is by no means necessary to play well to be an entirely acceptable golfing companion, but you must try. You must be able to keep the ball in play. You must not dillydally around. You must be ready to play your shot when your turn comes, and you must be aware of and respectful of the rights of others in your game.

If you can fill this bill, you need have no hesitancy about playing in any company. Indeed, the better players will be delighted to help and encourage you in the game. They like golf, and they will want you to like it, too. The better your partner, the more tolerant he is likely to be.

Experiment on the Practice Tee, Not on the Course

One of the greatest gifts golf gave to me was the enjoyment of many years of playful association with my father. We started to play the game about the same time, and from the time I was thirteen or fourteen, we had the same golfing companions. On one occasion he and I met in the final of the club championship. In later years we played together two or three times a week.

With my father on the East Lake course during spring vacation from Harvard. Dad appears well pleased with his game.

For many years the offices of our law firm were arranged so that there was an inside connecting door between Dad's office and mine. I used to stop by for him in the mornings so that we arrived at the office together.

Almost invariably immediately after we reached the office, Dad would appear through this inside door, carefully close the door from my office into the hall, select a club from several I had in a corner, and confront me across the top of my desk. "Here's something I discovered the other day. See what you think of it," he would say.

Whereupon, he would demonstrate, and I would comment, as briefly as possible, I admit, in order that we both might get some work done.

But Dad was a dedicated golfer. He always seemed to think he was on the verge of discovering the secret of the game. It cost him untold agony, but he loved it. The secret he had shown me in the morning never worked in the afternoon, but he always discovered a new one on the seventeenth hole and went home happy and with something to show me next morning.

There may have been other things wrong with these secrets, but the fact is that they were never given a chance. The golf course in the midst of a round is no place to experiment or try anything new. The only place for that is the practice tee, and Dad never went to the practice tee before a round.

We hear a lot these days about the repetitive or repeating golf swing. It seems to be a new term in the golfing jargon. Obviously, like the semiautomatic shotgun, it is a fine idea. If a golfer could only set himself in the same position each time and, by pulling a mental trigger, release the identical swing, he would be a happy fellow. Even though the swing might be bad, at least he would know where to look for the ball.

The struggle for good form in golf has purpose, because a sound, simplified swing can perform with greater regularity. But one of the eternal beauties of the game is that it will never be susceptible to such rigid control. The feel of the club is altered from day to day by changes in the weather, and the player's senses respond differently because of the myriad influences within his own make-up. It is important to test out this feel every day, either before the round or as early as possible in the play.

I stopped one day to chat with Al Watrous who, with a number of other contestants, was practicing the day before a tournament at Pinehurst. "Look at those guys wasting their time practicing that long, slow backswing," said Al. "Me, I'm snatching that club up and down like we'll all be doing tomorrow when the tournament starts."

That's a bit far-fetched, of course, as Al meant it to be. But even an average golfer can help himself a lot by hitting a few balls before starting a round, not really practicing in the sense of trying to learn anything, but merely in order to find out how his clubs and his swing feel on the particular day. In any case, he will do better on the course if he will try to play in the way that feels most comfortable instead of trying to remake his swing as he goes along.

Lacking the opportunity for this bit of practice, or even with it, I should always recommend that the start of any round be taken quietly. No matter what the length of the first hole may be, the first drive and the first few long shots should be struck well within the player's limit of power. He can always step up his rate of hitting as he gets the feel of his clubs. Some of the best tournament rounds I have ever played have started in just this way, with the first few drives kept down the fairway and the second shots played for the center or main body of the green. A long putt has gone down, or a second shot wandered up close. Then, with a stroke in hand and confidence assured, the rest can come quite easily.

If I should be limited to one bit of advice to offer to a golfer before the start of a round, it would be, "Take your time." And it would mean to take your time and to avoid hurry in everything; to walk to the first tee and from shot to shot at a leisurely pace; to pause before each stroke long enough to make a considered appraisal before deciding upon the shot to play; and, above all, to take a little more time if things should begin to go wrong.

On the Play Around the Green

The most exacting tests of a golfer's composure and judgment are provided in the play in the area on and around the putting greens, including hazards. In the short play it is easy not only to overlook making provision for that all-important margin for error, but also, after one misplay, to step quickly up to the next shot and play it impulsively or carelessly, even though it may be just as important as the one that went before. Skill, or at least a reasonable reliability in the short play, is not only the stroke-saver it is reputed to be, but also a tension-remover of the first magnitude. Bunkers and other hazards on a golf course affect play in two ways. Quite obviously, they punish the wayward shot by increasing the difficulty of the next. Less obviously, the threat of their presence adds to the pressure on the player as he plays toward them. This pressure is much relieved if the player has confidence in his ability to deal with bunkers and other short-approach situations. I have no doubt whatever that it is in this aspect of the game that thoughtful practice will pay the biggest dividends.

Taking the bunker play first, the first resolution of the average golfer upon finding his ball in a bunker should be to minimize the cost of his error. Not until he has acquired considerable skill in this department should he even think of completely retrieving the situation by his recovery. The main idea should be to make certain that the ball should come out of the hazard at the first stroke. Therefore, the only shot to be considered is a full blast.

The special-purpose sand wedge of the modern set was invented for just such use by the average player. The club has ample loft to get the ball up from almost any situation and extra weight for moving a considerable volume of sand. Unless the ball be deeply imbedded, all that is needed is a good healthy wallop downward into the sand behind the ball. The player only needs a few trials to learn how much sand he needs to take to adjust the range of his shot.

The important thing for him to remember is to strike downward to get his club under the ball, and to rely on the loft of the face to get the ball up.

As one progresses in the game, he will begin to appreciate that bunker play offers endless variety and opportunities for the display of artistry and talent. The delicate chip of a ball lying cleanly on soft sand, or the half-blast or severe backspin shot when the lie is almost clean, are in the realm of the expert. These can only be learned by much practice and by players with imagination and an understanding of the possibilities of controlling the behavior of a golf ball.

A strange thing to me is that I have never seen any but reasonably expert players practicing shots from sand. Those who visit bunkers most frequently in play show the least interest in learning how to deal with them.

I am almost tempted to recommend the recourse had by an Englishman I was told about who, unable to find a bunker in which he could practice, rented one for the season and spent four hours a day learning to get out. If he played golf for enough money, he might even have claimed the rent as a necessary business expense. I am sure it must have paid off.

The chipping and short-approach game is one place where the intelligent and experienced golfer can give himself all the best of it. Most good golfers are great chippers. They have to be, because they can't afford to go over par every time they miss a green with the proper shot.

A. C. M. Croome, a British golf expert of my day, once said that Walter Hagen was so hard to beat because he realized better than anyone else that "three of these and one of those still make four." The inference, of course, was that Hagen holed a lot of putts for pars. This was true, and Hagen was a great putter, but he was also one of the best short-approach players the game has ever seen. He gave himself a lot of putting opportunities.

When I try to tell a person something about how to swing a golf club, I am never quite certain that I am really helping him a great deal. But when I am on this present subject, I know I can give sound advice which anyone can apply, to take strokes off his score and add to his enjoyment of golf.

The main idea in the short play is to give yourself the benefit of all percentages. Never try to be unnecessarily fancy. Wherever possible, select a club which will permit the shot to be played in a straightforward manner and which will make all use possible of the most carefully prepared part of the golf course, the putting surface itself.

As must inevitably follow from the above, do not for one moment entertain the notion of playing all short approaches with one club. A chipper or run-up club has no place in today's limited set.

The rule to follow is this. Aim to pitch the ball in the air by only a safe margin onto the nearest edge of the putting surface, and strike it in a manner which will insure that it will take a full, normal roll—that is, without abnormal spin.

If your ball lies a foot or two off the putting surface on what would be called the "apron" of the green, use a number three iron and loft it just over the bit of apron onto the putting surface. The shot becomes only a long putt. From a few feet farther back you would use a five iron, and so on, but the shot would be the same. In any case, you are playing for the best possible average of results and not trying for anything spectacular. If you can consistently leave your chips within a radius of four to six feet from the hole, you won't suffer too much in the average golf game.

All this may sound pretty simple and obvious, but even in select company I have seen departures from it which proved costly. The most upsetting to me, especially if I happen to be sentimentally interested in the fortunes of the player, is the man who plays all chips from just off the green with a seven or eight iron, pitching the ball well onto the green, often halfway to the hole. Even in these days of advanced greenkeeping, putting greens do have soft and hard spots, and landing on either will throw the shot off. This risk must be accepted from farther out, but it doesn't exist for the ball that is always rolling.

On the other extreme is the player who habitually uses a putter from anywhere on the apron. Here the turf is usually well-conditioned, but the grass is a bit longer than on the putting surface. There is simply no way of knowing how those few feet of apron will affect the speed of the ball. If the ball hugs closely to the ground, the grass will have a braking effect, but if it bounces once, it may take off. A few feet of run, more or less, may mean the difference between a holeable putt and one that is not quite so.

One other rule should definitely be made for the average golfer. Let him never take his sand wedge from his bag except when his ball is in sand, or in such heavy grass that a prayerful escape is the ultimate hope. The pros do wonders pitching with the wedge, but the extreme loft and extra weight cause it to be a treacherous club in the hands of an inexpert player. It is so easy with it to leave a ball sitting or to scull it into tiger country beyond the green.

Putting

Often, too often I think, putting has been referred to as "a game within a game," implying that in some way the putting stroke is, or should be, different from that employed in playing other golf shots. I do not think this is true, and I know it is anything but a useful conception for the learning golfer. Somehow it conveys the notion that on the putting green, at least, one should be able to reduce the simple physical act into a precise routine of infallible accuracy.

To make a completely honest confession, I have myself been the victim of this delusion, and can be thankful that it only arrived after my serious playing days were over, and so only caused me a few temporarily painful experiences in the Masters Tournament.

It is remotely possible, I concede, that my jittery putting in Augusta may have been some early manifestation of the nerve affliction from which

I am now suffering, or some alteration of my attitude toward tournament play because of my earlier withdrawal from competition. It is my own conviction that my putting troubles began when I started to struggle for a precision in my putting stroke which I would never have considered possible in any other department of the game.

The fact is that the direction of the stroke in putting is so much more important than the exact alignment of the face of the putter. Any well-made golf club will seat itself in an approximately correct position when it is rested upon the turf behind the ball. The wiggling and twisting some players employ in an effort to make the alignment precise only serve to set up so much rigidity in the player that a smooth, rhythmic stroke becomes impossible. I think the very height of folly, or of imposition upon the credulous golfer, is represented by the spirit levels and sighting devices now being offered for sale as aids in putting.

The putting stroke should be thought of as just another golf stroke, except that it ought to be the simplest. The same requirements are to be met here as in driving from the tee. The posture at address should be comfortable and relaxed, the swing should move freely back and forth beneath a stationary head, and the blow should be directed along the line upon which it is intended that the ball should begin its travel.

I regard the putting stroke as so truly a miniature golf stroke that I think it is a mistake to try to exclude any members of the body from participation in the action. In other words I do not believe in trying to hinge the stroke upon either wrist, or in trying to restrict the movement to any sort of fixed base. Naturally, the shortest putt requires only the gentlest tap, actuated only by the hands; a putt slightly longer may require that the arms should swing a bit; and the long approach putt may need a stroke long enough to induce a little movement in the hips and legs.

In putting, and in chipping, too, it is important that the backswing should be long enough. Nothing can be worse around the greens than a short, snatching stroke. I have had some of the real masters of the short game tell me, and I heartily agree, that it is most helpful to swing back a little farther than needed on the first few chips or putts of any round. In this way, they may be certain of attaining that feeling of a smoothly-floating club so necessary for a delicate touch.

Actually, this touch is the key to good putting. Very few putts of any length are dead straight, so that no line is right except for one speed; and the player who tries to straighten even the shortest putts by charging the hole will miss a lot of those coming back.

I will guarantee that more putts under twenty feet, the kind you like to hole, will go in, and three-putt greens will pop up less often, if the player will forget about the precise alignment of his putter and learn to adjust his touch so that he may always keep his ball above the hole and always reach the hole with a dying ball. A ball dying on a slope above the hole often topples in, and always stops close; nothing is more disheartening than to watch a ball barely miss the lower side of the hole and then curl down the slope some five or six feet. And remember, even on the short putts, that the hole is of full size for the touch putter, while it presents only an inch or so to the charger who has to hit the exact center of the cup.

I like to think of putting as very much like rolling a golf ball from my hand across a green toward a hole. I know I should then not worry too much about the backswing of my arm. I think it would instinctively take care of itself. So in putting, I don't like to worry too much about the alignment of my putter at address or about my backswing, except that it be long enough. The picture I want uppermost in my mind is of the line I want the ball to travel on, and of how hard I want to hit it.

There occurs to me one other reason for saying that putting is a game within a game. It makes it much easier to say or to think, "I played very well, but I couldn't putt," or "He's a fine golfer, but he can't putt." I know—I have done it myself—but how can a man play golf well or be a fine golfer if he can't putt?

One thing is certain, you won't win any medals or many friendly bets if you can't get the ball into the hole. If you are not reasonably good at it, you had better learn.

If one is a close observer of golf, he will most likely take note that a number of the touring professionals and better amateur players make an alteration in their grip when taking a putter in hand. The most common golfing grip of today is that known as the "Vardon" or "overlapping grip," in which the little finger of the right hand to some degree rides upon or overlaps the knuckle of the index finger of the left hand. When putting, many players reverse this overlapping so that the index finger of the left hand rides on top. I doubt if any great number of those using this variation today could possibly tell where they got it from.

I think most, if not all, of them came by it, either directly or indirectly, from Walter Hagen or from me. We both used it, and I think I made the change before Hagen, but I can't be sure; and it doesn't matter anyway, because I am sure credit for the invention belongs to Walter J. Travis.

The Grand Old Man of the putting green, who certainly has better right than anyone to be recognized as the master putter of all time, taught it to me during the very early Twenties in the locker room of the Augusta Country Club. The lesson, by the way, was in the nature of an apology for one he had refused to give me at Merion in 1916 when I arrived at the club a few minutes late for an appointment we had made the day before.

Mr. Travis told me that he had found the change helpful because he relied upon the right hand to regulate the touch and speed of the putt, after taking the club back mainly with the left. He wanted to have the whole of his right hand upon the club. I won't say that this is the prime necessity for good putting, but somehow I seemed to do better after this little lesson.

Back some pages, when describing the proper swing for the longer strokes, I mentioned a pickup by the left hand that should be felt about halfway up in the backswing. Although this pickup is well known to expert players, most writers on the game hesitate to write about it for fear of seeming to approve the common inclination of the beginner to pick the club up from the ball without swinging.

Yet this pickup goes through the entire game into the short play as well, only in putting and chipping it is blended with the swinging of the arms, rather than with the windup of the player's whole body. It's the little pickup with the hands that keeps the head of the putter or chipping club moving straight back from the ball while the hands and arms are swinging to some degree away from that line; and it is the faintly or mildly slicing stroke so induced which carries the club freely through the ball.

Swinging the clubhead back in a flattened arc around the knees makes it inevitable that the stroking motion should become a rolling or a pushing action. The proper stroke, if I may say so, is a slicing action which does not slice across the line of play, but sends the club straight through the ball on the line to the hole.

PART TWO

Competition and the Grand Slam

CHAPTER *9*

The Education of a Competitor

The Raw Beginnings

o Many times I have been asked why I retired from competition in golf, but no one has ever asked how I got into the thing in the first place. Perhaps this is just as well, for there were reasons for quitting and none for starting. The beginning just began, as it often does.

In my view competitive golf has never been a term to be extended to sectional and local tournaments. These are fun affairs, pure and simple, and take place in an atmosphere relatively free of strain. To me, competition means the National Championships, Open and Amateur, both in this country and in Great Britain. Yet the tournament which set me off into National competition was the Georgia State Championship of 1916, and I think this tournament marked the beginning of my taste for and appreciation of real competition in golf.

I think it may be said that I was of the second generation in this country, having the opportunity to grow up in the game. Francis Ouimet perhaps belonged to the first. I do not mean to imply that Francis is old enough to have been my father. Actually, our ages are only eight years apart. But he was born about the time the first golf clubs were brought to this country and the game began to take root here, and I was born in the exact year marking the advent of the rubber-cored ball.

When I was playing around the East Lake course as a child, there were only two or three golf courses in Atlanta, where now the number is nearer twenty, and there were only a half dozen or so kids our age interested in the game at all.

Almost as soon as I was to be trusted to play a round of golf on the course under my own responsibility, I began playing regularly with

Perry Adair, the son of one of my father's good friends, who was about three or four years my senior. Perry, quite naturally, came along faster than I did; and by the time he was fifteen he was one of the best amateur golfers in the South. But I grew up a little faster physically than did Perry; and by the time I was thirteen, I could hold my own with him quite well. At that time, in the invitation tournaments around the South he and I were among the most favored competitors.

The first tournament I played in away from home was the Montgomery, Alabama, Invitation, in the year 1915 when I was thirteen years of age. Perry won this tournament, and I lost in the finals of the second flight to a left-handed player, which I considered at the time the ultimate of disgrace. Later that year, however, Perry and I met in the second round of the invitation tournament in Birmingham, and I beat him and went on to win the tournament.

In the following year, 1916, Perry beat me in Montgomery, but I won from him in the final of the Invitation at East Lake, and won a couple more tournaments in which Perry had been beaten by other players. At the end of this season we found ourselves again opposed to one another in the final of the Georgia State at the Capital City Club in Atlanta.

Up to this moment, despite the fact that I had won two out of the three matches in which Perry and I had met, I still considered that he was the better golfer. I looked up to him and thought that I had managed to win from him a couple of times mainly by accident. It was in this match at Brookhaven over thirty-six holes that I finally gained confidence in myself and in my game.

In the morning round I think I must have been tense, overanxious, and perhaps a little bit resigned. At any rate I played some pretty sloppy golf and came in for lunch three down. While I was having a few practice putts prior to the start of the afternoon round, the tournament chairman came up to me and asked that I play out the bye holes, with the obvious inference that Perry would beat me several holes before the finish, and he wanted the gallery to have the privilege of seeing a full eighteen holes of play. I replied that I would, without calling his attention to what I considered to be a rather obvious and unpleasant implication. Nevertheless, it appeared that he was right when I began the afternoon round by hooking my tee shot out of bounds and losing the first hole with a scrambling six, thus becoming four down.

But at this point I remember to this day that my whole attitude changed completely. Instead of being on the defensive and uncertain, I began to play hard, aggressive golf, hitting the ball with all the force at my command and striving to win hole after hole, rather than to avoid mistakes.

After halving the short second hole in three, I drove to the edge of the green on the third hole, something I had never done before, and from then on hit the ball as hard as I had ever hit it in my life. Perry played reasonably well, but he missed a couple of putts, notably on the eighth and tenth holes, and I finally won the match on the last green two up. I had played the eighteen holes in seventy, with the beginning six.

This was the match which gained for me my first opportunity to play in a National Championship, and also gave me what assurance I needed to enjoy taking advantage of it. I think what did most for me was Perry's remark as he put my ball into my hand on the last green. With understandable disregard for grammar, he had muttered, "Bob, you are just the best."

A few days later my father told me that Mr. Adair had come to him to say that he had planned to take Perry to the National Amateur Championship at Philadelphia, and would like to have me go along with them. Thus was I started into National competition.

Until that very moment, however, I am sure that I had never given even one thought to ever playing in a National Championship. I remember waiting on the front steps of our home at East Lake for my father to bring home the afternoon paper so that I could find out how Francis Ouimet had come out in his play-off for the National Open with Vardon and Ray. And I had read with much interest of Bob Gardner's winning the Amateur Championship the year before at Detroit; but somehow it had never occurred to me that I might one day be playing in tournaments of this kind.

It must be admitted that golf in those days was very little like golf today, especially in big-time competition. In 1915 when the Southern Amateur Championship had been played at East Lake, the two ultimate finalists, Nelson Whitney and Charlie Dexter, had tied for the medal with eighty-one. It is fairly revealing of the quality of golf in those days that Perry at the age of sixteen, and I at the age of thirteen should have been among the top competitors for the Southern Championship. Granting all possible precocity on the part of us both, one had to admit that we were so prominent because most other competitors had learned to play golf after reaching maturity. In the same manner most of them had per

In my first Amateur championship at Merion, 1916. Thank heaven I was somewhat more of a golfer than I looked to be.

My first Open, with Harry Vardon, the English master. This was Vardon's last appearance in our championship. He would have won except for being caught in a violent windstorm.

force learned to drive automobiles after reaching maturity, and few of them ever attained the facility with a motor car easily acquired by members of my generation who more or less grew up at the wheel.

This was true not only in the South, but, as was attested by the play at Merion, throughout the rest of the country as well. My first qualifying round on the West Course at Merion was a fair seventy-four, but my second was an eighty-nine, for a total of 163, and yet I qualified easily.

Since my seventy-four on the easier West Course had led all morning play, I was thus cast in the limelight at once. My eighty-nine in the afternoon before a considerable gallery probably convinced everyone that they had seen the last of the fourteen-year-old kid from Dixie. But I won in the first round from Eben Byers, a former champion, and from Frank Dyer, the Pennsylvania champion, in the second round. Dyer had been considered by many to be a possible winner of this tournament. In this second match, moreover, I had been five down through the first six holes, but had come on to even the match in the morning and win on the sixteenth green in the afternoon. So when I met Bob Gardner, the defending champion, in the third round, the match attracted quite a bit of interest.

Although I had no such thoughts at the time, I have since had emotions of sympathy for Bob Gardner on that day, and at the same time admiration for the gallant and courtly way in which he met and handled what must have been a very difficult situation.

Gardner was a tall, handsome, athletic young man who looked every bit the champion he was. He had even held the world record for the pole vault a few years before when he was at Yale. His victory in the Amateur Championship the year before had been his second, and he was now in quest of his third title.

On the other side was I, a pudgy school kid of fourteen, playing in my first National Championship. I was wearing my first pair of long pants, and I owned one pair of golf shoes, a pair of old army issue into which I myself had screwed some spikes.

Gardner was a good six feet; I a bare five feet four.

I have often thought since how little I should have relished being asked to play against such a kid in a National Championship. Truly, I realize now, as no one seemed to then, that all the advantage was on my side. What could I care about who my opponent was? I was having the time of my life, with nothing to lose, and thinking of nothing to gain except playing golf. And I was doing that about as well as anyone in the tournament.

Anyway, we had a really good match; not flawless golf exactly, but good and bad. Gardner messed up the first two holes and handed me a two-up lead; he took these back, then went ahead himself; then, came my turn and I was again two up through seventeen. But Bob won the eighteenth, and we went to lunch with me one up.

Of course, that was enough to bring out the crowd for the afternoon round, which I began, as Gardner had in the morning, by losing the first two holes, putting me once more a hole behind.

The fourth hole was mine, but Gardner won the fifth, so that I was again one down as we stood on the sixth tee. In the next three holes I experienced as much excitement as I can remember on a golf course. All that registered at the time was the excitement, and perhaps frustration, because I hadn't yet thought of anything such as a golfing career. But I have since looked back on that little stretch and realized how unfortunate it might have been for me had things happened differently on those three holes.

Here is the way Grantland Rice described this sequence in his column the next day:

> After the fifth, there came three holes in succession that broke the kid's heart, and that would have broken the heart of almost any golfer alive.
>
> Coming to the sixth after the drives, Jones placed an iron within twelve feet of the pin. Gardner's second was ten feet above the green with a ridge to pitch over and a fast downhill slope awaiting his shot. No one believed he had even a chance to get the ball close, but by a wonderful recovery he stopped the chip shot within four inches of the hole and got a half in four.
>
> This was the first shock. The second came at the 210 yard seventh. Jones was on the green twenty feet away, while Gardner's long iron had carried over into the rough. Once more, he had to call upon his nerve and skill for another chip shot over a ridge to a fast, downhill slope, and this time the ball stopped only a foot from the cup for another half.
>
> But the kid was still fighting. At the eighth, he was on the

> green ten feet from the cup in two. Gardner's second struck the back of the green and bounded well over upon a neighboring tee. He had saved two holes, but how could anyone save this situation? No one but a champion could. This time, Gardner pitched back fifteen feet beyond the cup, but he sank his putt for a par four, getting another half.

As ever, Grant's description was accurate. Even so, words simply could not describe the amazing quality of these recoveries. Because of the severity of the slopes and the speed of the shining greens, the first two at least were authentic miracles.

After all these years I remember exactly how I felt as I walked onto the ninth tee, and I remember exactly what I did. I felt that I had been badly treated by luck. I had been denied something that was rightly mine. I wanted to go off and pout and have someone sympathize with me, and I acted just like the kid I was. I didn't half try to hit the next tee shot, and I didn't half try on any shot thereafter. In short, I quit. Ten years later, it might have been different, but it wasn't then.

It is the keen, poignant, and accurate recollection of this episode which has caused me so often to be thankful it happened just as it did. If I had won those three holes, or even two of them, I probably should have won the match. And it is not inconceivable that I might even have won the tournament. I hadn't had any experience, but neither had I any fear or self-consciousness. There was no tougher competitor than Bob Gardner in the tournament. If I had beaten him, I might well have beaten the others.

Yet if I had won, what would have happened next? Not giving myself any the worst of it, I think I was a fairly normal kid of fourteen. But how many of us today can look back at ourselves at that age and be completely proud of the picture? I must admit that I had already become a bit cocky because of my golfing success in play against grown men. Had I won that championship, I should have been Amateur Champion for not only the next twelve months, but, because of the suspension of play for the period of the war, for three whole years. I shudder to think what those years might have done to me, not so much to my golf, but in a vastly more important respect, to me as a human being.

I think of some of these things today as I see fathers enraptured by precocious sports accomplishments of their offspring. To take pride in these things is normal, but let me admonish these fathers to be not too unhappy when their youngsters take a beating now and then. The chastisements are bound to come sometime. The boys will fare much better if they get some of this bitter taste early in the game.

O. B. Keeler

Despite the fact that the Georgia State Championship of 1916 hastened by at least three years my arrival on the national golfing scene, quite the most enduring reward I got out of that tournament was my association and friendship with O. B. Keeler.

O.B. at that time was a very recent fugitive from a clerkship in a railroad office in a small town near Atlanta. Having found the confinement of this job intolerable, he had attached himself as a reporter to one of the Atlanta newspapers, but had not yet arrived at or been given any field of assignment. He was writing anything and everything.

But he covered that State Championship, and he wrote a glowing and impassioned account of the final match. He told me later that he decided that day that he wanted to make a career of writing about golf in general, and my golf in particular.

The paper did not send Keeler to Merion that year, but during the war years he reported a number of Red Cross matches in which I took part and one Southern Championship. And when, after the war, the play of National Championships was resumed and I became an accepted part of the National picture, Keeler and I became inseparable.

By Keeler's estimate we traveled 120,000 miles together, in which travels he watched and reported on my play in twenty-seven National Championships in this country and abroad, in addition to countless less formal appearances. At these tournaments we lived together in the same room most of the time, except when either or both of us had his wife along, and the play and result were as personally his as mine. Indeed, I think he suffered in defeat and reveled in victory even more than did I.

It is difficult to put into words an appreciation of the full value to me of this association. There was so much meaning for us in golf matches and tournaments; so much to talk about before and after the play. There were so many other times when golf was the last thing to be mentioned.

Whatever the mood, Keeler was the ideal companion. He had read almost everything and remembered most of it; he could, and frequently did, recite verse for hours; I found the opportunities for a liberal education as we lolled about our hotel room or on a train letting our thoughts wander around. Above all, he was an acutely sensitive, instinctively gallant, and wholly unselfish friend whose loyalty and devotion could never once be questioned. There is no way to measure the worth of such a companion when one is in the midst of a taxing endeavor.

I think I have said that I have never felt so lonely as on a golf course in the midst of a championship with thousands of people around, especially when things began to go wrong and the crowds started wandering away. It was then that I began to look around for Keeler, and I always found him.

The ebb and flow of a player's confidence is one of the strange phenomena of competitive golf. I have discussed this angle with all the great players of my own and later eras, and none deny or can explain

With Perry Adair, Chick Evans, and Ned Sawyer (left to right) in one of those Red Cross matches during the First World War. Perry and I lost the sartorial contest by a good margin but we did better at golf.

the periods of uncertainty that occasionally come in the midst of the most complete assurance.

In the first qualifying round for the Amateur Championship at Minikahda in 1927 I posted a seventy-five. I never wanted to win qualifying medals—a sort of superstition, I suppose—and I had tried to coast along and do a modest, comfortable score. But I had slipped a stroke here and there and perhaps had been lucky to score seventy-five. Suddenly I began to see that another slack round with a stroke or two more gone might leave me out of the tournament.

So I set out to find Keeler.

"O.B.," I said, "the only way for me to get out of this thing is to go out this afternoon and try to win the medal, and I need you to walk with me for a few holes until I get calmed down."

I wanted just the satisfaction of having an understanding soul with me to get over that feeling of aloneness which comes when your confidence is gone. It worked like a charm. I let O.B. go after the fifth hole, finished the round in sixty-seven for a course record and the medal, and went on to win the championship.

This is just one of the things I owe to Keeler. The bigger thing no one knows better than I or than the boys who were writing sports in those days. To gain any sort of fame it isn't enough to do the job. There must be someone to spread the news. If fame can be said to attach to one because of his proficiency in the inconsequential performance of striking a golf ball, what measure of it I have enjoyed has been due in large part to Keeler and his gifted typewriter.

The "Seven Lean Years" of Keeler

The only fault I ever had to find with Keeler, and it was anything but serious, was what I considered his overplay of the "seven lean years." He was always fond of the idea of some sort of preordained symmetry he thought he could discover in certain aspects of golf. He first became fascinated by his analysis of my sixty-six at Sunningdale in the qualifying for the British Open in 1926. He always broke it down into thirty-three out, thirty-three in; thirty-three long shots, thirty-three putts. So when he found that from 1916 to 1923 I had played in ten National championships without winning one, he loved to call these "the seven lean years." I know he was happy when I quit in 1930 so that the "seven fat years" could not possibly be stretched into eight. I am glad, too, because I owed him more than that.

Actually, though, those first seven years didn't seem so lean. At least, they gave me the experience without which the "fat years" would never have come.

One trouble was that in the first two, my only play of consequence had to be in exhibitions, usually for the benefit of the Red Cross. This was fun, but not of much value as competition. I did learn, though, rather bitterly, that my childish displays of temper had to be dispensed with.

I think the low point I reached in this regard came in a match at Brae Burn in Boston when I was fifteen. Perry Adair and I were on a Red Cross tour with Alexa Stirling and Elaine Rosenthal. Alexa, with whom I had grown up at East Lake, had won the Ladies' Championship the year before. She was one of the truly great woman players of all time. After the war she won the championship twice more in succession, so that she held her championship for a total of five years.

Although I should have known that Alexa, not I, was the main attraction, I behaved very badly when my game went apart. I heaved numerous clubs, and once threw the ball away. I read the pity in Alexa's soft brown eyes and finally settled down, but not before I had made a complete fool of myself.

That experience had its proper effect. I resolved then that this sort of thing had to stop. It didn't overnight, but I managed it in the end, at least in tournaments. To the finish of my golfing days, I encountered golfing emotions which could not be endured with the club still in my hands.

But the other years could not have been so lean, because I look back upon them as the years when I most enjoyed competition. Certainly I took some beatings, but I also won some good matches, and some I lost deserved to be so classified.

When the Amateur Championship was resumed in 1919, I was runner-up, losing a good match to Dave Herron in the final.

That same year I finished in a tie for second in the Canadian Open and a clear second in the Southern Open. True, in Canada Jim Barnes, Karl Keffer, and I were sixteen strokes behind Douglas Edgar's record score of 278. But in the South, Barnes beat me by only a stroke.

In 1920 I won the Southern Amateur for the second time and lost a really fine match to Chick Evans in the semifinal of the Western. Chick beat me on the thirty-sixth green. I had been three down with

O. B. Keeler and I hold a thoughtful conference on the practice green at Oakmont during the 1925 Amateur championship.

seven to play, but had then won three straight holes to even the match.

Francis Ouimet beat me in the third round of the National. In those days, if you wanted to pick a couple of guys to lose to, you couldn't do better than Chick and Francis. They were the best.

I admit 1921 was rather dismal. My first venture in the British Amateur ended in the fourth round when Allan Graham beat me. This was all right, except that he did it with an old-fashioned (even then) brass putter.

Then followed the most inglorious failure of my golfing life—when I picked up my ball in the British Open at St. Andrews.

In 1922 I won the Southern the last time I played in it, and tied for second in the U. S. Open one stroke behind Gene Sarazen. Jess Sweetser beat me eight and seven in the Amateur, but things could have been worse.

The main point is that it was definitely not true, as has been often said, that I probably should have quit tournament golf had I not won the Open at Inwood in 1923. Such a thing had never once entered my mind. I was enjoying playing for a good showing, or to win as many matches as possible. Tournament golf only began to gall when anything but an outright win looked like failure to me, and to everyone else.

Keeler and I were certainly impatient for the actual winning of an important title. But when I look back and find that I first won the Open at the age of twenty-one and the Amateur at twenty-two, I can't feel that we were too badly treated by fate. Of one thing I am certain. I started winning every bit as soon as I deserved to.

The "Seven Fat Years," also Keeler's

According to Keeler, the fat years began in 1923, because in June of that year I won the Open Championship after a play-off with Bobby Cruickshank. But because of my studies at Harvard, I had not been able to go to Britain for the Walker Cup Matches and the championships over there. Anyway, it is not of the nature of golf that once you start winning you keep on winning. Even fat years have moments of gloom.

So when I arrived at the Flossmoor Club in Chicago for the Amateur Championship of 1923, I bore what for me was the most impressive title of Open Champion. When in the second round I stood on the seventeenth tee needing only two fours for sixty-eight on a long, tough golf course and standing four up on Max Marston, I must have thought that Marston, too, should have been impressed. But Max played the next nineteen holes in five under par and beat me two and one in one of the best matches I can remember.

I won the Amateur in 1924 and 1925, finished second in the Open in the former year, and tied for the championship in 1925, losing by one stroke in a double play-off with Willie MacFarlane.

In early 1924 I had my first failure in one of those "challenge" matches against a professional. Arthur Havers, British Open Champion, quite neatly took me, U. S. Open Champion, over my home course at East Lake.

Nineteen twenty-six was a funny year. It began and ended with a defeat. The first loss was a lopsided drubbing from Walter Hagen in a special seventy-two hole match we played in Florida. Although this match involved no championship, it did carry a sizable load of prestige, and I wanted badly to win it. The last was a narrow defeat by George Von

Elm in the final of the Amateur at Baltusrol. This turned out to be the last thirty-six-hole match I was to lose to an amateur.

In between these two, an unknown young Scot, Andrew Jamieson, beat me over eighteen holes in the British Amateur at Muirfield.

Naturally I have heard a lot about that match with Hagen and read a lot about it, too. I do not, as one might think, mind in the least having it recalled to memory. When you play a lot of intense and interesting competitive golf with and against a man, you develop a real affection for him. The respect and admiration you have for him as an immediate adversary ripens through the years because of the memory of the tense and thrilling experiences you have shared. I have always been grateful that I was lucky enough to come along at a time when there were so many players of competence, color, and personality. It isn't necessary to name them all, but Hagen on all counts stands near the very top of the list.

A few years back Hagen, too, wrote a book. At least, he produced one with the aid of a writer to put the words on paper for him. Somehow I can't imagine Hagen ever taking the trouble to write anything himself. The labor of writing in some ways seems too menial for a guy like Hagen. He wasn't called Sir Walter for nothing.

With Hagen in Florida about the time of our special match in 1926 which he won by 12–11 (we're still friends).

As I scanned through the book and read Hagen's account of that match in Florida, there came into my imagination a picture I found amusing. Two very old geezers are sitting before the fire on a cold winter night. Each is clad in smoking jacket and slippers, and each has a snifter of brandy beside his chair. For a while nothing has been said. Finally one of them comes out in a high-pitched sort of nasal voice, "Bob, do you remember that match we had down in Florida 'way back in 1926? Say, I'll never forget how I fooled you on that first hole. That got me off to a good start. You remember how I took a strong iron and let up on the shot so you would overplay the green?"

"Now come on, Walter," drawled the other, "when I read that tale a few years ago in a magazine story about you, I thought, 'Well, the old boy has read that yarn so many times he's come to believe it himself.' I never was that stupid, even in 1926. Don't forget, that was on the Whitfield Course where I had been playing almost every day, and you know we could always judge how far a ball was traveling by how long it stayed in the air, and we always got help in judging distance by observing the apparent height of the flag stick and the apparent size of people and other objects around the green.

"But you were smart that day in always favoring the short side in playing to the greens. All those putting greens sloped up from front to back, and it was easier to be always playing up to the hole.

"And I remember also that it was not until the middle of the afternoon round that I discovered you were using a three wood off the tee. You said you were doing it to stay out of the trees, but I think you did it so you could play the second shot first and leave me looking at your ball up by the hole as I played my own second. I'll tell you that had some effect. You were playing those iron shots mighty well."

"But," continued the one with the drawl, "I had to laugh when I read the description in your book of that shot that ran through the bunker at the sixth hole of the afternoon round. You said you had to slice around a tree and that you half-topped the shot but hit it with so much spin it bounded through the bunker.

"Now, my memory isn't as good as it used to be, but that hole made a lasting impression on me. I was three down at the time and had pitched onto the green about ten feet from the flag. I have a very clear recollection of you playing that shot from the exact middle of the fairway. You hit the ball squarely on top, and it ran along the ground all the way to the bunker, through it, and on up within six feet of the hole. I missed my

Finish of a three-quarter iron shot from a tee in the 1923 Open championship. The strain of the competition shows rather plainly.

A free finish to a full iron shot. Note the toe of the club pointing straight down.

putt and you holed, so that instead of being two down, I was then four down. That made a big difference."

"Well, anyway," parried Hagen, "I thought I wrapped you up on the twenty-seventh green. You remember, you chipped in for a deuce while my ball was about thirty feet away. As your ball went down, I said to Grant Rice, 'Look at the lucky stiff. He gets a half after all.' I knew I could make mine."

"I guess that was it," said Jones a bit woefully. "You had command of the match, all right, and I had to take all the chances. You finished the first thirty-six holes eight up; and even though I played fairly well the last day on your course at Pasadena, I couldn't hope to make up any sort of deficit against your fine golf and wonderful putting.

"But you have to admit you were pretty ornery on that finishing hole. You were dormy twelve, and I canned a forty-footer trying to keep the match alive. And then you dumped in a thirty-footer to wind it up."

"Well," said Hagen, with a wide grin, "I had you in a sack and I couldn't let you make it look respectable."

The winning margin of twelve–eleven does look anything but respectable. Two things a golfer most dreads are failing to qualify and losing a match by "double figures." Yet the latter can happen at thirty-six holes—and even more easily at seventy-two. In this match Hagen secured command by the twenty-seventh hole. In the last nine of the first day, he broke away with some fine golf to open up a big lead. The last thirty-six, like the second round of some thirty-six-hole matches, was strictly no contest.

Yet with all this spectacular lack of success in match play during the year 1926, it is nevertheless a fact that in one period of three weeks I managed to win both the British and United States Open Championships for the first "double" in golfing history. In a way, an analogous combination of circumstances was produced by Hagen a few years later when he lost a special match in England to Archie Compston by eighteen–seventeen and the next week won the British Open, in which Compston was second, by three strokes.

It had become fairly obvious by this time that my play was a good bit more effective at stroke competition than at match play. Keeler and I did a lot of talking about it.

I have often said that I never learned anything from matches or tournaments I won, because of the inclination, natural, I suppose, to accept successes as altogether fitting and proper. Whenever I lost, I would analyze the play and try to figure out if I had made any mistakes that might have been avoided. Mechanical misplays were not considered, because a certain number were to be expected. Keeler and I agreed that in most of these lost matches there were identifiable instances when different tactics, usually more conservative, might have produced better results. But I think we agreed, too, that the main trouble was to be found in the fact that I simply did not play match golf so uniformly close to my capability as I played medal. Keeler, at least, figured that if I played as well as I could, I should not lose many matches.

To Keeler, this meant that at match play I should play the card, or against "Old Man Par," as he put it, so that I should occupy myself only with getting the figures and let my opponent do what he would. I cannot deny that on occasions I had been guilty of playing a slack shot when my opponent had played one, and then watched him make a recovery I could not match, or had unwisely attempted a daring shot when the risk was too great. I accepted Keeler's prescription, but the following of it seemed to require a bit more.

I was very acutely aware that my mental attitude and nervous attunement toward the two forms of competition were quite different. I was nervous before a match, but it was more an eager sort of nervousness or impatience to go out and see who could hit harder and make the most birdies. Before a medal round, my nerves would be even more tightly wound, but the eagerness gave way to apprehension and caution. I always had that hollow feeling in the pit of my stomach, and my concern was to get the agony over, rather than to have the conflict started. I never had any sensation of fear before a match, but more of it than anything else before a medal round.

I suppose I never became as good at match play as at medal, but I did make progress in the former department by the ultimate achievement of the realization that after all, a round of golf in either form was still a complete structure to be built up hole by hole, that restraint and patience paid off in either form, and that consistent pressure would subdue an opponent just as effectively as an opening salvo of birdies.

It was not precisely playing the card or against "Old Man Par" hole by hole. It amounted more nearly to setting out in complete detachment from surrounding circumstances to produce a fine round of golf. An opponent might do some damage at one stage or another, but he was not likely to surpass the entire production.

CHAPTER 10

Preliminary Skirmishes

o The Grand Slam, according to Keeler—or as George Trevor christened it, The Impregnable Quadrilateral of Golf—was accomplished or constructed, in harmony with the metaphor you prefer, in the year 1930. As I write this in September 1958, that was almost exactly half my lifetime ago. Up to the present writing, it has not been duplicated. Whether or not it will be in the future has been, and may continue to be, the subject of some discussion. For me, at any rate, that year marked the culmination of my golfing experience, and into it went all the knowledge, skill, resourcefulness, and character I had gained in the first twenty-eight years of my life. It is possible that I might have become a better golfer had I kept on. But I am certain I could have added nothing of significance to the record.

The important happenings of the year are, of course, indelibly imprinted in my memory. But there are some aspects which I did not care to discuss entirely frankly at the time.

I have been frequently confronted with the question, "Had I started out the year 1930 with the expectation, or even hope, of winning the four major championships?" I did not feel like saying that I had, because I felt reluctant to admit that I considered myself capable of such an accomplishment. At this point, separated from the fact by so many years, this reticence seems a bit silly. Actually, I did make my plans for that golfing year with precisely this end in view, and so prepared myself more carefully than I had ever done before.

I first got the idea that the Grand Slam might be made during the campaign of 1926.

This may seem a bit odd, since the British Amateur Championship was normally the first of the big four to be contested, and this had always been the toughest one for me to win. In 1926 I had been beaten in the fifth round of this tournament and had come nowhere near winning it. That is, from all appearances. But I had gone on to win the British Open and the American Open, and had reached the final in the United States Amateur, to lose by a close score of two and one over thirty-six holes in the final to George Von Elm.

My reason for regarding my failure in the British Amateur of 1926 as having been not so dismal involved another circumstance which I have never mentioned until now.

I had been playing fairly well in the early rounds of this tournament and had had a truly exciting streak against the holder, Robert Harris, in the fourth round. My putter had been especially hot, and I had played the first nine holes in thirty-four or thirty-five, despite a double bogie on the seventh hole. Although Bob Harris had played reasonably well, I had won by a considerable margin. My confidence was quite high, and I feared no one left in the field except Jess Sweetser, who was in the opposite bracket and could not be encountered before the final round.

This confidence was to get a rude shock when I awoke on the following morning, for in the act of lifting my head off the pillow, I pulled a grievous crick in my neck. I had been sleeping on my left side, and as I lifted my head, I felt, and I am sure heard, the muscle up the left side of my neck give a loud, rasping creak like a rusty hinge. I realized in a flash that this was likely to be the end of my participation in that tournament.

Then came what I think was the most difficult decision I ever had to make with respect to a golf tournament—whether to play the match or default. Keeler and I were rooming together, so I told him of my trouble, making him promise that on no account would he ever say anything about it. It would certainly not be fair, should I decide to play, to impose upon my opponent the burden of playing against a disabled man, nor would it be sporting to deprive him of the credit for a victory should he gain it. I only feel it justifiable to mention the matter now because my opponent that day, Andrew Jamieson, played exceptionally well, two under par for the number of holes the match lasted, and would probably have beaten me anyway; and because I think it illustrates an interesting point with respect to golfing competition.

I still had not made up my mind when I arrived at the golf course.

Naturally, I did not relish the prospect of playing a tournament match when I knew that I should be severely handicapped. But I hated to give up after having come so far, especially when I had been playing well up to that point. If I should manage to scramble through this round, there was a chance, although a slim one I admit, that the trouble in my neck might abate some by the next day.

There being no practice ground at Muirfield, I took Keeler and my caddy with me and walked a hundred or so yards down the eighteenth fairway to hit a few balls back toward the tee in order to test my neck. A congested muscle in either side of the neck, or in either shoulder, is bad enough, but this one was in the left side, which is the ultimate because of the stretching produced by a full windup in the backswing. I could not lift my hands as high as my neck, and I am sure that the abbreviation seemed much greater to me than it appeared to an onlooker.

Just hitting a few balls with a brassie told the story. I was being called to the tee, and there was no need for further delay anyway. So the decision had to be made while I walked that last hundred yards. I resolved it in this way. A golf tournament has to be played on dates fixed well in advance. A golf match cannot be postponed like a boxing match until both contestants are fit for competition. It is the player's business to come to the tournament not only in proper practice insofar as his golf is concerned, but also in proper physical condition. If I had failed in either respect, it was the fault of no one but myself. I would go out and do the best I could, so long as I could lift the club at all.

As I have said, Jamieson played a beautiful round of golf, so much as was needed to beat me four and three. A little-known player before, his performance at Muirfield won for him a place on the British Walker Cup Team, in which capacity he again acquitted himself nobly at St. Andrews, during the following week. It was certainly no discredit and no accident to be beaten by a player of his ability. On the other hand, I was left with some reason for believing that things might have been different had I remained fit.

After 1926, the first opportunity to play in all four championships would come in 1930, when the United States Walker Cup Team would return to Great Britain. I think the Grand Slam idea must have been somewhere in the back of my head from that time on.

In 1929 the Amateur Championship was played at Pebble Beach in California. In connection with this tournament there were two happenings which may have had significance for me in the 1930 year.

One, of course, was my defeat in the first round of the championship by Johnny Goodman. The other was a visit to Douglas Fairbanks, Sr., at his studio while he was at work on a picture.

I assure you that it would have been very difficult at the time to convince me that my defeat by Goodman might in any sense be regarded as a blessing in disguise. Yet I am not so certain that it was not. I had always had a dread of eighteen-hole matches because I considered the run to be too short. On a good many occasions I had barely escaped being eliminated in the early rounds by players not regarded as having much chance to beat me. So when the thing I had feared so much became a reality, I felt that I had sort of gotten something out of my system and found in fact that it was not so bad after all. It may seem a nebulous thing, but golfers are funny that way, and I feel that it is entirely possible that this may have helped a great deal in adjusting my attitude toward eighteen-hole matches in the following year.

Also from this Goodman match, I think I had come to a realization that even though eighteen holes did not provide as long a run as thirty-six, at the same time eighteen holes constituted a round of golf, and there was still ample time within that round for the assertion of any superiority a player might possess.

I had been more than normally nervous at the beginning of the Goodman match and had failed to shake this nervousness as quickly as had been my experience before. It endured to a disagreeable degree through the first three holes, all of which I lost, the first two on my own misplays, the third on a good birdie putt by Johnny; but on the fourth tee, or going to it, I gave myself a very brisk mental shaking-up, and from that point on, I managed to play a semblance of what I had a right to call my game. Yet, in looking back on it, I realized that I really lost the match because I was in too big a hurry to overcome Goodman's lead and to seize command. After winning back two holes of the next three with birdies, I went too resolutely for a putt for a two at the short seventh, ran past, and missed coming back. So instead of being one down at this point, as more conservative play would have assured, I found myself again two down. I got these back by the time we finished the tenth hole, but threw away another opportunity on the twelfth by again being too bold, this time with my second shot, so that a hole I should have won finally resulted in a half, only because I was successful in jumping a stymie. Then came the crusher at the fifteenth.

The fifteenth hole at Pebble Beach is a very long par five dogleg to the right. I hit two good wood shots, leaving me fifty or sixty yards from the green. Goodman hit a short drive and pulled his second off into the rough under a tree. It seemed that the hole was in my pocket. Johnny played a very good recovery shot from the rough, a low, running shot which was the only chance the presence of the tree allowed him. But he was still some twenty yards short of the green in three. It was here that I cooked my own goose.

The hole was cut very closely behind the bunker in front of the green, and I had to play over it to get close. Johnny had an open shot from the right side, and I had become accustomed to seeing him regularly get down in two from such positions. I wanted desperately to get my nose out in front, because I figured once there, I could stand off any challenge Goodman might make. So I elected to try to get close to the pin over the intervening bunker. I got the shot a little heavy and dumped it into the sand. Johnny, as I had feared, pitched up quite close, and when I failed to get down in two from the bunker, it was he who went ahead instead of me. As I look back at it now, I know it was impatience as much as anything else that caused me to lose the match—impatience born of my feeling that eighteen holes was too short a run. Had I been merely content to keep the pressure on, the holes might very well have run out on my opponent.

Whether or not Johnny Goodman should be thanked for the result, it is true that never afterward did I face an eighteen-hole match with fear and trembling just because it was at eighteen holes. I was to feel nervous again, and there would be times when I found the short route distasteful, but from that day on, I was able to play all matches in the same way.

From Douglas Fairbanks we picked up a game which I think played an important part in getting me into acceptable physical condition a bit earlier in the year than was my custom.

I have never believed in going into any sort of severe or strenuous training for a golf tournament. The condition of one's nerves and mental attitude is so much more important, within reasonable limits, than the state of his physical condition. I think it is a mistake to be too finely drawn at the beginning of a tournament, and that it's a good idea to have a few extra pounds available as a sort of nerve cushion. I discovered long ago that it was far more helpful to me to spend the last day before a tournament lolling about my hotel room reading a book and taking things easy, rather than being out at the golf club playing the course and listening to all the chatter. Obviously, though, it is not helpful even to a golfer to carry fifteen or so extra pounds into the start of a strenuous campaign.

It had been my habit for years to give up any sort of regular golf-playing in the fall of the year and to begin again in April or early May. Golf in raw weather, which we have even in the South, is not much fun, anyway. So the necessity for exchanging golf clubs for schoolbooks or law-books was never too irksome.

But in this year, 1930, the fireworks were to begin in May with the Walker Cup Matches, rather than in mid-June with the Open Championship. It behooved me, therefore, to avoid picking up the usual extra weight during the winter layoff. The game we had seen Fairbanks playing seemed ideal for the purpose, and he had sent me a complete set of equipment as a much appreciated gesture of friendship.

The game had been christened "Doug," in honor of its inventor. It was played with light tennis rackets and heavy shuttlecocks, and was quite obviously an adaptation of badminton. The court was of somewhat larger size, and the net a bit lower. Several alterations in badminton rules encouraged longer rallies, and so made for a good bit more movement. The old Atlanta Theatre was in disuse, and being owned by one of my friends, its stage provided an ideal site for our court. We played this game for an hour or so almost every afternoon after work and often in the evenings after dinner. It did not make me a race horse, but it did keep my weight down.

Throughout all this period, although I was not playing golf, golf was my paramount concern. I was thinking about the coming year, and since I needed to be at top form a couple of months earlier than usual, I determined to make another departure from my normal habits. I decided to play in two winter tournaments against the pros as a sort of warmup, one in Savannah and the other later in Augusta.

My first venture in Savannah was the only unsuccessful sally of the 1930 season. I did well enough for a first try, but was beaten out in the end by Horton Smith.

Horton had been very much the hot rock of the winter tour up to that point, having won a great many tournaments, several in succession. It was obvious that he was the up-and-coming young professional.

I have forgotten exactly how it came about, whether Horton invited me or I him, or one of our mutual friends arranged it. In any event, Horton and I shared a room at the hotel during the practice and the tournament, a circumstance for which I have long been grateful. It was the beginning of a long and close friendship, which has been a rich experience for me. Both on and off the golf course, Horton has always been a model of his profession and a credit to golf.

Of course, we two roommates had a very good time together. I think we both liked one another from the beginning, and we had a lot of fun talking golf, practicing swings, and exchanging pointers in the room and going to movies in the evening after dinner. But the tournament soon developed, if it had not been so from the very beginning, into a very keen personal duel between Smith and me. To the others it may have been just another golf tournament, but to us it was a great deal more than that. We were never paired together, even for one round, but we were each at all times acutely aware of the other's presence on the golf course.

I began with a sixty-seven, which was at that time the record for the course, while Smith was doing seventy-one. In the second round he lowered my record by one stroke with a sixty-six, and I had a misadventure with a tree on the second hole, which cost me a seven, with the result that I posted a seventy-five.

On the morning of the final day in the third round, I got a few putts down, holed one chip shot, and again lowered the record with a sixty-five, while Horton with seventy came in to lunch just as I was going out, with the totals deadlocked between us.

He beat me on the last two holes. The seventeenth was a par five, and in trying to reach the green with my second, I hooked the ball out of bounds and wound up with a six. I managed a birdie three on the last hole, but Horton, coming along some thirty minutes later, finished with two fours to beat me out by one stroke—278 to 279. My prize, incidentally, was a handsome Parker 12-gauge double-barrel shotgun which gave me a lot of pleasure for many years afterward.

My next encounter with Smith and the rest of the pros on the tour came in the Southeastern Open in Augusta in March of 1930. In this tournament I played the best golf I ever played in any tournament before or since, and even after an appalling finish on the last three holes, won by thirteen strokes.

It must be said, however, in all fairness, that Horton in this tournament was performing under a tremendous handicap. The sponsors had been so eager to renew the duel between Smith and me that they had managed to persuade Horton to return for the tournament, even though his schedule had not included it. There was a financial inducement involved, of course. Nevertheless, Smith had to fly by small open airplane from Washington, D.C., to Augusta and was forced to play on two different golf courses, neither of which he had ever seen.

The two courses used for this tournament were both good golf courses and good tests. The main difficulty, however, lay in the putting greens, which were so keen they positively shone in the bright sunlight. Someone remarked that when he walked out on the green he was fearful that his feet would skid out from under him. The test was fully as much one of self-control and a putting touch as it was of ability to play the other shots.

This time Smith and I were paired together for the first two rounds. We had a nice time with golf which, while not scintillating, was quite good and adequately appreciated by a large gallery. I was more than well satisfied with my game, which was marred only by a stupid performance off the sixteenth tee. I had just drawn a full brassie shot past the corner of a bunker and holed a good putt for an eagle three at the fifteenth and was really beginning to feel my oats. I stepped quickly up to the sixteenth tee and promptly hit a very solid, perfectly straight shot out of bounds. I realized that I had hit the drive without ever once looking down the fairway—just the sort of thing that can happen when you relax your alertness or concentration for one instant.

Anyway, my seventy-two–seventy-two gave me a short lead which I increased with a sixty-nine the following morning at Forest Hills. Smith again had to bow to the exigencies of a tight schedule and take an early starting time so that he could fly back to Washington to resume his professional chores. He had just finished his final round when I arrived at the course to start my own.

At this point it was apparent that I had only to do a reasonable round in order to win. After I had played the first three holes the question of winning became of no consequence. I had started with three threes, the first and last of which had been birdies and the middle one an eagle. I dropped a stroke at the short fourth, but picked up another on the way to the turn, which I reached in thirty-two. I began home with a birdie three at the tenth, hit the flag on the twelfth with my tee shot for a two, and finally arrived at the sixteenth tee needing three pars for a sixty-six and a clear lead of eighteen strokes.

At this point I got another golf lesson, though this time not from a golfer. The sixteenth hole was a short hole of approximately 175 yards. Play had become quite congested at this point so that there were three or four pairs ahead of us on the tee waiting to play. Being understandably not vastly disturbed about the progress of the tournament, or rather the result of the tournament, I lay down on the ground under a tree to chat with Grantland Rice and Ty Cobb. Every few minutes Ty would urge me to get up, swing a club, keep warm, do something, all of which very good advice I would laugh off and then keep on talking to and listening to Grant.

But the wait stretched on and on until it exceeded a half hour. I finally got on the tee, hooked a tee shot into the woods, pitched into a bunker, and wound up with a five. With great difficulty, I achieved a par five on the seventeenth and again hooked into the woods for a finishing six on the last hole.

From there we went to Ty's house for a drink, where I got the dressing-down of my life. It was not Ty's idea just to win, but to win by the most you could. That's what had made him such a great baseball player. He was wrong this time, though. My trouble had not come from a muscular chill, but mental complacency.

So the preliminary skirmishes were out of the way in reasonably satisfactory fashion. One had been lost and one won, but the one I had won was exceedingly gratifying. In particular, I had picked up a little trick from Horton Smith that had worked a considerable improvement in my short-iron play, especially with the mashie-niblic. The trick was to give my wrists a little extra cocking at the very beginning of the downward stroke. Almost miraculously, this barely perceptible movement seemed to assure that I would strike the ball a crisply descending blow. It is a fact that from Augusta onward during the 1930 season, my pitching was better than it ever had been before.

Since this was a Walker Cup year, the team match at Royal St. George's Sandwich provided the first order of business on the other side of the water.

Although this was not an individual competition and had no relationship at all to the goal I had set for myself, a team competition such as this imposes a strain all its own. One feels very keenly his responsibility to his teammates. Especially is this a bit punishing in the foursome matches.

The foursome form of play is not well known, nor well appreciated in this country. The form provides that the two players on a side alternate from hole to hole in playing the initiating stroke from the tee, and on each hole, play alternate strokes on the same ball. To my way of thinking, it is a far better test and a more enjoyable method of play than the four-ball match so popular in this country, in which each player plays his own ball throughout, counting the better ball of the side on each hole. The testing quality of the foursome arises from two factors: first, through the green the player probably will be playing shots of unaccustomed length, because of having had someone else do the driving; and second, because, although you may not be concerned too much to put your own ball into a bunker, you dislike to impose the recovery obligation upon your partner. Since the relatively slow pace of golf allows so much time for thinking, imagining, and worrying, responsibilities such as these immeasurably increase the pressure on the player. The effectiveness of a partnership in foursome play depends in large measure upon the degree of understanding between the partners.

As Captain of the United States Team, it was my duty to assign partners to the foursome play, as well as to decide in what order the pairs should be placed. This is about the only place where the captain of a golf team has an opportunity to affect the play in one way or another beyond his own participation in the matches. Perhaps I was just a wee bit grateful to the foursome idea for providing some reason for my existence.

Yet here again, most of the pairings were obvious. The only one for which I care to claim any least degree of inspiration was in my own pairing of myself with Dr. Willing. Doc was the most inclined of all our boys to be a bit unorthodox. He was a short hitter but very straight, a very good man around the greens, with an aggressive, competitive attitude. If there should be any question of any two of our players working well together in double harness, the problem would involve Dr. Willing. I, therefore, resolved to take him myself because I happened to like Doc very much, and I thought he liked me.

As a matter of fact, we probably made the most effective team on the side, insofar as the scoring was concerned, for Doc Willing's play was absolutely flawless, and to him goes most of the credit for the result we obtained. Although we were playing in third position, I think we would have acquitted ourselves just as well at the head of the parade.

The other pairings were pretty obvious. Von Elm with Voigt playing number one, Johnston and Ouimet playing number two, and Moe and McKenzie playing number four. As a matter of record, our side lost only two matches, one in the foursomes when Von Elm and Voigt were beaten two up by Cyril Tolley and Roger Wethered, and Francis Ouimet lost in the singles to Tony Torrance.

There was a brief interlude between the Walker Cup Matches at Sandwich and the Amateur Championship at St. Andrews. This provided an opportunity for the members of both teams to join with a number of other very good British amateur golfers in a delightful one day competition for the Golf Illustrated Gold Vase at Sunningdale. There was nothing serious about the competition. Players were allowed to choose their own playing partners, and within certain limits, their own starting times. I had the good fortune to play with my old friend Dale Bourne, who had a year or two before won the English Amateur Championship and was a delightful playing companion.

There is a story about Dale which I should doubt if it were told with respect to anyone else, but for him it seems perfectly plausible.

The story goes that Dale had reached the final of the French Amateur Championship being played on a course near Paris. He had been out quite late the night before the final, which was to be played at thirty-six holes. On going to bed he had failed to leave a call, so that he only awakened at ten o'clock, the exact time at which he was due on the first tee.

In the most apologetic manner he rang the club, got his opponent on the telephone, and said, "Terribly sorry, old chap. A bit late, you know. Tell you what, I will concede you the first nine holes and meet you on the tenth tee in an hour and a half." The story does not relate the result of the match, or even whether the proposal was accepted.

In the morning round this day at Sunningdale, I am afraid that Dale and I were enjoying ourselves a little too much. Our golf was not good, the play was very slow, and our attitudes anything but competitive. Certainly I was not playing Sunningdale as I had in 1926. My morning score was a very poor seventy-five, and Dale's several strokes higher.

At luncheon I got to thinking that it was a pretty silly thing to play in any sort of golf tournament without trying hard to win it. Yet I realized that I was going to have a hard time shaking myself out of the lethargy of indifference I had permitted to take possession of me. The Walker Cup contest, although not exactly grueling, is nevertheless of considerable importance and takes something out of the reserve nerve supply. I was looking forward to a tough week at St. Andrews and was enjoying a little relief from the competitive strain. Nevertheless a very good young Irish golfer, the former Honorable Brownlow, then Lord Lurgen, was leading the field at the halfway point with a sixty-nine. It was obvious that if I were to overtake him, it would require some doing.

So, not that the amount of money was important, but merely to give me some sort of focus for the recapture of my concentration, I made a bet of one English pound, a "quid" he called it, with Dale that I would "break seventy" in the afternoon round. It worked quite well. I managed to get back into an aggressive attitude toward the game, and after hitting two very good wood shots to the green on the first hole, managed to get around in sixty-eight with a five at the last hole when the issue had already been settled.

The morning leader, playing just a couple of holes ahead of me, had come in with one stroke more than my total. This was just another example of the futility of trying to play golf in a casual way. Even though the competition was more for good fellowship than for the record, it was nevertheless pleasant to have another trophy.

CHAPTER *11*

The British Amateur—The Most Important Tournament of My Life

O So to St. Andrews to begin in earnest the quest for the Grand Slam. If, with respect to this tournament, I should adduce more detail than appears to be warranted, it is because I have soberly concluded that this was the most important tournament of my life. Without it, I should never even in a lifetime have won this one of the four major championships of the golf world and the Grand Slam would have died aborning. Besides, the winning of it included more interesting, dramatic matches than any tournament in my experience.

Beginning with the puzzled dislike I had felt for the Old Course when I first played it in 1921, by 1930 I had come to love it. I thought that I appreciated its subtleties. I had taken great pains to learn the location of all the little pot bunkers and felt that I had a complete familiarity with all the devious little slopes and swales which could deflect well-intended shots in such exasperating ways. I may have been flattering myself, yet I felt very confident that I should encounter no opponent having an advantage over me on the score of local knowledge. Truly, if I had had to select one course upon which to play the match of my life, I should have selected the Old Course. Whether or not this confidence was justified was really beside the point; it was unquestionably good for my morale.

A few days after the conclusion of this championship O. B. Keeler said to me, "Son, it took you a long time to win this thing, but when you did win it, you managed to extract every possible ounce of drama from the performance."

I don't recall exactly what I replied, but it could have been that my concern had not been to extract the drama, but to extricate myself from the many perilous situations I encountered on the way. Certain it was that on four of the five days on which I competed, I had had to fight for my golfing life, and a bad turn of the ball either way would have dashed my hopes in no uncertain fashion.

It all began for me on Monday of the tournament week in the first round. I was drawn against a player from Nottingham named Sid Roper. About all anyone seemed to know of Roper beyond his habitat was that he was a very ordinary golfer. And I was told by one of my friends who professed to know him that he would most likely not play any hole better than five.

Throughout all the years I had engaged in golfing competition, I had held a notion that I could make a pretty fair appraisal of the worth of an opponent simply by speaking to him on the first tee and taking a good measuring look into his eyes. I don't mean that I could form any opinion as to his ability to hit golf shots, but I thought I could tell whether or not he would be likely to play his best game under pressure.

What I observed of Mr. Roper in this respect was not at all reassuring. He had a very clear, steady look in his eyes; his manner and his bearing were quite composed, and he had the look not only of a competitor, but of a golfer as well. When he struck his first tee shot, he looked even more like both. His swing was polished, compact, and assured. I knew right then that I was in for a real game, and how glad I am that I did have this knowledge!

At the very beginning of play for the Grand Slam, I had one great stroke of good fortune. I started my first round 3, 4, 3, 2, 4 against par figures of 4, 4, 4, 4, 5. I holed a good putt for a three at the first, pitched almost dead for a three at the third, holed a shot of 120 yards from a bunker at the fourth for a double-eagle two, and reached the long fifth in two to pick up another birdie. Roper played each one of the five holes very precisely in four each; so at the end of five holes, I was five under par, and only three up. What's more, my opponent had not turned a whisker and was playing fine golf shots as though he could keep on doing so forever.

After this blazing beginning it was only humanly expectable that I should falter some. The very fortunate thing is that I did not falter much. With a five on the par-three eighth hole, occasioned by being laid an unmakable stymie, I was out in thirty-three. And when the match ended on the sixteenth green, I had two fours left for sixty-eight, which, even with the stymie, would have equaled the amateur record I had set three years earlier.

Mr. Roper, who had been expected to play few holes under five, had actually required that many strokes on only one, the sixteenth, which he three-putted. The other fifteen he played in four each. On the basis of comparative scores I think he would have won from any other player in the field in that round. I know he would have beaten me on any other day of the tournament, except possibly on the morning of the final match.

And there you have one of the major uncertainties of a golf tournament. In order to win you must play your best golf when you need it most, and play your sloppy stuff when you can afford it. I shall not attempt to explain how you achieve this happy timing.

From the start, and even before play commenced, everyone around St. Andrews seemed to be looking forward to the possible meeting of Cyril Tolley and me on Wednesday afternoon. Of course, we both had to win two matches in the interim, but this had seemed quite likely of accomplishment when we expected Mr. Roper to shoot fives. Cyril, too, had a narrow escape in the first round, but he also managed to make it.

This was very definitely one eighteen-hole match, into which I went with the complete realization of its vast import and difficulty. I had won from Cyril by a very wide margin over this same course in the Walker Cup Matches of 1926, but that had been over thirty-six holes. Jimmy Johnston had also beaten him in the singles of the Walker Cup recently completed at Sandwich.

But no one had any illusions about Cyril. He had always been a fearsome competitor in this championship. He had won it for the second time the year before, and so would carry with him the very considerable prestige and responsibility of the defending champion. He was a big, powerful player with an exquisite touch in the short game, and in my opinion the most dangerous man I could possibly meet in an eighteen-hole match at St. Andrews.

Added to this, on the dawning of the day upon which the match was to be played, the conditions of nature were precisely those to cause me greatest concern. The greens were hard and fast and the wind was blowing toward the sea at something more than half a gale. Sand was

With Tolley at St. Andrews. Waiting for a large gallery to be cleared from the fairway increases the pressure on the players. This was no tea party.

being whipped from the bunkers, and spectators and players alike were seeking refuge behind the dunes and whins whenever a lull in the play developed. St. Andrews was in real truth St. Andrews on such a day, and the test was more of resourcefulness in maneuvering than of regularity in playing standard golf shots.

Some years later, Bernard Darwin wrote of the match:

> Yet even this, paled before his battle with Cyril Tolley. Every man, woman and child in St. Andrews went out to watch it, and Mr. Gerard Fairley was quite right to set the scene of the murder in one of his stories on the afternoon of that match. There would have been ample opportunity to commit several murders and escape undetected through the lonely streets, though stained with the marks of crime. Never was there more perceptible the silence of expectation, that lull before the storm in which men speak instinctively in whispers, and Cyril gave it, if possible, a more thrilling emphasis, since he began with a full-blooded top from the first tee. It was ominous, but it was no presage of disaster, for he played finely afterwards and a dog-fight on a magnificent scale ensued which delighted everyone, save other poor wretches who were trying to play their own insignificant matches. Each man, seeing the mighty flood approach him, must needs crouch over his ball,

The green of the famous 17th or Road Hole at St. Andrews as it appeared in my day, except that the restraining fence across the road was not then in existence.

guarding it as best he might, and pick himself up again when the torrent had swept over him. The most discussed shot in the match was Bobby's second to the Road Hole, as to which hundreds are prepared to take their oath that the ball would have been on the road if it had not hit a spectator, and an equal number of witnesses are quite certain that it would not. I was there, but was running for my life, with my head well down at the moment, and can offer no opinion. The hole was halved, so was the last, and Bobby won at the nineteenth where his adversary played a rather loose second and was punished by a stymie. Exactly how good the golf was, I cannot now remember, for there are occasions when that is of secondary importance. It was the devil of a match.

Nor have I any real recollection of how good the golf was, that is, in total, but I have graven on my soul, I think, the completely brutal ferocity of that man-to-man contest. Cyril and I had been very good friends for many years before that day, and we have remained fast friends ever since. I know that that match still stands in his memory, as it does in mine, as an afternoon when each of us called upon every resource in an all-out effort to beat the other. There was nothing of the dilettante in either one of us. I think we both have found at other times something of the aesthetic in golf, but we would have none of it that day. I know I felt the same exultation and desperate urgency I should expect to feel in a battle with broadswords or cudgels. And after it was all over, when I said I felt six years older, I was perpetrating a masterpiece of understatement. It was the kind of match in which each player plays himself so completely out that at the end the only feeling to which he is sensitive is one of utter exhaustion.

As for the golf, I have the score cards before me. They are not exciting. They are as follows:

JONES	4	5	4	5	5	4	4	3	5	39		
TOLLEY	5	4	4	4	5	4	5	4	3	38		
JONES	4	4	5	3	4	3	5	4	4	36	39	75
TOLLEY	4	5	4	4	3	5	4	4	4	37	38	75

Yet I also have the cards of other leading matches played at the same time. The figures of our match look very good in comparison. The truth,

I think, is that our golf from a match-play standpoint, under the harrowing conditions, was fully as good as could have been expected. There is no way to exaggerate the difficulty of the Old Course on that Wednesday afternoon. As the match itself was primitive, I think the playing conditions must have been also.

As a few examples, Tolley drove the ninth green, 306 yards; we both overdrove the twelfth, 314 yards. With the gale at our backs, neither was able to hold the green with the tee shot at the short eighth, the ground being just as hard, in another sense, as the wind. Playing the short eleventh, in the opposite direction, Tolley hit a strong iron which at one time was hovering above the green, yet was blown back to the fairway short of Strath bunker, where he found it half-embedded in wind-blown sand. In my effort to avoid a similar fate I played too strongly over the green onto the bank of the Eden River. I remember watching Cyril playing from this loose sand-on-turf and thinking how simple it would be for him to fluff the ball into Strath bunker. Actually he fluffed it only a few feet, and then into the bunker, whence he emerged with a great shot to get a five but lose the hole to my four.

The putting, too, was as difficult as could be imagined. The greens were as keen as glass and had been somewhat scarred by the heavy traffic of players. On every putt, account had to be taken of the wind effect, as well as of the breaks and irregularities in the putting surface. In consideration of all circumstances, I think neither Cyril nor I has reason to be ashamed of the figures we produced.

In sixteen holes the match had been brought back from one down to even six times, with the two players alternating in taking the lead. The play on the seventeenth, the famous Road Hole, is still being discussed. That it was a break for me is undeniable. Just how colossal a break it was will perhaps never be known. The facts, as agreed by Cyril and me, along with all observers known to me whom I consider to be competent because of their opportunities, are as follows:

The two drives, with the wind behind, were long, with Cyril out in front. My ball lay near the left side of the fairway, his about center, or maybe a little right-center.

The hole was cut back of the road bunker so that it was entirely shut off from my position and only barely open to Cyril.

Playing the odd, my second was an iron to the left of the road bunker which bounded into the mass of spectators, and dropped on the apron at the back of the green, a few feet off the putting surface.

Great Britain in 1930. Even in championship play, the attitude indicates naturalness and physical relaxation, no matter how taut the nerves may be. The lady in the front row on the left is Diana Fishwick, then British lady champion.

Tolley's second was short and curled off the slope at the front of the green, stopping in a position leaving the bunker between his ball and the flag.

I, being away, chipped to a distance of approximately eight feet from the cup.

Tolley's little pitch dropped exactly on the only possible spot, barely over the bunker, at the top of a slope running down to the hole. His ball stopped within two feet of the cup.

I holed the eight-footer and Cyril, of course, holed his for the half.

The point of controversy was and is, "Where would my ball have finished had it not been stopped by the crowd? Would it have finished on the eighteenth tee or in the rough beyond the eighteenth tee, or would it have gone into the road?" No one knows, or ever will.

If the ball would have gone into the road, the stopping of it definitely saved for me the hole and the match. If the ball would have stopped either on the eighteenth tee or in the rough beyond, I think in all reason I could have approached as well as I had chipped.

I think, though, that the really interesting part of the situation lies in having a knowledge of the mental processes of the two players.

Long before this fateful afternoon I had gained a great respect for the famous Road Hole. In the Open Championship of 1927, when in every round it had been within range of the second shot, I had four times played short, relying on a chip and a putt to get a four and refusing to take any risk with the road or the bunker. This time two circumstances were different. A gale of wind was blowing and the ground was quite hard and fast.

With my long tee shot, in order to reach a spot in front of the green from which I could chip to the hole clear of the bunker, it was necessary to play very close to the road and almost directly at it. A small error in judgment or a little extra run on the ball would surely put it into the road. A little less, and I would not have a clear shot at the hole.

I had never heard of anyone playing intentionally past the Road bunker on the left, but after more study than I normally give to a shot I concluded that this was my best chance. At least I should not be playing directly toward the road. If I should succeed in merely sneaking the ball past the Road bunker, I should have a very short, easy chip; and I expected to have an adequate margin for error on the long side.

At least one observer thought that I had played directly into the crowd, knowing that they were packed so densely that the human barricade must stop my ball. This was very definitely not the case. I should never have been so heedless of the possibility of inflicting injury upon a spectator. I made completely audible requests to the stewards to move the crowd back on the left side, and even mounted a high piece of ground to motion them back myself. I played only after several minutes, and after it had become apparent that the crowd could be moved no farther.

I attempted to play a soft shot with a number-four iron, designed, as I have said, barely to pass the bunker. I have a very distinct recollection that as I swung the club I was acutely aware of the prime necessity that the ball should pass the bunker. If it did not, my situation would be hopeless. I know that I gave the shot a little extra nudge. I saw the ball land about even with the bunker and take a bound forward. I know it was strong, but I don't know by how much. Yet I did see it strike a spectator and drop near the green.

Tolley, seeing my ball so well located, decided that in order to save a half, he must go for the flag. This was a more reasonable prospect for him, because he was playing more nearly down the length of the green. But I think as he was swinging, an unwelcome thought intruded. I think he must instinctively have flinched from the road, and so his shot, being a bit weak and with a little curl to it, did not finish as he had intended.

It cannot be stated as a fact, but it is nevertheless my conviction that Tolley's third shot on this hole has never been surpassed for exquisitely beautiful execution. I shall carry to my grave the impression of the lovely little stroke with which he dropped the ball so softly in exactly the right spot, so that in the only possible way it finished dead to the hole. Tolley himself, after the passage of twenty-eight years, confirmed to me that this was the finest shot of his life. I am sure that it was.

It certainly put the seal of necessity on my eight-foot putt. If I had not holed this one, I would not be writing this story. Although it had been as tense a hole as I had ever played in my life, the result only served to increase the pressure. Coming now to the eighteenth all even, there was no room for either of us to make a mistake.

Two long drives down the big wind left us both some ten yards short of the green, with Tolley ahead as he had been all day. Being a bit on the left side, I had to play a run-up through the Valley of Sin, since pitching was out of the question under the conditions. I made too certain of getting through the big swale, which is the Valley, and overran the hole some twenty-five feet. Tolley played up to within a little more than half my distance. I missed my putt but left the ball very close, and then I went through, I think, the most agonizing moments of that entire year.

Tolley was one of those players who had a flair for the spectacular. Although he did it in a different way, he played the game, like Hagen, in the grand manner. As I watched him putt, I remembered that he had holed one longer than this on the thirty-seventh hole at Muirfield to beat Bob Gardner for the 1923 Championship. I fully expected him to hole this one, and there was nothing I could do about it. But he missed, to relieve my agony, and we headed for the nineteenth.

I have always regretted that such a splendid, exciting match should have been decided by a stymie, yet the stymie was an accepted and important part of match-play golf in those days, as indeed I think it should be today and always. And as Tolley himself said, generously but truly, he had left himself wide-open to it. A slack second to the left of the green and a weak chip had left his ball seven feet short of the hole in three, whereas mine in two lay only ten feet away. Since the two balls were on the same side of the hole, when my very careful putt stopped only a couple of inches short, the hole was completely shut off to anything but a miracle.

The great battle had ended and the release from the tension was almost unbearable. I was neither exultant nor elated, just very, very tired. I suspected that Cyril felt the same way.

That seventeenth hole, the playing of which I have described so painstakingly, proved to be a decisive hole in every one of the perilous

Police escort back from the 19th hole of the Tolley match. It seems I am being carried, as I am sure I wished to be.

A beautiful and cherished view of the Old Course, St. Andrews. The 18th hole of the Tolley match. I am playing a running approach through the Valley of Sin, while Andrew Kirkaldy holds the pin. The stream in the left background is the Swilken Burn, and the spectators are behind the first green. The course turns right at the second hole and goes out and back between the whins and the railroad tracks. The sheds at the upper left are those over which we drove on the 17th hole. The Eden River is in the far background. The beach belongs to St. Andrews Bay.

matches I had to play in this championship. It is such a famous hole, and so justly so, that I think it merits a full description. I hope the accompanying scale drawing will help the reader to visualize the hole, but nothing except the actual playing of it in a championship can bring one to a full realization of the havoc the road can inflict nor the terror it has for the players.

As will be seen from the drawing, the drive must be over a low-lying shed. In my day, the side of the shed nearer the tee bore the name "D. Anderson" in letters more than a foot high. The proper line on

17TH HOLE OLD COURSE ST. ANDREWS 466 YDS. PAR 5

most occasions was over the "d" in Anderson. Playing in the Walker Cup foursomes in 1926, Andrew Jamieson plunked his tee shot solidly into the side of the shed, out of bounds, so that his partner, Cyril Tolley, had to return some hundred yards from the corner of the fence, which he did in majestic grandeur, exuding indignation from every pore. This started a comical sequence which ended when my partner, Watts Gunn, and I won the hole in seven.

In golf there is a fairly general aversion to blind shots. I don't especially mind blind tee shots such as this one, because the "d" in Anderson and a familiarity with the skyline of the town provide sufficient guideposts. Blind shots to the green, when it is not possible to know the exact location of the flag, are entirely different.

The tee in those days was in the very corner of the fence alongside the railroad. Now, in order to provide passageway for spectators in connection with the modern "Crowd Control," the tee has been moved nearer the second green. The hole may be as good, but it simply is not the same to me.

The green is very narrow, and when the ground is firm, a most precarious target. The irregular terracing in front and on the left side is capable of deflecting the second shot in bewildering directions. The surface of the road is always hard and gravelly, so that to pitch from it with assurance is almost impossible, and the bank separating the road from the green, though only a few feet high, is normally covered with matted grass so that a running attempt is most uncertain. When a ball is played onto the road or into the bunker, the player needs only a very little imagination to see himself going back and forth from one to the other. It has been done more than once in important championships. In most circumstances, even though the green is easily reachable in two shots, the wisest course is to play for the short edge.

It seemed that in this championship all of my troubles came in the afternoon. Maybe that was the reason O. B. Keeler made his comment about the drama I had extracted from the tournament. My morning matches were all uneventful. Perhaps Keeler meant to accuse me of waiting for the afternoon crowds to arrive before getting myself into trouble.

After my ordeal with Tolley on Wednesday afternoon, I was glad to be permitted to survive Thursday morning with no more than ordinary pressure. I was to play Jimmy Johnston, the American Amateur champion, that afternoon and was completely aware that I would have to be at my best to win.

As a member of the U.S.G.A. committee, I had refereed the match in which Johnston had beaten George Voigt on the thirty-eighth hole on his way to winning the Amateur Championship at Pebble Beach. As Captain of the American Walker Cup Team at Sandwich, I had had no qualms about awarding the number-one spot in the singles to Jimmy and had had my judgment vindicated when he beat Cyril Tolley. I was, in truth, looking for another bout like the one the day before.

It seemed for a long while, though, that Jimmy was going to be reasonably co-operative. I was out in even par, playing well enough, but not holing any putts. At this point, I was one up. Starting for home with a birdie three at ten, I won three of the first four incoming holes, and so stood four up with five to play. No one could blame me, I think, for feeling fairly comfortable at this stage.

But then Jimmy began to put on one of his characteristically strong finishes. He took the fourteenth with a well-played birdie four, accepted the fifteenth, which I messed up badly, holed a good putt for a half at the sixteenth, and then won the seventeenth with a daring four, while I left my ball short, with the Road bunker between it and the hole. Again it was that seventeenth getting into the act, but this time not on my side.

Going to the eighteenth hole one up is better than being all even at this point, but anything can happen at St. Andrews and I was not too happy. I was less so when I needed a curling, eight-foot putt to avoid having to go to the nineteenth hole. It was a very pretty sight when I saw my ball take the last break in the green and run precisely into the center of the cup.

On Friday morning, the last day of the eighteen-hole matches, my opponent was a very good young English player, Eric Fiddian. I played quite well against Fiddian, being one under par for the first nine, at which point I was four up. With every hole exactly in par coming home, the holes ran out at the fifteenth green, where I won by four and three.

But here I made a mistake off the golf course which almost cost me the championship between rounds.

Never before had I touched a drop of alcohol before playing a tournament round. I had occasionally played a friendly round, or even an exhibition, after taking a cocktail or two before lunch. But I had never even thought of doing such a thing when playing in a tournament.

But this time I was tired. My morning match had ended early and my afternoon opponent, George Voigt, had started his morning match somewhat later than I. It was going to be a long wait before this very important semifinal. Since it was the last eighteen-hole barrier between me and the title I had coveted for so long, the afternoon match held even more than the usual significance. I guess I was just plain nervous.

Anyway, when I got to the hotel and met Mary, my wife, I suggested that we go up to the sitting room on the second floor overlooking the eighteenth green and have a glass of sherry. I felt that it might steady my nerves, quiet the butterflies, or rid me of some of that tired feeling. I knew it was an experiment, but I thought the wine might do when I would not have risked anything stronger. I could not have made a greater mistake. I suppose my keyed-up condition had much to do with it, but the wine flushed my face and caused me to be very keenly aware that my eyes were the slightest bit out of focus. I really began to get panicky as our starting time approached and the condition continued.

I honestly and solemnly declare that I could not get that sherry out of my eyes until more than half the round had been played. George and I halved the first hole in birdie threes, and I holed about a fifteen-foot putt in order to get mine. But the ball slammed into the back of the cup much too hard, and I remember taking a worried practice swing or two afterward in an effort to figure out what was wrong. I played well enough from tee to green, but I kept missing putts all over the place and finally even fluffed a short pitch at the thirteenth hole. When George holed a good putt there to win the hole, I found myself two down with five to play.

There is an old saying that two up with five to play never wins, but I can offer complete assurance that as I walked from the thirteenth green to the fourteenth tee, I held no faith whatever in this maxim. I did not think that Voigt was the kind of player who would toss away this sort of lead, and I was quite certain that I was not capable of the golf needed to wrest it away from him. All I could do was what I did, namely, resolve to swallow the medicine, whatever it might be, and to keep on trying as best I could.

I don't think I can describe my feeling on the next tee when George, driving first into a strong left-hand wind, cut his tee shot over the stone wall, out of bounds. With the stroke and distance penalties, this was just exactly the same as handing the hole to me on a silver platter. Never was a gift so unexpected nor so eagerly accepted. With that one stroke I was hauled back into the golf game. One down with four to play is vastly different from two down with five to play.

Voigt slipped again at the fifteenth, and I had a putt of six feet to square the match, but missed it. But at the sixteenth, another cut tee shot put my opponent in the Principal's Nose bunker from which he could not recover. Now it was all even coming again to the famous Road Hole.

The state of the match was exactly the same as it had been at this point with Tolley on Wednesday. However, the weather conditions were more nearly normal and, without the elements to contend with, there was no need or opportunity to employ anything but ordinary tactics.

In the normally accepted way, therefore, George and I each hit good drives and each played for the front of the green. With the conservatism I usually practiced on this hole, I left my second about five yards short of the putting surface. George, being a bit bolder, almost pushed his ball up onto the top level of the green. It teetered a bit on the brink and then rolled slowly back down to the bottom of the bank, but still lay on the putting surface. My chip down the long green was on line, but I failed to judge the distance accurately, leaving myself a good four yards short. This was not good, but neither was it disastrous, because it was a long way from being certain that Voigt could get down in two.

The uncertainty endured for only a few moments, however. George's ball still lay on the putting surface where he could use his aluminum putter, and he rolled a beauty down the length of the green, stopping it within two feet of the hole.

Again on that seventeenth green I found myself putting for my life. Again it was do or die, sink or swim, now or never, and again the putt went down. As I told Keeler later, I had a strange feeling as I stepped up to make that putt. I suppose it was because I had had so many crucial shots to make during that week and every one had come off. At any rate, when I stepped up to this one, I could see the line as plainly as if it had been marked on the green. I knew before I swung the putter that I would surely hole that putt.

This time the wind was against at the eighteenth and Voigt's shorter drive left him a little too much to do with the second shot. He tried to bang it up to the hole, but again caught the top of the slope so that his ball rolled back to the bottom of the Valley of Sin. My shorter pitch was good, two yards from the flag. George ran up just inside me, I missed for the win, but so did he for the half.

I had had about as hard a week as I could imagine, but had now reached the final and needed only to win one more match over thirty-six holes. This was my game. I held the utmost respect for my opponent, Roger Wethered. But I had to know that all factors, both physical and psychological, were on my side. I felt that I could wear Roger down over the long route simply by keeping up an unremitting pressure. Now that I had come through the eighteen-hole matches without encountering a hot burst of irresistible fireworks, I felt that I could handle any pyrotechnic displays over the long route.

I honestly felt that Roger himself held very little hope of winning. I was not even certain that he cared very much. Roger was a fine golfer and a wonderful sportsman who could be counted on to give his best at all times. But he was also a completely charming person without any semblance of aggressiveness on the golf course. I recall so well the evening in 1921 when he, an amateur, had surprised everyone by finishing in a tie for the Open Championship with Jock Hutchison. I had stood in a group of Roger's friends near the eighteenth green below the cement steps going up to the clubhouse and had joined in an effort to persuade him that it was more important for him to remain over to participate in a play-off for the Open Championship than to return home for a neighborhood amateur cricket match in which he had agreed to play the next day. Our arguments finally prevailed, but remembering that little session convinced me that Roger thought golf championships were very nice things, but it was plain that he did not want to win them as badly as I did.

The final match went as nearly according to plan as any match I ever played. I began by looking a bit silly on the first hole when I hit my mashie-niblic pitch a bit fat and left the ball short of the burn. No harm resulted, however, because I chipped the next one close and holed the putt for a half in four.

After that one lapse at the beginning, I played along as smoothly as I could have wished. I didn't hole any putts, but I made no costly mistakes, nor even any which caused me concern. The first nine was taken in eight fours and one three, all being pars except the four on the long fifth hole. The match was even. Roger slipped once on the third hole, but made up for it by playing his second to within a foot of the hole, from the heather on the right of the sixth fairway. It was the kind of match I enjoyed. I was not getting anywhere very fast, but I was playing easily and most of the time leaving my opponent to do the work.

The break I had been expecting came on the tenth hole. After I holed for a four from about six feet, Roger missed from a foot closer. As he turned after picking up his ball, I thought I read in his face his belief that he could not keep this up much longer. Two pars on eleven and twelve resulted in halves, then a string of four fours was good enough to win four holes in a row, so that I came to the Road Hole this time five up. Again the famous hole produced an incident, but this time more amusing than otherwise.

The wind was against, and Wethered, after hooking his drive, played a magnificent brassie shot right onto the middle of this treacherous green, five yards from the hole. This left me with nothing to do but take the chance myself. My wood second rolled into the Road bunker.

Someone had told me that the Old Course had never been played in competition without at least one five on the card. As I neared the finish of this round with nothing but fours and threes, I began to have an ambition to be the first to accomplish this feat. The seventeenth was now the last remaining problem.

My ball was lying quite cleanly on the white, powdery sand and the hole, cut between the bunker and the road, was only a short distance away. It was the one shot in golf I could play better than any other.

Since the shot required no study and no preparation, as soon as I saw the position of the ball, I pulled a niblic out of the bag and stepped up to play without any hesitation whatever. This must have taken the gallery stewards by surprise, for suddenly they rushed over and began moving spectators off the edge of the green near the road. The angle that appealed to me as funny was that the rush of the stewards had been so spontaneous and ingenuous that it was quite obvious that there was absolutely no hint of the ulterior purpose of upsetting me. I could appreciate that with the lurid history of the hole, it was unthinkable to them that a man should be allowed to play from the Road bunker without having every opportunity to play into the road, as he might be expected to do. I could not suppress a smile as I stepped back from the ball to allow the stewards to complete their work. Seeing my smile, the crowd and the stewards, too, caught the humor of the situation and all had a good laugh.

When we had had our fun and things had quieted down, I popped the ball onto the green and watched it trickle down the slope and stop four feet from the hole, whereupon I missed the putt and acquired my first five of the round. It was a bitter disappointment.

At the outset of the afternoon round a stymie forced me to take five on the first hole. I picked up another five at the fourth without any aid from the enemy, got it back with a birdie four at the long fifth, and so reached the turn this time one over par and five up. A birdie three at the tenth made it six, and two more pars closed out the match. I was quite well satisfied with my play in the final. Although my golf had not been devastating, to play thirty holes at St. Andrews in two under fours could certainly be regarded as satisfactory. The figures on the card of five threes, three fives and twenty-two fours were a fair reflection of the round, with nothing stolen and nothing thrown away.

Seven eighteen-hole matches, four of them grueling, and one at thirty-six holes represent a fairly busy week of golf. The British Open was coming up in two weeks, but what I needed most was rest on the physical side and a change of scenery mentally. So Mary and I took off for a week in Paris, where my only golf was a pleasant little round with Jimmy Johnston as my partner against France's best amateur, our friend Andre Vagliano, and the country's leading professional, Marcel Dallemagne. I think Jimmy and I managed to win the match by one hole, if anybody cared.

Winning the British Amateur had meant a lot to me. At St. Andrews immediately after the tournament was over, I must have been too tired to be aware of any sensation except one of relief. During the few days in Paris, though, I had realized that this championship had taken a big load off my chest, or back. Now, even if I should fail to win the British Open, I felt I should be entitled to consider that the expedition to Britain had been a complete success. Even if this should be the only championship won during the year, with it I had now won, at one time or another, all four major championships. I should, therefore, henceforth feel no obligation to myself, or even to Keeler, which was about the same thing, to continue playing in competition unless I felt like it. Finally, the inescapable fact was that I could not win all four without the first one, and this first one had always been for me the most difficult. This one tournament had put me more than one-quarter of the distance on the way to my goal and, in effect, might be said to have put a price support under my crop.

Keeler told me later that he had wondered if I would be able to get myself keyed up for the British Open at Hoylake. I think he could not have been seriously concerned. To my knowledge I have never taken a golf tournament casually. It did not make sense to me to travel three thousand miles for a lark.

CHAPTER *12*

The British Open

O Mary and I came back from Paris about a week before the beginning of the championship at Hoylake. Quite irrelevantly, I remember thinking on the boat coming back across the Channel how good it would be after all that rich French cooking to get back to some cold mutton and boiled potatoes.

Back in England the first order of business was to get through the qualifying for the British Open, which I had a right to expect would be something on the order of a formality. The qualifying was, as before, in two sections. But this year the two courses in use were the championship course, Hoylake, and another nearby, Wallasey.

Here, I should like to adduce a quote I have just run across in an old scrapbook belonging to Mrs. O. B. Keeler. I had not seen it before, but I like it because it so accurately sums up what I think was the true nature of my golf during the eventful year of 1930. It was written by Bob Howard, a top London golf writer of the time. It was written after I had completed the second qualifying round with a total of 150, nine strokes behind Archie Compston and seven behind Henry Cotton, but safely within the necessary limit.

After praising Compston's fine play, Howard wrote as follows:

> Bobby Jones took a turn among the ordinary mortals by compiling a score of 77. It was plenty good enough for qualifying purposes. But although he said he was very dissatisfied with his golf, I am quite sure he could have done considerably better if the need had existed.

Jones on a highly important occasion somehow creates the impression that he is trying about twice as hard as anybody else, and it is precisely this element that seems to produce his world-beating golf.

Today he was playing golf, rather than slaving at it. I dare say he will be as tense as ever when the championship proper begins tomorrow.

His worst patch came when he took 5, 5, 6, for the sixth, seventh and eighth holes. Here, he made just about as many mistakes as he could make in so small a compass.

Next day, however, was the first round of the tournament proper and at its conclusion I found myself with a score of seventy, tied for the lead with Henry Cotton and MacDonald Smith.

I remember being somewhat startled late that afternoon upon returning to Liverpool, where we were staying at the Adelphi Hotel, to see a banner headline in an afternoon paper, "Eight Inches Off a World's Record." To my surprise I found that the headline was related to the round I had played that day. I confess that I had some difficulty appreciating the relevance of it.

To be sure, I had accomplished a very satisfactory round. After the first three holes my shots to the green had been reasonably good, and my putting had been of the kind that at least made for comfort, if not for a very low score. With my first putt I was always leaving the ball so that, as Keeler liked to describe it, "You could cover the ball and the hole with a derby hat." As a consequence I had not had to go through any agonizing struggles with the three- and four-footers. But I had been grateful that I had only had to tap in so many putts for pars, rather than being disappointed, as the British headline had suggested, that more of the longer putts had not gone in.

Hoylake has always been a long, testing course, but singularly lacking in subtleties. I think it could be said to be a long hitter's paradise, because, although the distances are considerable, the ground, on the whole, is quite flat. The whole course is there for the player to see, and I should think that the first time around he ought to know as much about it as he could ever learn.

In some strange way, though, my experience with the course seemed to be precisely opposite to that of my fellow competitors. I seemed to have my trouble where everyone else was holding his own or building up a cushion, and contrarily, I managed to make my hay on the holes that caused others the most trouble.

The first three holes at Hoylake were good holes, but of no extraordinary difficulty. The first two were par fours of moderate length, while the third, of something like 480 yards, could be called a par five, but was in reality easily reachable in two shots. Yet in the first three rounds, the total of my scores on these three holes, played three times, came to a matter of eight strokes over an average of fours. In effect, I had in every round, except the last, hung a weight around my neck before I had fairly got started.

The last five holes at Hoylake averaged over 450 yards, with two of them over the 500 mark. This was at that time reputed to be the most difficult finishing stretch in the world. Others had their trials with it, but for me the contrariness continued, and in every round except one I managed to improve on the card on these holes. Yet because of the first three, every round of this tournament was a struggle.

The second day I added a seventy-two to the seventy of the first round, so that at the halfway point I was leading the field, although only by one stroke over Fred Robson and three over Horton Smith. I had a margin of five over Compston, who had played so well in the qualifying.

Five strokes sounds like an awful lot, but here is what can happen. On the morning of the final day I began my third round 4, 5, 6, and Compston, starting about an hour later, did these first three holes in 4, 3, 4 and then added a 2 at the short fourth where I had taken a par 3. In four holes, my lead of five strokes had vanished completely.

Beginning with the fourth hole, I had managed to settle down and had played the next ten holes with five fours and five threes, so that three over-fours had now become two under, and the prospect of seventy-one or seventy-two for the round quite reasonable.

I can't say whether it had any effect or not, but I do have a very vivid recollection that all during the latter half of that round the cheers from Compston's gallery were ringing in my ears. The American domination of the British Open had been unbroken for a number of years, and it was quite natural that a British crowd should lustily cheer Compston's great play. They must have been confident that the long drought was about to be broken.

In any event the final five holes, which had been so good to me up to this point, for the first time caused me trouble. This time I needed four fives in the stretch of five, and so turned my seventy-one or seventy-two into a seventy-four.

I thought I had done pretty well starting home 3, 3, 4, 3, but Compston went 3, 3, 3, 2 and finished in sixty-eight to take the lead from me by a stroke at 215 to 216.

I can still see the awesome figure made by Compston toward the finish of his round. One of the British writers said that he was playing "like a frenzied giant." A tall, powerful man, Compston was truly striding after the ball as though he could not wait to vent his fury upon it. Watching from the clubhouse as I saw him sweep past the sixteenth green, I had the feeling that spectators, tee boxes, benches even, might be swirled up into his wake. As he left the eighteenth green after his great sixty-eight and made his beaming way to the clubhouse through a myriad of well-wishers, he was about as happy a figure as I have ever seen. At the time I was heading for the first tee to start my final round.

Never, it seemed, at least during that year, was it to be given to me to simply play an ordinary round of golf and then wait to see whether or not it would be good enough. Things just could not be that simple.

Yet it did seem a good omen when I managed for the first time to get past the opening holes in decent figures, especially so, perhaps, because of one outrageous piece of good fortune.

After an uneventful four at the first hole, I hit a high towering drive off the second tee, which I saw coming down a yard or two off the right edge of the fairway into the heavy rough. As I watched the ball descending, I also saw that it was going to land very close to one of the gallery stewards wearing his identifying red skull cap. I have often wondered what that fellow's head had been made of. He was in no wise injured by the impact, but my ball, landing on his head, careened some fifty yards entirely across an adjoining fairway, and finished in a bunker intended to be a hazard for players approaching the fourteenth green. I am unable to say whether or not the accident resulted in my ball being nearer the hole than it would otherwise have been. I do know that it found a very clean lie in the sand which was infinitely preferable to one in the deep rough for which it had been headed.

This second shot from the sand was almost exactly the same shot I had holed on the fourth hole at St. Andrews in the match against Sid Roper. I played the same club and, as nearly as possible, the same shot. This one did not hole out, but it finished about twenty feet from the hole, after which I holed the putt for a birdie three. It was a most auspicious start for the last round.

Having this time safely passed the early holes, I continued on a very comfortable way until I arrived at the eighth tee, needing two fours, which were entirely reasonable, in order to be out in thirty-five. This was the best I had done to this point during the tournament, and I must admit that I was feeling most optimistic. I felt that Compston must inevitably suffer some reaction from his great round of the morning (actually he put himself completely out with an eighty-two), and no one else was close enough to offer serious challenge if I could but put in a reasonably good round.

The eighth hole at Hoylake was of some 480 yards, but I had been consistently either on, or just off, the green in two shots. This time was no exception. After a good drive my spoon second just missed the left edge of the green and rolled off some ten or fifteen yards down an innocent slope. It lay still in the fairway with absolutely nothing between it and the flag.

The events of the next few moments caused much wonderment among the spectators and golfing authorities present. Mr. Darwin said later that a nice old lady with a croquet mallet could have saved me two strokes from this point. Yet I will swear that I took seven on that hole in the most reasonable manner possible.

First, to describe the situation, my ball lay some ten or fifteen yards off the putting surface. The hole was located another five yards, perhaps, beyond the edge of the green. From my ball the fairway sloped upward to the putting surface, and then dropped off in a fairly fast slope to the hole and beyond. The green was quite keen.

I felt that I had done quite well up to this point. I wanted desperately to get that four so that I could take things a bit more easily from that point in. I tried to let my first chip die just onto the edge of the green, hoping that it would roll down close to the hole. I was not willing to play conservatively past the hole with the idea of settling for a five.

The first chip was underplayed and did not quite reach the putting surface. Still, with the same respect for the keen green, I left the second chip some ten feet short of the hole. Trying very hard to save a par at least, I slipped the first putt a foot past the hole, and then, a bit unsettled perhaps, hurriedly tapped the next one—and it didn't go in.

The whole thing was at once so unbelievable, and yet so supremely simple, that it comprised the most perfect example of the potentialities of torment ever-present for the contestant in an Open Championship. I have had a number of such experiences, yet never one which I had any reason whatever to anticipate. Always, it has been possible to look back and to see how they have happened without the commission of any real atrocities. Almost always, they have resulted from a succession of strokes which have not been quite precisely played, plus a tiny relaxation of concentration, or perhaps a little carelessness or petulance.

However possible it may be to rationalize or minimize the occurrence, it is certainly not possible to exaggerate its impact upon the player. As I walked to the ninth tee, I was in a daze. I realized that in one brief span of only a moment or two, all the effort of the past three days had been just about washed out. I wasn't looking at any Grand Slam, only at the one championship. If ever a person could be made groggy by a blow entailing no physical consequences, I had been made so by that seven.

I should like to say that this disaster caused me to rise up in all my might and resolve to win out at all costs. I should like to feel that from that point on it was my blazing spirit that carried me on to victory. The fact is, though, that I did anything but that.

My reaction was precisely this. I had been badly shaken and I knew it. I was even confused mentally. At this point I was completely incapable of making any calculation either of what score I might ultimately achieve or of what it would be necessary to do to stave off the challenge of others. Since I could not think, I did what I think nine persons out of ten would have done under similar circumstances. I simply resolved to keep on hitting the ball as best I could, to finish the round in an orderly fashion, if possible, and let the result be what it would. I had no more thought of attacking or defending or of being over par or under par, but merely of finishing.

Only one stroke of all the rest has left any definite impression. I know that I did the next five holes in four each, but two of them were par threes. And then I faced those five long finishing holes.

I remember getting a four at the fourteenth. At the fifteenth I played my second a bit short of the green, chipped up to within a half-dozen feet, and missed the putt. And so to the sixteenth, which produced a shot that was one of the best I ever made in my life. As it turned out, it won the championship for me.

The sixteenth hole at Hoylake in 1930 was 532 yards in length. It was a dogleg to the right around the corner of a dike, at about 270 yards from the tee. The green was wide and flat, and whatever may have been on the right-hand side, there was a bunker at the left-front corner of the green. Going all-out for a four, which I knew I needed desperately, my long wood second was pulled just enough to finish in this left-hand bunker.

When I reached my ball, I found it lying cleanly on the smooth sand, but very close to the left-hand wall of the bunker, that is, the wall on the side opposite the hole.

The slope of this wall was quite abrupt, so that there could be no thought of playing an ordinary blast or half-blast, or even a chip. The ball could only be struck by a sharply descending blow, and my right foot had to be placed almost at the top of the bank behind me. The hole lay at some twenty to twenty-five yards across this flat, shining green.

Putting on the 11th green at Hoylake in the final round of the British Open.

I had not used for any important shot during the whole year the massive, concave sand-sedge which Horton Smith had given me earlier in the year. At St. Andrews I had hacked a ball out of a gorse bush with it, and in this tournament at Hoylake I had used it for a routine shot on the first hole in one of the earlier rounds. But as I looked at this situation on the seventieth hole of the championship, I could see that this was the only club with which this shot could be played successfully. If I could drop the club just behind the ball so that contact would be made just above center of the face of the club, the loft should be just about right to play a running shot across the green. I knew it was dangerous to use a club with which I had so little familiarity, but it was the only hope. The shot came off precisely as intended, the ball popped over the forward bank of the bunker and crept slowly across the green until it just tickled the edge of the hole and stopped two inches beyond.

That did it. I had to hole a reasonable putt for a four at the seventeenth. But I finished with another four at eighteen and was safe from pursuit. Leo Diegel, coming along an hour later, took six at this same sixteenth hole and so lost to me by two strokes. MacDonald Smith, just as happened later in the American Championship, needed a two at the par-four eighteenth to tie me. The par four, which he got, left him tied with Diegel for second.

These last two British championships were the hardest ones of any I could remember. I might say they still are.

Looking back on the Grand Slam year, I find that there is one little episode that was of absolutely no importance, yet it is one that I still have a great deal of pleasure in remembering.

During the Open Championship at Hoylake, Ted Ray, who won our Open in 1920, asked me if I would be willing to play a charity match at his golf club, Oxhey, sometime between the conclusion of the championship and my departure for home. There was something in Ted's manner of extending the invitation which led me to believe that he had not intended that he himself should take part in the match. To me, however, the proposition immediately suggested the possibility of having a most enjoyable game. So I said, "Sure, Ted, I'll be delighted to play, provided you'll play and that you'll get any two of Vardon, Braid, or Taylor to complete the match." These three, of course, comprised the Immortal Triumvirate for which I had long had so much admiration and respect. Ray himself, with his boisterous good humor and slashing play, could not fail to make an attractive addition to any exhibition.

For my part the occasion could not have had a happier result. Ted got Vardon and Braid to join us. I played one of those easy rounds which are possible only when every sort of thing is working smoothly and right. My score for the round, with a bogey five at the last hole, was sixty-eight, which I understood at the time was the lowest eighteen-hole total ever returned for the golf course. It was not a record, though, because the British quite properly only recognize as records scores made in formal stroke-play competition.

Above all else, I like to recall an incident of the seventeenth tee. With my newly-acquired skill with the mashie-niblick, I had played a tee shot to within a yard of the hole. As Vardon stepped forward to play, I heard him say in his very quiet, soft voice, "Ah, Master Bobby's 'ot today." Since we had first played together in 1920, he had always addressed me as "Master Bobby." I liked it very much, and I liked also the combination of American slang and Channel Island accent. Old Harry was a very great player and fine gentleman. Every round I played with him was an event in my life.

On the boat train a few days later on our way to Southampton to board a ship for America, Mary, Cyril Tolley, and I were in a compartment together. At one point Cyril said reflectively, "Bob, how long have you been over here?" "About six weeks," I replied, not seeing very much point to the question. "Do you suppose," Cyril continued, "you have ever played so badly for so long a period, and yet you have won both our championships?" I confess to being a bit astonished by this comment. Yet I was certain that Cyril had not meant it in an unkindly way. He was not that kind of person.

As I considered the question, I was quite aware that to agree would very obviously imply a disparagement of the opposition I had encountered. Yet I knew Cyril had not meant this either. He was trying to emphasize what I knew so well to be a fact, that I had managed by the hardest possible kind of labor to win these two tournaments when my game was never once anywhere near peak efficiency.

For the most part I had been able to produce satisfactory figures, but there had not been one competitive round, save perhaps the Amateur final against Wethered, when things had gone smoothly. One day it would be the long game, another the putting. On other days there had been stretches of very excellent play in all departments nullified by incredible lapses in concentration or effectiveness of alarming proportions. It was a little difficult even for me to believe that this kind of play had carried me unbeaten through a Walker Cup Match, the competition at

Sunningdale, and the two championships. I had been very lucky. Of that I was quite sure; but the recollection of the game at Oxhey was a very good thing to take onto the boat with me. There I had played entirely up to the form I had had in Augusta. Perhaps I should not have to work so hard in the tournaments back home.

We arrived in New York to one of those ticker-tape receptions made famous by Grover Whalen and Jimmy Walker. A special train had brought a number of enthusiastic Atlantans to New York for the occasion. My very wonderful old friend Harry Atkinson had chartered a river excursion boat, the *Mandalay,* upon which he loaded the entire Atlanta party and a band, and had it steam gaily around our ship with the band blaring "Valencia." I really did not know what all the commotion was about until I made out the great sign of welcome to me on the side of the boat.

Our party was taken off our ship at Quarantine onto the city's boat, the *Macom,* landed at the Battery, and paraded to City Hall, where Mayor Walker made his usual, graceful little speech. That night, a big dinner at the Vanderbilt Hotel, and next day Mary off to Atlanta to resume her charge of the children and I to Minneapolis for the United States Open.

An amusing sidelight on that New York welcome only came to my knowledge many years later. It has since been one of my favorite stories. The proof was convincing that not everyone in New York had been quivering with delighted excitement at my triumphant return.

The intelligence reached me more than ten years later in the form of a letter from a man whose acquaintance I have not yet made. He said that he had told the story many times with so much success that he thought he should not longer keep it from me.

It seems that my friend had been walking down on the Battery on that day in July at the time when our party was being landed from the *Macom* and the parade was in process of formation. The day was very warm, and a number of New York policemen in their dark-blue uniforms were laboring vastly to clear away curious onlookers and to marshal the various automobiles into an orderly procession. My friend had approached one massive policeman, sweating profusely under the heat and his heavy uniform, and asked, "What's the parade for?" The policeman, giving him a look of eloquent disgust, replied, "Oh, for some goddamned *golf player!*" In a way it's too bad that policeman could not have had the solace of knowing that for all my thankfulness, I was suffering just about as much as he.

Reception in New York, 1930. This is what followed the profane protest of the policeman on the Battery.

CHAPTER 13

The United States Open

O A restful, but for me tedious, Atlantic crossing climaxed by the inevitably exhausting tension of that New York welcome quite definitely does not constitute the most effective way of preparing for an open golf championship. I found this out when I reached Minneapolis. With only three or four days of practice available, my clubs had a strange feel, and I was finding it difficult indeed to get back into the habit of thinking about golf. I was not playing really badly in practice, but I was very definitely aware that the keenness was not present.

Ordinarily I liked to spend the day before a tournament in bed, reading a book or just doing anything not connected with golf. This time the heat was so great that a hotel room held little attraction. So I induced Jimmy Johnston, whose home was in Minneapolis, to take me fishing on Lake Minnetonka. But the fishing was not especially exciting, at least not enough to keep me from a sort of vague concern about the state of my golf game. And so Jimmy and I knocked off at the lake early in the afternoon and went out to the club for a nine-hole spin.

The first round of that 1930 Open at Interlachen was played on the hottest day I can ever remember. I never knew what the official temperature was, but it was certainly well over a hundred degrees on the golf course, and the air was so humid that it must have been only a very little shy of liquidity. I started the round clad in light-gray plus-fours (I started to say knickers, but remembered that in Britain these are worn only by the fairer sex), a shirt with collar, and a red foulard four-in-hand tie. I carried a dozen or so red wood tees in my trousers pocket.

When I finished the round, my plus-fours were so saturated that they appeared to be black. The tie had run all over my shirt and the red from the tees had stained one leg of my trousers. Neither Keeler nor I could loosen my tie, so he cut it off with a pocket knife. The heat was too much for a good many players, among them my friend Cyril Tolley. I am sure the big Englishman had never dreamed of encountering such a combination of temperature and humidity.

Despite it all, though, I managed to get off to a fairly good start—out in thirty-four and back in thirty-seven, with a couple of slips. My seventy-one was good enough to be tied for the lead until late afternoon when MacDonald Smith and Tommy Armour came in with a pair of seventies.

I suppose the best way to take the heat was to joke about it, and my companions on the round gave me a couple of chuckles.

In those days the players were not protected from the galleries as they are today. Spectators were permitted onto the fairways and were only restrained, by ropes and other means, around the greens and tees, and behind the players when they were making their strokes. In walking down the fairway and from greens to tees the players found themselves in the midst of the milling throng, and were thus accessible to conversationalists and autograph seekers who meant well enough but were not aware of the intense concentration demanded of a tournament golfer.

In order to protect myself from these distractions it had long been my habit to ask a couple of friends to walk with me, one on either side, during the course of the round. At Interlachen I had two lifelong friends with me. They were Chick Ridley and Charlie Cox, both of Atlanta. Both were my constant golfing companions, with complete understanding of my needs.

I have never felt more alone than I have on a golf course in an Open Championship in the midst of thousands of people. It is good indeed under these conditions to have companions with whom one can talk, or not, as he chooses.

The drinking fountains around the course were understandably in constant use. It was quite impossible for the players to get to them without causing delays on the next tee. So Chick and Charlie equipped themselves with small vacuum bottles, each of about a half-pint capacity, from which they supplied my liquid requirements.

On the twelfth hole, a par five, I had played my third shot, a pitch, some eight or ten feet past the hole. As I was awaiting my turn to putt, standing behind my ball looking over the line, my eye happened to wander up to Chick, who was in the crowd below the green, just as he was taking the water bottle down from his lips. A big, boyish-looking fellow anyway, he feigned the shamefaced grin of a little boy caught with his hand in the cookie jar, and daubed the front of his shirt several times with the stopper of the bottle. Somehow in those circumstances his performance seemed so perfectly ludicrous that I still enjoy it as though it were yesterday.

Charlie at that time was Adjutant-General of the State of Georgia, and so took great interest in the fact that many of the tees around the course were being guarded by Minnesota Militiamen. It was inevitable, of course, that Charlie should make friends with them and make known to them his interest and station in the Georgia National Guard. On one of the tees, while waiting to play, I heard one guardsman say to another, "I don't know what sort of golfer this fellow Jones is, but he's got the goldangest highest-ranking water boy I ever saw."

This might be the best spot at which to insert a firsthand account of what really happened on a shot that ever since has been the most discussed stroke in the tournament—my second shot to the ninth hole in the second round.

This ninth hole was a par five which could be reached by a spoon second across a pond, the green being situated some thirty yards beyond the edge of the water. My drive had been down the right side of the fairway, so that I had to play directly over the pond. I half-topped the shot so that the ball skipped a few times over the surface of the water before it hopped up into the grass on the bank of the lake. From this point I pitched to within a yard or so of the hole and made the putt for a birdie four.

The shot soon came to be known as the Lily Pad shot, in keeping with the notion that the ball had bounded from a lily pad onto the bank. Actually, no lily pad was involved, and the action of the ball was precisely that of a flat stone being skipped across the water.

As I was playing the shot, the gallery was lined up behind the ropes along the right and behind me. I was playing as though down a human fence. Just as I reached the top of my swing and started down, my eye caught a sudden movement in the gallery several yards in front of my position. It developed that two little girls had made a break as though to run across the fairway. My involuntary flinch caused the half-top.

There is no question but that it was a considerable stroke of luck that my ball should have escaped the water and found such a good lie on the bank. Had it remained in the water, a six would have been the best score expectable. That the stroke of luck actually decided the championship, I very much doubt. Everyone who has played in a competition of this kind knows that no one stroke can be removed with the assurance that everything else would have remained the same. The problem of constructing a seventy-two-hole total is itself altered by everything contributing to that total.

Nevertheless, I was grateful for the saving, and so ended the round in seventy-three, one over par, which gave me a total of exact par for two rounds.

Of course, I don't intend to pretend that I now remember all such things. The following scores of the leaders after the first two rounds of this championship have been taken from O. B. Keeler's *Boy's Life of Bobby Jones* published in 1931 by Harper & Brothers. According to Keeler's figures, and I am sure they are accurate, the standing of the ten leaders starting the third round on Saturday morning was as follows:

HORTON SMITH	72-70=142
HARRY COOPER	72-72=144
CHARLIE LACEY	74-70=144
JONES	71-73=144
MACDONALD SMITH	70-75=145
TOMMY ARMOUR	70-76=146
WIFFY COX	71-75=146
JOHNNY FARREL	74-72=146
WALTER HAGEN	74-73=147
JOHNNY GOLDEN	74-73=147

The scoring, perhaps excusable because of the heat, was not very good, but I had no doubt that I was surrounded by a group of contenders which was plenty formidable. Yet my position was not too bad, because I was never too keen about being in the lead at the start of the final day. I had found that I always felt more comfortable when I lay in good position to move to the front, instead of being oppressed by that feeling of having something to protect. From a spot a couple of strokes back, a really good third round could be counted on to pick up a lot of strokes.

Precisely this happened at Interlachen. Although my second-round seventy-three had been two strokes off my first-round seventy-one, I was beginning to hit the ball more nearly in the Augusta fashion. I felt that

A little practice during the Open at Interlachen in 1930. The gallery is just the right age for beginning golf.

my game was coming at just the right time, and I did not have much doubt that I could give the boys a real run for it on that last day.

I began that morning swinging smoothly and comfortably in the way I liked to start a championship round—not pressing for anything at first, but taking things quietly and easily until I could play myself into a good feel of the swing, then gradually increasing the tempo until by the middle of the round I was hitting at full power.

The first break came at the long fourth, where I came out of a bunker short of the green and holed a putt for a birdie four. Two more birdies at six and seven, and I was out in thirty-three.

Two more birdies, both fours, at the long holes eleven and twelve, and another one, a three at sixteen, and I was set for the best round I had ever played in a championship, and I believe what would have been the lowest score ever turned in at the United States Open up to that time.

This was the one time that I played at my very best in a championship. I felt as I think a good halfback must feel when he bursts through a line of scrimmage and finds the safety man pulled out of position, sees an open field ahead of him, and feels confident he has the speed to reach the goal. Most of the dangerous people were behind me in point of time, but I did not think it likely that they were holding this pace.

I did not get the sixty-six that seemed so certain. I went one over par on each of the last two holes. The four at seventeen was pardonable,

Driving from 10th tee of the final round of the U. S. Open, 1930. No worries about a lost ball here.

Playing a short iron at Interlachen in the Open of 1930. For better control, these shots are always played at less than full strength. That's my playing companion, Jock Hutchison, in background.

because at 262 yards it was about as long as a par three could get. The five at eighteen came when I pushed my drive to the right among some trees and had to waste a shot playing out.

Even so, the sixty-eight started me off on the last round five strokes ahead of Harry Cooper, who had moved up to second position. But now, if I had been that halfback in an open field, I stumbled so many times before I got to the goal line that I am sure my coach would have made me turn in my uniform before taking himself off to the hospital to recover from a heart attack.

In that last round, three times I took five on a par-three hole, thereby kicking away six precious strokes. These lapses were only partially redeemed when I followed the first and last each with a birdie, and the middle one with two birdies.

It was not possible to know precisely what those behind me were doing, although I was aware that the two Smiths, Mac and Horton, were doing quite well. It was obvious that the round which should have been a breeze was likely to become sticky indeed.

After the second double bogie five on the thirteenth, I managed to get hold of myself and for a while it seemed that I should, after all, win going away. A good drive and an iron to the fourteenth green was followed by a putt of about fifteen feet for a birdie three. A better drive and iron to number fifteen left a putt of eight feet for the birdie, which I missed. But at sixteen, my mashie-niblick pitch stopped a foot from the hole for another three.

Just when everything seemed nicely settled, I got all tied up within myself in trying to hit a wood tee shot to the par-three seventeenth, and the ball wheeled far off line to the right into a marsh whence a local rule permitted me to drop into the fairway, but many yards short of the green. With the penalty, this brought the third par-three five.

It is easy to guess that these events had been somewhat unsettling. My drive and second to the eighteenth were at best tentative and left my ball on the very front of the green at least forty feet from the hole. The crowd was milling around in great excitement, and it was only with some difficulty that I myself was able to maintain some composure. More than for any other reason in order to settle my nerves a bit, I walked up to the flag and went through the motions of looking over the putt with great care. The green sloped gradually upward for about half the distance to the hole, whence a somewhat steeper slope carried up to a small table, upon which the hole had been cut.

As I stepped up to the putt, I was quivering in every muscle. I confess that my most optimistic expectation was to get the thing dead. It is impossible to describe the sensation I felt when I saw my ball take a small break five or six feet from the cup, so that I knew it was in.

Hats were tossed into the air all around the green, and I know the great shouts must have been heard by my adversaries still on the course. I had a long wait in the clubhouse before the result became official, but I felt pretty confident that I could not be caught. Actually, again as at Hoylake, Mac Smith came to the last hole needing another eagle two to tie. That final putt had again closed the door.

It had been a long two months of golf from Sandwich to Sunningdale to St. Andrews to Hoylake to Interlachen, and after another welcoming celebration in Atlanta I was more than ready to get back to my office to do a little work and to my normal routine of playing three or four rounds a week for fun. There was left only the U. S. Amateur, and it was a long way off.

The final stroke of the U. S. Open, 1930. The ball topped the slope, took a small break to the right a few feet short of the hole, and went into the center of the cup. My, what a relief that was.

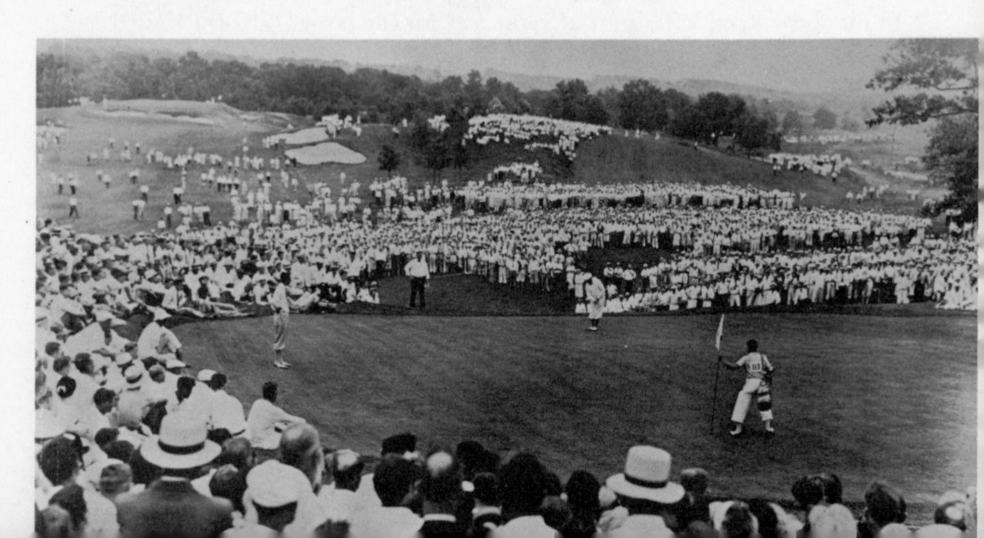

CHAPTER *14*

The U.S. Amateur

o With all due respect, but at the same time in all frankness, I had for a long time felt that the American Amateur was the easiest to win of the Big Four. To be sure, there were a number of first-class amateurs in the country, but with a semiseeded draw I was not likely to catch one of them in the first or second round, and after that all matches were at thirty-six holes. To be completely honest, I recognized that the major part of the problem would be behind me once I showed up at the tournament all in one piece and in fit condition to play. I was shortly to find out that the fulfillment of this condition was more dubious than I should have liked to think. Between July and September I had the two closest brushes with death of my entire life up to this writing.

The first one came on the golf course. One afternoon at East Lake, as we crossed over between nines, a summer thunderstorm seemed to be building up in the southwest. We debated a while whether we should wait at the clubhouse until the thing made up its mind. But after some moments we decided to chance it. If the storm developed and approached us, we could come back in across the lake from the twelfth green.

While coming down the twelfth hole, it became obvious that we were not going to make it. But the storm had given no hint of more than minor severity. Only a few drops of rain were falling as we putted out on the hole. Suddenly a bolt of lightning crashed into the ground in the middle of the tenth fairway, not forty yards from where we stood. I felt a little tingle through my spikes. Having had much experience with them, I had long since ceased to be terrified of thunderstorms. But this one was a little too close, and I suggested that we make a run for the clubhouse.

As we started to leave the green, another bolt hit a small tree at the back of the thirteenth tee, every bit as close to us as the other, but on the opposite side. It struck exactly where we should have been, had we been a minute or so earlier. That did it and ended all discussion.

As fast as we could make it, we set out across the bridge over the lake to the clubhouse. By this time lightning was popping all around, almost as rapidly as we could count. I had taken one of my companions under my umbrella so that he could give his to the caddies.

As we hurried across the driveway in front of the club on our way to the locker-room entrance, we were dazed by a monstrous explosion, as a heavy bolt hit a big double chimney immediately above our heads. I did not feel a thing, except that somehow my umbrella had suddenly collapsed and draped around my head. When I got into the clubhouse, someone discovered that the back of my shirt had been ripped down to my waist and I had received on my shoulder a scratch some six inches in length and just deep enough to break the skin.

After the storm we found the spot where we had been hit littered with masses of brick and mortar, any one of which could have killed a man had it struck him on the head. Fragments of the chimney had been blasted as far as the eighteenth green, which, upon pacing off the distance, I found to be more than three hundred feet away.

It was only a few weeks after my brush with the chimney at East Lake that I had my second narrow escape from a serious accident.

One day I had walked the seven or eight blocks from my office to the Town House of the Atlanta Athletic Club, where I had a luncheon engagement. I had turned the corner from Cone Street into Carnegie Way, and was proceeding along the sidewalk toward the entrance to the building. The entire block ahead of me was devoid of pedestrians.

I must have been thinking about something far removed from the present scene, because I was aware of nothing until, having reached a point about midway between the corner and the club entrance, I heard a voice behind me call, "Lookout, Mister." Startled, I turned quickly and saw an automobile actually mounting the curb headed directly toward me. I made a broad jump that would have done credit to Jesse Owens, and the automobile crashed into the wall of the clubhouse, having passed exactly over the spot from which I had jumped. There was no doubt that I would have been crushed between the automobile and the building had not the lone pedestrian warned me.

There was no one in the car. Apparently it had been carelessly parked near the top of the hill some one and a half blocks away.

By this time I was beginning to see that there might be many things other than missed putts to interfere with the completion of the Grand Slam. I began to wonder what other things might happen and how I might protect myself against them. I could think of only two against which any safeguard might be erected.

I had heard of one prominent golfer, I believe it was Craig Wood, who had been forced to withdraw from a golf tournament because he had impulsively snatched out of the air a bare razor blade he had dropped in the act of shaving. I resolved to still my normal reflexes during the morning session in the bathroom so that if I dropped a razor blade, I should be prepared to let the blamed thing fall.

I thought, too, of seeing a photograph of myself leaping across the Swilken Burn on the first hole at St. Andrews during the play of the British Open Championship of 1927. Now at least, I thought, I can deny myself the privilege of inviting a sprained ankle by any such childish carelessness. This was not going to be just one more Amateur Championship. At this point I had made no decision that it would be the last one in which I would compete. Nevertheless, I knew that there would never be another which would present the same opportunity, and it could not be postponed if I happened to be unable to compete on the dates upon which it had been scheduled.

I think some thoughts of this nature must have been in my mind throughout the week of that championship. I knew that no American golf course could be more to my liking than Merion. Besides being a good course, it was one for which I had come to have a good deal of sentimental affection. It was at Merion in 1916 that I had first played in the Amateur Championship. It was there that I had first won in 1924. I could not have picked a more propitious setting for this final event of the most important golfing year of my life.

I was playing fairly well, too, hitting the ball with enough freedom and power and scoring well enough in practice. Yet I felt all week a sort of vague uneasiness. It was not that I felt any lack of confidence on the golf course, but I was constantly running into patches of mediocre golf just when everything seemed to be going quite well and easily. And for the first time in my life I was finding it difficult to get to sleep at night.

Keeler professed to know what the trouble was. An old baseball writer himself before taking up the golf trail at about the same time I did, he had been hobnobbing around the club with Mickey Cochrane, Cy Perkins, and several others of the Philadelphia Athletics baseball team who were also pretty good golfers. Mickey had said that my position seemed to him to be very closely analogous to that of a baseball team needing to win that fourth game in a row to make a clean sweep of a World Series. There was just no way in which a build-up of pressure could be avoided.

As the tournament got under way, however, the only disturbing aspect that could be found lay in the superstition I had always had about winning the qualifying medal. Too often, it had seemed, the low scorer in the qualifying rounds had lost out in the tournament, apparently because he had come upon his best game too soon. I knew from experience that it was not an easy matter for me to hold to a peak rate of performance throughout an entire week, and I preferred to reserve any extraordinary effort for the closing rounds of the tournament when the important prize was at stake.

I was entitled to take some comfort, however, from the undeniable fact that my qualifying scores, although low enough to tie the existing record, were in fact achieved without any drain of nervous energy or pressure upon my game. The sixty-nine in the first round might have been several strokes better had my putting been really effective, instead of merely safe and sound. The second-round score became seventy-three, instead of seventy-one, because after a long wait at the seventeenth tee I failed to get a par three on the hole, and then overplayed the eighteenth green, mainly because I drove farther down under the hill than I had ever done before.

I have always thought that the first round of that championship saw the real turning-point of the tournament for me. In much the same way as at St. Andrews, I managed to play my best golf in the very first match. And again as at St. Andrews, it proved, and unexpectedly, too, that it was here that I needed it most.

As I was making my way that morning from the locker room to the first tee, I stopped to have a word with Jess Sweetser, who was going in to change for his match. After an exchange of greetings, Jess asked, "Who have you got this morning, Bob?" "Sandy Sommerville," I replied. "Phew," said Jess, "what a guy to get in the first round!" "I know," said I.

Ross Sommerville, the Canadian champion, better known to his friends as "Sandy," was at that time probably the least-appreciated amateur golfer in the world. In this country it seemed that only the golfers knew how good he was. But those of us who had played with him had no doubt about the effectiveness or soundness of his compact and very beautiful and regular method. Above all, in his quiet and unspectacular way, we knew him as a competitive athlete of the first rank, not only in golf, but in a number of other sports. I believe that about this time Sommerville was recognized as one of the best amateur hockey players in Canada. The American press and public came to know him better when in 1932 he became the first Canadian to win our Amateur Championship.

Most likely, it was a good thing for me to catch a first round opponent for whom I had such a high respect. After halving the first hole in par fours, we each hit big wood second shots just off the edge of the green at the long uphill second hole. We each chipped very dead, and it became even more obvious that I had a battle on my hands.

Sandy missed his par three at the third, after which we halved three holes in par figures. At the next hole, the seventh, came the break of the match, and as it turned out, the break of the tournament for me.

In 1930 the seventh hole at Merion was a drive and pitch affair, with the pitch, after a normal drive, being a little more than a hundred yards. Sandy and I both pitched our seconds to the right of the hole, and a little less than hole high, he about seven feet, I about eight. The two balls were only a little more than a foot apart, although no stymie was involved. I was one up at the time.

This was definitely not one of those occasions the importance of which is appreciated only in retrospect. As I walked up the green to finish the hole, there was going through my mind a very well-remembered sequence of thoughts. "There is a chance right here," I was thinking, "for this match to swing one way or the other. Sandy has been hitting right along with me on every shot. On every hole it has been just a question of who would make a putt. I've got the first go at it this time. If I can get my ball into the hole, Sandy's putt will become a lot tougher; and if he should miss, it might mean the match. If I miss first, almost certainly he will hole and we will be even. If that happens, with Sandy in the mood he is in today, I will be playing for my life from here in."

I will swear that I never worked any harder on any putt than I did on this one. The green was very keen, and there was a little break from right to left which was very difficult to read. I putted the ball very gently. The touch was exactly right, even if the line had been a bit too conservative. The ball hesitated on the upper edge of the hole and then dropped.

Sandy played the same line, but too strongly by a hair. His ball touched the top of the hole, but passed it by an inch. I was very certain that by getting my ball into the hole first, I had gone two ahead instead of being hauled back to even. A little thing like that can make so much difference in a golf match.

With a little more margin to work with, I holed a fair putt for a birdie three at the eighth, and a really good one of twenty-five feet past a partial stymie for a two at the ninth, and so reached the turn four up, and my opponent had played seven pars, one birdie, and one bogie.

I won from Sommerville in the morning by five and four, and in the afternoon from Fred Hoblitzel, another Canadian, by the same score. In the morning I played the first nine in thirty-three, four under par. In the afternoon I played the first nine in forty-two, five over par. What a difference in the two matches, with the winning margin the same!

Unfortunately, this was to be typical of my progress through the entire tournament—very good golf, day after day, was to be mixed up with some very bad golf. I cannot say whether it was luck or the strain of that fourth championship, or whether I was playing so well, but was just so tired that my game would respond whenever I called upon it, and yet was not equal to a steady performance. In every match I would play quite well for a while and then, having gained what looked like a comfortable lead, I would lapse into something worse than mediocrity and manage to get rid of most of it. But always when it got to close-running again, my play would improve. I should have ended every match more quickly than I did. Yet I was never down to any opponent and never in any sort of trouble.

When Gene Homans stroked that last putt on Saturday afternoon on the eleventh green and, before the ball had stopped rolling, came with a big smile to shake my hand, all at once I felt the wonderful feeling of release from tension and relaxation that I had wanted so badly for so long a time. I wasn't quite certain what had happened or what I had done. I only knew that I had completed a period of most strenuous effort and that at this point, nothing more remained to be done, and that on this particular project, at least, there could never at any time in the future be anything else to do. I am certain that many others have enjoyed this feeling—that the project, no matter what its importance, has been finished, and ahead, at least for a time, lies nothing but rest and cessation of worry.

The completion of the Grand Slam. Gene Homans, my opponent in the final of the Amateur championship, extends his hand on the 29th green at Merion.

PART THREE

And After

CHAPTER *15*

Reflections and an Appraisal

o Immediately after this final trick of the Grand Slam, of course, came the question, "What would I do now? Would I continue to play in tournaments, or would I retire?"

I answered, as truthfully as I could, that I did not know. At this point, I truly did not know. I had started in the first place to play in golf tournaments for fun, and I had continued to play because I enjoyed doing so. But when I began to win, I also began to feel a certain responsibility in connection with competitive golf. Each year had ended with speculation upon the future. It had seemed to be expected by others, as well as myself, that this thing would go on indefinitely, and that I would always be beating my brains out trying to win either the Open or Amateur Championship.

At the conclusion of the Merion tournament, in response to these queries, I said what was on my mind and in my heart, namely, that I intended to settle down to the practice of law, and that I could henceforward recognize no obligation to play in any golf tournaments. I thought it would be nice to feel free to play in a tournament now and then if I felt like doing so at the time, but I thought it would also be nice if I could merely neglect to send in my entry for a championship and let it go at that. I had never played golf with any idea of making a career of the game. Above all things, I wanted to avoid ever getting myself into such a position that I would have to keep on playing. Now seemed a good time to make this position clear. So, still at Merion, I allowed myself to be quoted as follows:

I expect to continue to play golf, but just when and where I cannot say now. I have no definite plans either to retire or as to when and where I may continue in competition. I might play next year and lay off in 1932. I might stay out next season and feel like another tournament the following year. What I want most right now is to be free of any obligation, express or implied, to continue playing each year in both major championships.

In my mind today the accomplishment of the Grand Slam assumes more importance as an example of the value of perseverance in the abstract than as a monument to skill in the playing of a game. I am certain that in those moments when the success of the project was most in doubt, the decisive factor in each case had been my ability, summoned from somewhere, to keep control of myself and to keep trying as hard as I could, even when there was no clear indication of the direction in which hope of victory might lie.

In at least two matches, those with Tolley and Voigt at St. Andrews, I had been outplayed throughout; and in the final round of each of the two Open Championships I had made mistakes of grievous proportions. On several occasions I had lost control of my game. But having once found myself in these dire predicaments, I had managed, from the point of realization, to drive myself to the end, when it would have been easy, even pleasant, to play the "give-up" shot.

Every one recognizes that form in golf runs in cycles. It can be seen even today if one watches the results of the weekly tournaments. No one player can hold to top form for a run of more than two or three weeks. During such a period, he is operating under a formula which he has played himself into that enables him to play well, thinking of the two or three moves in the stroke that he can consciously control. Ultimately he will begin to overdo one of these or something will go wrong in another place and he will have to work out another pattern.

The only tournament of 1930 I was able to hit in top form was the one in Augusta that didn't count. The campaign extended from May to September and it was not to be expected that the whole route could be smooth.

In winning both the British and American Open Championships as one-half of the Grand Slam, I returned the lowest score of the field in only one of the eight rounds played. Obviously then, I was not winning because of the overpowering excellence of my play. I could have won only because, despite some very disastrous and unaccountable lapses, I did manage to keep up some sort of organized effort to the end, and so prevented major setbacks from developing into utter rout.

The margin of victory in each tournament was a bare two strokes. These might well have been those saved by a sort of desperate hanging on in the closing holes.

The one most important thing for the tournament golfer to learn is that golf championships are not won merely by having greater mechanical skill than the other players. It is not rewarding, of course, to harbor a real weakness on the mechanical side. But in most tournaments including players of the first rank, there is little difference in shot-making ability among the top echelon. Some may be able to keep it up longer than others, but in the main, the decisive factor will be found in the relative abilities of the various players to perform under the strain which all must feel.

The toughest and most conclusive test in golf is the Open Championship. Match play can be a pretty game and exciting, but it can never exert the relentless pressure of the card and pencil. In match play you can lose only one hole at a time, and that only to an opponent you can see. In stroke play you can blow a comfortable lead with one careless or misplayed shot; and the most phlegmatic player is always plagued by rumors or imaginings of what others are doing.

You learn very soon, I think, in tournament golf, that your most formidable adversary is yourself. You win or lose according to your own ability to withstand the pressure. You must learn to keep on playing your game despite all the disturbing thoughts that may keep crowding in upon your consciousness, and above all, you must keep on fighting the awful pressure, no matter how much you would like to give in to it. In a well-played tournament round, you will play at the rate of a little more than three minutes for every stroke, including the shortest putts. That gives you a lot of time to think. Too much, I am sure you will find.

In the beginning I had one lesson to learn which, fortunately, does not confront everyone. It has been long and well advertised that in my early years I was frequently guilty of displays of temper on the golf course, throwing and breaking clubs, and the like. Outbursts of this nature are too puerile to merit any notice here. I realize, of course, that I should not have been competing in adult company so long as I failed to appreciate the grossness of these improprieties. Nevertheless, no one at the time seemed to recognize, as they have since, that I was only fourteen and fifteen years of age when most of these offenses occurred.

It was part of my golfing education to learn that these outbursts, however much they may have offended others, were in fact harmful only to me. I think I began to realize that the cause was only partly anger at myself for having missed a simple shot; the other part was a childish effort to make known publicly that such a misplay was not to be tolerated by a player of so much ability. Inevitably, the sense of guilt and shame immediately ensuing would affect my play for an important interval thereafter. Given this awakening, it was not difficult at all to refuse to yield to these ridiculous impulses and to assume an attitude of composure and calm. It even helped sometimes to admit to myself how really inexcusable the shot had been.

Playing one day in Augusta, I hooked my drive into the trees on the left of the tenth hole. I found my ball under a tree in the dense woods. I looked the situation over very carefully, taking more time, I think, than on any shot I ever played. I could see an opening leading out of the trees toward the opposite side of the fairway. I thought I could hit the ball through that opening and hook it back onto the fairway just short of the green. As I swung at the ball, my club caught in a bit of stubble I had not seen, so that I moved the ball only a few feet.

I looked up into the faces of an embarrassed group of spectators who had followed me into the woods to witness the miracle. Since they seemed to expect some comment, I said, "Well, I believe I could have done that well with a lot less preparation." Not the most brilliant humor, perhaps, but better than a broken club.

There is a school of Oriental philosophy, I am told, which holds that the aim of life should be the perfection of personality or character, and that sufferings, joys, and achievements mean nothing except as they influence the development of this personality or character. I hope the analogy will not appear too ridiculous, but it has been thinking along such a line that has uncovered the only real regret I have ever had about quitting competitive golf when I was only twenty-eight years of age.

I have never been sorry that I did not try for a fifth Open or a sixth Amateur, for after adding one of either, there would always be the question of another. What I have regretted at times was that I did not keep on until I might have achieved, in my own estimation at least, the status of "Compleat Golfer," to use Isaac Walton's spelling.

Whatever lack others may have seen in me, the one I felt most was the absolute inability to continue smoothly and with authority to wrap up a championship after I had won command of it. The failing cost me the eventual winning of more than one, and made several others look a lot more fortuitous than they should have.

Let's just take these instances in the United States Open Championship:

In 1923 at Inwood, after three rounds I was three shots ahead of the field, and with three holes to play, I had the championship as clearly won as could be. Yet I finished 5, 5, 6 against a par of 4, 4, 4, and was subsequently tied by Bobby Cruickshank. I only won after a rousing battle in a play-off.

In 1928 at Olympia Fields I began the last round leading by three clear strokes. I played the first six holes in two under par and was hitting every shot with complete confidence. Standing on the seventh tee, I knew that the championship was in my pocket. Yet I hit a tee shot far off line to the left into a ditch and wound up with a double bogie five on the par-three hole. Beginning with this hole, I dropped seven strokes to par in a stretch of five holes.

This left me in a tie with Johnny Farrell, which resulted only because poor Roland Hancock finished with two sixes. Farrell beat me by one stroke in a thirty-six-hole play-off next day.

In 1929 at Winged Foot I again began the last round leading by three strokes, and again I played the first seven holes quite well, and again I had that feeling of having won the championship; but after my second to the eighth hole had taken a nasty kick into a bunker, I played back and forth across the green to wind up with a seven. I took another seven, quite inexcusably, on the fifteenth, and so had to hole a twelve-foot putt on the last green to tie Al Espinosa for a championship I should have won by at least six strokes.

Holing the twelve-foot putt on the last hole at Winged Foot to tie Al Espinosa in 1929. Al Watrous watches at right foreground.

I have already recounted the near debacle in the last round at Interlachen in 1930, as well as the seven on the eighth hole of the final round at Hoylake.

The only open championship I ever managed to win easily was the 1927 British Open at St. Andrews. Here, I again began the last round with a three-stroke lead, and again I started as if I intended to get rid of that, too. But after taking three fives in the first five holes, I hit a hot streak and picked up five threes in the next six holes around the famous Loop, and so came home easily six strokes ahead.

I have no means of accounting for this sort of thing. It was not, as some have said, the result of overconfidence or of a desire for "coasting." Both explanations would appear reasonable, but I think either is more charitable than I deserve.

As nearly as I can analyze my own state of mind, up to the point of becoming aware that I was the winner I had been possessed of a singleness of purpose driven by an intense desire to win, which had of itself focused my concentration upon playing golf. Up to that point there had only been the determination to wring the best figures possible out of my game.

Having reached a stage where I suddenly knew that I should certainly win with any sort of ordinary finish, I became fearful of making myself look ridiculous by kicking the thing away. At this point, I think I began to be conscious of my swing and began trying to make too certain of avoiding a disastrous mistake. I was no longer playing the shots for definite objectives, but was rather trying to keep away from hazardous places.

The one American championship I won with the fewest qualms and the least unhappiness in the final round was the 1926 event at Scioto. In this tournament I began the last round three shots behind, rather than three ahead. Although I would never voluntarily seek the trailing position, it is a fact that I found it much more pleasant to be coming from behind. The excitement of chasing Joe Turnesa through the closing holes of that tournament is one of my best-remembered experiences in golf.

Joe was playing just a couple of holes ahead of me. There was a very good wind, which added importantly to the difficulty of the play.

I had collected one of my customary sevens on the eighteenth hole of the second round, which had given me the very generous total of seventy-nine for that round, and a total of 149 at the halfway point. Joe had been at 145, and with a seventy-two against my seventy-one for the third round he led by three as we started after lunch. He picked up another stroke on the way out in the afternoon.

Starting the last nine four strokes behind, I first began to make progress when I picked up a birdie four at the eleventh and was told that Joe had needed six there. From then on word kept coming back to me hole by hole of Joe's progress, and I was aware all along as I managed to get a stroke here and there. Finally, a birdie four on the last hole put me a stroke ahead at the all-important point.

It was a most satisfying victory, but the significant thing to me was that at no time during this round did I feel the fear that I have known when leading the field. Maybe this was Joe Turnesa's burden that day.

I have often wondered whether or not I could have overcome this weakness had I played longer in competitive golf. I think perhaps I could have, had I learned to play safe by merely choosing a safe objective and playing as definitely for it as I had for the flag in driving into the lead.

I like to think that I could have done this, because then I would have scored within reasonable distance of some of our modern geniuses.

I always felt that O. B. Keeler had earned a full partnership interest in the Grand Slam. Since I had captained the Walker Cup team of 1930, the U.S.G.A. awarded to my home club the custody of the Walker Cup to go with the other four. Thus we were able to display together the five major trophies of golf.

CHAPTER *16*

No Longer a Competitor

o Even though the distinction between the amateur and the professional is so important in golf, the basic reason for making the distinction is not always kept in clear view. It is, in the simplest terms, merely that the amateur, who presumably must find time for golf outside his more necessary and ordinary activities, ought not to be asked to compete on equal terms with the professional, who is free to devote his entire time to the game. It is true that it may have been born of snobbery, as evidenced by the older terms of "gentlemen" and "players," but this aspect has long since lost its importance. Indeed, the professional of today is every bit as jealous of his status as the amateur.

In recent years the United States Golf Association has been much troubled by the frequency with which its amateur champions have been lured into the professional ranks. Obviously the temptation is great for the young man, having proved his proficiency, to set out on the tournament circuit in quest of a share of the money prizes. Equally obviously, he has a perfect right to do this if he is so inclined.

The only trouble is that in some cases the action has been so precipitate as to leave little doubt that the intention had been there all along. And so the U.S.G.A. has taken the position that it is the state of mind that counts, and that once the golfer has decided upon a professional career, he is no longer entitled to compete as an amateur, even though he may not yet have performed any overt act of professionalism.

Of course, it will never be possible for anyone other than the player himself to know of his intentions until he expresses them. There is no way that this ephemeral thing can be acted upon.

Yet the idea has very definite merit, because the young men themselves are intended to be beneficiaries of any rules made for the betterment of the game. Once an individual has decided that he wants to become a professional golfer, it is to his ultimate advantage for him to begin as soon as possible to learn his trade. On the other hand, if he intends to enter business or a profession, he should not waste important years of his life chasing around to golf tournaments, especially if he is able to do so only by having his expenses paid by someone outside his immediate family.

Throughout all the period when I was competing in golf tournaments, I played as an amateur. My father was not a rich man, and I have no doubt that the expense of even the little traveling I did to golf tournaments sometimes became troublesome. But there had never been any thought in the mind of either of us that I should ever play golf as a professional. Even the accomplishment of the Grand Slam made no change in our attitudes upon this point.

After Merion I went home with very definite intentions of settling down closely to the practice of law. I even felt a sense of relief that at least a large part of this golf business was behind me for good—that I could escape from competition in the Open Championships which had taken so much out of me. At this point, I truly thought that if I should ever play in another championship, it would be the Amateur.

Back in 1925 when Keeler and I were returning from Oakmont, where I had won the Amateur for the second consecutive year, I had said:

"O.B., I suppose it is inevitable that anyone who engages in championship competition in any sport should become aware of the record book and should have a desire to leave something of importance in it. Just now I have won either the Open or the Amateur in each of the last three years. I am now twenty-three years old, and I can't keep fooling around with this thing much longer. I think if I could win one of these championships in each of the next three years, I'd be willing to call it quits."

Now, five years later, I had managed to improve a bit on that ambition and the Grand Slam seemed to leave nothing lacking. By keeping on I might add one or more championships to the total, but it seemed that even the most I could hope for would be anticlimax. I knew I could never do another Grand Slam, nor would I ever try.

During the tournament at Merion I had been approached about

doing a series of motion pictures on golf, but I had declined even to discuss the subject. But it happened that in Atlanta one of the closest and warmest friends of my father and of myself was Y. Frank Freeman, then of S. A. Lynch Enterprises, a chain of motion-picture exhibitors, later and most prominently of Paramount Pictures.

Frank was in our offices almost daily, sometimes on business, more often visiting about Georgia Tech football, the Atlanta baseball club, or about nothing in particular.

One day we started talking about my doing some motion pictures designed to teach people how to play golf. The more we talked, the better we both liked the idea. The game was growing in popularity; both it and I had been well advertised on the front pages; this would enable us to reach millions in theaters and perhaps present the game to them in an attractive manner. It was an engaging prospect and the money involved for me would not be inconsiderable.

The most important problem, however, concerned my amateur status. To give it up would be like giving up part of myself. For some years I had been writing golf stuff for a syndicated newspaper column. For this I had received the prior approval of the U.S.G.A. on the basis that the columns would be in fact written by me. I could not see that there was any vast difference between a newspaper column and a motion picture. Yet I realized that there was really very little difference in using either to teach golf and in doing so in person on a practice tee. In all honesty I would have to relinquish my amateur status if I undertook the pictures. The resulting decision and my reasons for it were set out in a public statement I made at the time:

> Upon the close of the 1930 golfing season I determined immediately that I would withdraw entirely from golfing competition of a serious nature. Fourteen years of intensive tournament play in this country and abroad had given me about all I wanted in the way of hard work in the game. I had reached a point where I felt that my profession required more of my time and effort, leaving golf in its proper place, a means of obtaining recreation and enjoyment.
>
> My intention at the time was to make no announcement of retirement, but merely to drop out quietly by neglecting to send in my entry to the Open Championship next Spring. There was at that time no reason to make a definite statement of any

kind; but since then, after careful consideration, I have decided upon a step which I think ought to be explained to the golfers of this country, in order that they may have a clear understanding of what the thing is and why it is being done.

On November 13, 1930, I signed a contract with Warner Bros. Pictures to make a series of twelve one-reel motion pictures, devoted entirely to exhibiting and explaining the methods which I employ in playing the shots ordinarily required in playing a round of golf. These pictures are to be purely educational in character, and it is the ardent hope of both parties that they will be of some value, first by improving the play and thereby increasing the enjoyment of the vast number of people already interested in the game, and, second, by creating an interest where none exists now among the many who may find enjoyment and beneficial exercise on the golf course.

The talking picture, with its combination of visual presentation and demonstration, with the possibility of detailed explanation, appeals to me as the ideal vehicle for an undertaking of this nature.

Of course, the matter of monetary compensation enters into the discussion at this point, and it is for numerous reasons that I wish to be perfectly understood on this score. The amateur status problem is one of the most serious with which the United States Golf Association has to deal for the good of the game as a whole.

I am not certain that the step I am taking is in a strict sense a violation of the amateur rule. I think a lot might be said on either side. But I am so far convinced that it is contrary to the spirit of amateurism that I am prepared to accept and even endorse a ruling that it is an infringement.

I have chosen to play as an amateur not because I have regarded an honest professionalism as discreditable, but because I have had other ambitions in life. So long as I played as an amateur, there could be no question of subterfuge or concealment. The rules of the game, whatever they were, I have respected, sometimes even beyond the letter. I certainly shall never become a professional golfer. But, since I am no longer a competitor, I feel able to act entirely outside the amateur rule, as my judgment and conscience may decide.

When these pictures have been made, I expect to return to the practice of my profession, unhampered by the necessity of keeping my golf up to championship requirements.

Frank and I made a call, together, on Harry Warner of Warner Brothers in New York. At the end of the day Mr. Warner seemed pleased with the deal, as was I. He asked Frank and me to work out the details with Dan Michalove, a young Warner executive who was also an ex-Atlantan and good friend of ours.

I went back to New York a week or so later to sign the contract. After the signing Dan took me to see *Once in a Lifetime,* George Kaufman's and Moss Hart's hilarious lampooning of the motion-picture industry of that time. As we were leaving the theater, Dan grinned at me and said, "What do you think of that contract now, Bob?"

I confess to having had some misgivings at the time. The Kaufman and Hart show had made the thing look so ridiculous. But I never had a more delightful experience. Jack Warner assigned George Marshall to direct the pictures and gave us an entirely free hand; and apart

O. B. Keeler mans a typewriter as I work out script and action for a shot for a Warner Brothers series.

from the inclusion of a "story line," which was then considered necessary but now appears more than a little corny, I think we did a pretty good job. At least the pictures "sold" very well, and I think made some contribution to the development of the "theory" of golf, if not the practice.

Although I had not the least suspicion of it at the time, the most important part of my public statement turned out to be that bit about feeling free to "act entirely outside the amateur rule." It was to change my whole life.

Once the motion-picture contract had been signed and announced and my statement released, I was surprised and delighted that I experienced a new sense of freedom. Suddenly I realized that there had been considerable strain attached to the job of maintaining a strict amateur position. So many well-meaning persons were coming up with ideas for promotions, advertising gimmicks, and business ventures, it was not always easy to know and explain to them just why these things would not fit into the amateur picture. Present also was the need for eternal vigilance lest unauthorized activities of others lead to compromising situations. It was really good to be free of it all and able to consider various proposals on their own merit.

It was, of course, very clear that the next year was going to be well occupied by the pictures; and since the contract with Warner included an option for six additional pictures, which option was in fact exercised, it seemed that the job would require nearly two years for completion. There would not be much law business for that time.

But the pictures were merely the beginning. Next came the offer of a radio series from Lambert Pharmacal Company for "Listerine." Since the sponsors were top-flight people in every respect, and because the general idea of promoting golf seemed to fit in quite well with the pictures, I accepted this as well. This has been the one "business," or golf venture, which has caused me anguish over the years.

Jack Lambert never complained, but I knew he could not have been pleased with the result. Nor was I. When we went into the thing, we had no very clear format, but the general idea was that the series should be instructional. But when I got into the production of the scripts, I found that it simply was not possible to fill so much time with instructional material.

After the first broadcast Jack got O. B. Keeler to help me, and we did our level best, but I fear it was not too good.

By this time, though, being free to direct my thinking along practical lines, I began to realize that golf was the only thing in the world I really knew very much about. And since all phases of the game had interested me, why should I make an effort to put it away from me? It was not necessary to play for money, or to teach, or to run a golf shop. I could serve the game in other ways and let it serve me.

A man does not become a golf professional merely by becoming a nonamateur. The pros themselves have something to say about that. You have to have certain qualifications and sign a "Player's Agreement" to compete in P.G.A.-sponsored tournaments, and you have to serve an apprenticeship to become a P.G.A. member. But I could find other ways to use my knowledge of the game. One of the most obvious of these was to devote my attention to the design and manufacture of golf clubs.

My father had for many years been General Counsel of Atlantic Steel Company in Atlanta, and its President, Robert Gregg, was one of the closest friends of the family. Soon Bob, my father, and I began discussing setting up in Atlanta a company to manufacture golf clubs.

I have already told of my interest in golf clubs from the player's angle. In addition to my visits to Tom Stewart's forge at St. Andrews, I had designed a few of my own clubs and had them made up for me by A. G. Spalding. One in particular had been a driver with which I had driven yards longer than with any club I ever owned.

This club was conceived one night in my room at Harvard when I should have been catching up on some reading in English history. But I had learned a little something about mechanical drawing while earning an engineering degree at Georgia Tech. I began idly to sketch out the plan view of the head of the driver.

Suddenly I became aware that this was the most beautiful driver I had ever seen. I just wished that I could take the grip in my hands and see that lovely head resting behind a real ball.

The history reading was completely forgotten. Quickly I got out another sheet of paper and sketched out two other views—one of the face of the club, the other of the toe. It was beautiful from every angle. Having made the drawings actual size, I sent them off next morning to Victor East at Spalding to have several clubs made up.

The face of the club was one and three-quarter inches in depth. It was a monstrously powerful implement with which I could drive many yards farther than with any other. But its great depth and lack of loft caused it to be most demanding with the small ball. It was born a few years too soon.

While Bob Gregg and I were still talking, I was approached by two of the more important manufacturers. The first I saw only through courtesy. I knew he could have nothing of interest to offer. The second was M. B. Reach, Vice President of Spalding. M.B. and I started a friendship, and Spalding and I began a relationship that has endured for almost thirty years.

Prior to that time there were no satisfactory iron clubs made in this country. The American-made irons were too long from heel to toe and had a "tinny" appearance and feel. Striking the ball off center produced a most unpleasant shock in the hands of the player. A satisfactory iron could be had only by using a British-made hand-forged head.

The first set of Jones irons reached the market in 1932. M. B. Reach, W. F. Reach, Victor East, and I had designed them, working from my own hickory-shafted set as a base. By making the blades more compact, with a thicker top line, and providing a flange sole on the back of the head, we succeeded in bringing the center of gravity of the head more nearly behind the center of the striking surface, or "sweetspot." I cannot resist declaring my honest opinion that these were the first really fine matched sets of irons produced in this country.

A form of flange back had been used in the Old Country on occasional hand-forged heads, going back many years. But I think we were the first to make use of the flange as the dominant feature in the design of a matched set. Today, expressed in some way, it is present in all top-grade iron clubs.

My playing set as it appeared in the late twenties—shafts all of hickory and heads all hand-fashioned.

CHAPTER *17*

Then and Now

O The one question put to me most often is "Were the golfers of my day as good as those of the present time?"

There can be no question more impossible to answer. Yet if golfers insist upon speculation on this topic, there is no reason why they should not have that privilege. And since it seems to command so much interest, perhaps I may join in the discussion.

In 1927 when I won the British Open at St. Andrews, one of the old-time professionals, described as "the grand old man of Scottish golf," was quoted in the newspapers as follows:

> "I knew and played with Tom Morris, and he was every bit as good as Jones. Young Tom had to play with a gutty ball, and you could not make a mistake and get away with it. St. Andrews then had whins up to your head and the fairways were half the width that they are now. This rubber-cored ball we have now only requires a tap and it runs a mile."

So, you see, the controversy is not new. Young Tom had died some thirty years before I was born. Yet there is, of course, much substance in the above quotation; that is, if one must pursue the controversy.

Perhaps it is fortunate, so long as we care to remain friends, that the players and personalities involved in the discussion do not take it too seriously.

When Ben Hogan won the British Open in 1953 in what has been until now his only try, I happened to be in New York on business. I certainly had not planned it that way, and equally certainly, after spending an afternoon harassed by newspaper people and photographers, I shall certainly plan it any other way, should Hogan make another try for the British title. Anyway, I could not escape, and the papers next day were filled with the usual controversy as to who was the better golfer, Hogan or I.

I went on up to the Spalding factory in Chicopee, Massachusetts, to continue my business, but returned a few days later to attend a luncheon in honor of Hogan upon his arrival in New York. As we sat together at the head table, I said, "Ben, I want you to understand very clearly that I had nothing to do with the controversial stories about you and me, and I certainly didn't project myself into the picture with any idea of detracting from your enjoyment of the glory which you had so well earned." "Bob," said Ben, "you may be sure I understand. I have always felt and said that a man who can be a champion in one era could be a champion in any other era because he has what it takes to reach the top."

That was good enough for me, so we left it there.

I think we must agree that all a man can do is beat the people who are around at the same time he is. He cannot win from those who came before any more than he can from those who may come afterward. It is grossly unfair to anyone who takes pride in the record he is able to compile that he must see it compared to those of other players who have been competing against entirely different people under wholly different conditions.

It is human, I suppose, for every man to think that his days were the best. It is completely natural for him to recall with high respect the capabilities of other competitors of his day, to remember the sufferings and trials his triumphs had cost him, and so to convince himself that his were the days of the giants. Not many months ago Lincoln Werden, writing in the New York *Times*, quoted Tommy Armour as saying that he would "hate to see what Jones would do with this modern equipment." Since I have always considered Tommy to be a good friend of mine, I must assume that he meant to be complimentary, even though a bit extravagant.

The proponents of the modern era, at whatever time it may be, have always pointed to the lower scoring accomplished in the big tournaments, and those who argue for the past have always countered by citing the improvement in clubs, balls, and golf-course conditioning. The nearest thing to a resolution of this controversy is obviously to say that both are right.

The first thing to point out is that there is nothing absolute about scoring in golf. We all know how the same golf course can change, even from day to day, depending upon weather conditions. It is entirely possible that on the first day of a tournament the greens may be hard and impossible to hold, even with well-played second shots, and the wind may be blowing so hard that to score anywhere in the seventies is quite creditable. A good rain at night and a complete laying of the wind may produce conditions the next day which will lower the scoring by a good many strokes. These things, unfortunately, do not appear in the record books.

Neither is it possible to deny that over the longer range there has been a steady improvement in the conditioning of our better golf courses. When I first played in England at Hoylake in 1921, the country was in the grip of a record-breaking drought and there existed no means of applying artificial watering. Many of the greens, notably the sixteenth and eighteenth, were impossible to hold, even with the shortest pitch. Nowadays, it can be counted on that any course where a big championship is played has means of artificial watering from tee to green throughout.

Then there is the matter of weed control, in which tremendous progress has been made. I remember quite well that when the 1929 Open Championship was played at Winged Foot, we found the golf course almost completely covered with clover. There is nothing a golfer hates worse than clover. The ball, of course, settles deep into the lush growth so that the effect is of having all pitching clubs covered with a coating of lubricating oil. Without the clean contact between the face of the club and the ball, control of iron shots is not possible. In response to urging by me and others, some of the fairways at the more exacting holes were closely mown in order to alleviate the condition. This helped some, but was not a complete cure. Today we have the means of eradicating clover, crab grass, and a good many other unpleasant golf-course pests. On a properly conditioned course today, it is almost impossible to get a bad lie.

To think of golf in the days of Young Tom Morris, we have only to recall the paintings and early photographs, wherein it is difficult to distinguish the point at which the fairway ends and the putting green begins, or to examine in the Royal and Ancient collection the number of iron clubs especially designed for playing out of ruts and cart tracks.

By some sort of coincidence, I suppose, I was born in 1902, the year of the advent of the rubber-cored ball. The first golf ball had been produced by stitching up horsehide with a stuffing of feathers. The result looked something like a miniature baseball. Later, this was superseded by the ball molded of gutta-percha. By virtue of some experiments being conducted in the early Thirties, I had the dubious privilege of playing a few rounds with a gutty. I have no difficulty in summoning up a considerable admiration for some of the scores accomplished with it in the late Nineteenth Century.

Yet, even the rubber-cored ball has been constantly improved throughout the years. We have learned more and more about various things, including methods of construction, and even respecting the efficiency of various kinds of markings. Perhaps the greatest progress has been made in producing balls of greater uniformity. When you consider that a difference of five yards in the driving power of two different balls may make the difference between having a putt for a birdie and playing the next shot out of a bunker, the importance of this may be appreciated.

Freddie Tate was a gallant young Scottish golfing hero who died in the Boer War. On the morning after the Open Championship of 1927 I was called on at the Grand Hotel in St. Andrews by a brother of Freddie. He had with him some old clubs which he said his brother had used, and which he would like to present to me. He asked that I come out in front of the eighteenth green and play some run-up shots with the irons. This, of course, I was delighted to do, although I did not acquit myself with any great distinction. Nevertheless, he gave me the clubs, and after a while I presented them to the U.S.G.A. for its museum in Golf House, where the clubs now repose. If you could take a look at these clubs with their mammoth grips, clumsy hosels, and shovel-like blades, you would understand that immense progress has been made in golf clubs during the present century.

When I retired from competition in 1930, I was very proud of my golf clubs. There were some eighteen of them which I considered to be on the active list, and I suppose they represented a selection from almost two hundred that I had bought, tried, and discarded over a period of some fifteen years. All, of course, were of hickory shafts.

After my retirement, and in response to requests, I gave my favorite driver to the Royal and Ancient of St. Andrews, my brassie to the James River Museum in Virginia, and the putter, Calamity Jane, II, which I had used from 1926 through 1930, to the U.S.G.A. museum. The remainder of the clubs have been, and are now, on display at the Augusta

National Golf Club. When I look at them today in comparison with modern clubs, I wonder why I was so proud of them.

The big difference, of course, between clubs of today and those of my time is in the steel shaft, which was just beginning to gain acceptance at the time I quit competition.

A hickory shaft of average length, say for a number-two iron, would weigh a little bit over seven ounces. The same shaft in steel will weigh four and one-quarter to four and one-half ounces. Obviously, this feature alone provides more latitude for the distribution of weight in order to achieve the optimum balance.

Hickory, too, possessed another weakness in that it would yield in varying degrees to twisting or torsional stresses. In other words, with the head of the club held in one hand and the grip end in the other, the shaft itself could be twisted through perhaps a quarter turn. Thus, there was introduced into the play an element of variation or uncertainty against which the player had always to be on his guard.

It is noticeable and often the subject of comment by players of my era that the players of today seem to hit the ball harder. Actually, they do, and consistently attain lengths which are really stupendous according to our standards. I think it is fair to say that players of my day hit the ball really hard only when there was something definite to be gained by doing so. On holes of the ordinary drive and pitch variety, the opportunity for profit seemed not to exist, and the matter of placement for position seemed to be of paramount importance. Today, with the deadly pitching wedge used so proficiently by our better players, even on these holes of medium length, a long drive can be of advantage, and it seems to me to be very definitely true that with steel shafts the players are able to hit more nearly all-out without too much risk of having the club betray them. I think this point is amply supported by the fact that I know several of my friends and former golfing companions who are today driving the ball appreciably farther than they did twenty-five years ago. I know in all reason that they are not any stronger or more effective in their swinging.

All of my 1930 set had been "handmade." Most of the irons bore the famous "Pipe" trade-mark of Tom Stewart of St. Andrews. Some had been picked up as completed clubs in golf shops in this country. Others had been assembled from heads made especially for me in Stewart's forge. Whenever I had visited St. Andrews, I had gone to Stewart's to look over his shop and occasionally would stand with the finisher to be certain that he completed the head according to my taste. In those days "club-making" was part of a club professional's job. Having got my heads from Stewart, I brought them home for shafting by whatever pro we had at East Lake. This operation would involve selecting a shaft from available stock, planing and sanding it to proper size and feel, fitting it and securing it into the hosel, applying lamp black to bring out the grain and shellac to give it a polish, and finally winding on the grip and listing under it. It was an exacting operation requiring several days, and if the player happened to be as interested as I was, he took pains to check on every move.

In the case of the wood clubs, too, the skill of the maker was most important, for he always started with a block only roughly of the desired shape. Working from this with rasp, file, and sandpaper, he produced the final head, which he finished himself with stains and shellac. The marvel of these old clubs was certainly not their perfection, but rather that they were as good as they were. By no conceivable act of charity could they be compared with the precise instruments produced by modern methods, which work to close tolerances with quality control fully up to the highest engineering standards.

It seems to me that the net effect of all these things—improvements in balls, clubs, and golf-course maintenance—has been to make the game easier. A better ball, better lies through the fairway, more regular and smoother putting surfaces, clubs better suited to their intended purposes, and perhaps above all, the more perfect balancing and matching of sets, all must contribute to the making of lower scores.

Some may argue that all this has had an unfortunate consequence of reducing the skill requirements of the game. For my part I feel very strongly that these developments have helped the average golfer more than the expert and are therefore important influences for the growing popularity of golf. I am certain that the cumulative effect of all these factors is reflected in the noticeably lower scoring in ordinary amateur or club play.

Actually, the top-rank professional player has the ability to overcome difficulties. He can work the ball up from a close or cuppy lie, and he can in time, by means of his highly trained senses, assemble a fair set of matched clubs. Of course, he can hole more putts on good greens. But anything making the game easier must be a leveling influence and cause it to be that much more difficult for a person to excel. Anyway, I am in favor of anything which will ease the troubles of the average golfer.

Apart from the obvious progress I have already mentioned, I think there has been one very great change on the psychological side which has had its effect upon scoring in our big championships. In a way, I think, it bears close resemblance to the psychological barrier that apparently was once erected against the four-minute mile.

In my day every player set out in an open championship with some sort of feeling—often well defined—that he had to have at least one bad round. There was even a saying that became trite to the effect that "those who do not blow up in the third round will in the fourth," and it usually turned out to be true, except for those who had already had their troubles on one of the first two days.

In the same way, we talked for so long of the "mythical" four-minute mile and wondered if anyone would ever run it. Then Roger Bannister did, and almost immediately John Landy. Now I think five men have run the distance in under four minutes.

I award to Ralph Guldahl the credit for breaking the barrier in golf. First at Oakland Hills in 1937, and again at Cherry Hills in 1938, Ralph made it clear that in order to win, you had to play four good rounds, not just three.

It has been that way ever since. That difference of from four to six or seven strokes accounts for most of the improvement in championship scoring since the Thirties.

I do not believe that I should have needed seventy-nine for the last round at Winged Foot or seventy-five at Interlachen if I had gone out on those afternoons feeling that I still had to win the championship, rather than just to protect it.

As I appraise the efficiency of modern golf-club manufacture and the excellence in balance and design of today's matched sets, I am often reminded of a period of considerable anxiety I experienced back in 1929.

It was just two weeks before the Open Championship was to be played at Winged Foot, and I had had to make a little trip to New York on business. As I frequently did, of course, I had taken an afternoon off to have a game with some friends. We had played a course over in Jersey, had had dinner at Dinty Moore's, and had gone for an evening of bridge to the apartment of a friend. While we were so engaged, our chauffeur had left the car in a garage. And when I was delivered back to my hotel, it was discovered that my golf clubs had disappeared. Had such a thing happened today, it would have been of little consequence. Either I should have had another set available at home, or it would have been possible to obtain satisfactory replacements almost immediately from the Spalding factory, where my specifications would have been of record. At that time, though, I saw the loss of something wholly irreplaceable.

It was fortunate indeed for me that one of my companions was Bill Nye, who had not too long before retired from the United States Secret Service, and who had been assigned to protect the Prince of Wales on his visit to this country. Bill went to work immediately, I believe through Grover Whalen, who was then Police Commissioner of New York, and was able to telegraph me in a couple of days that my clubs had been recovered. They had been stolen from the trunk of the automobile.

With all these changes in equipment and golf-course upkeep, it is not unnatural that the question should often occur, "What changes have come about in method? Is there a modern method, a modern golf swing which is essentially different from that of twenty-five or thirty years ago?" Actually, I think not, and I believe that so long as man is constructed as he is, which seems to be a fairly reasonable prospect for the predictable future, the order of the movements necessary to the complete, sound golf swing are not likely to change. In two respects only am I able to find any difference, and these are not of the nature which can be called fundamental.

The first difference I note is in the length of the backswing, and perhaps in the speed of it as well. In my day and before, the virtues of a long, leisurely swing had come to be fairly well accepted. Writer and players alike extoled the value of rhythm.

I still think that the long, leisurely swing is best for the average player. I think he should always try to make certain that he gets the club back far enough and that his change of direction at the top of the swing should take place in a leisurely manner, because nothing can so upset his timing and execution as hurry at either one of these points.

If there is a new method in golf, it seems to involve a more careful, even meticulous, "sighting" of the shot. While we still have many graceful, comfortable-looking players, there are a number who have the appearance of being excruciatingly stiff. In some cases the traditional waggle of the club designed to promote smoothness of movement has been replaced by a waggle of the player's behind as he strives to place himself in precise alignment for the delivery of the blow.

Some of these players are very effective. Once they have settled into a satisfactory position, the quick, convulsive stroke seems to send the ball very straight indeed toward the objective. But the method involves a complete disregard of the amount of time consumed, and so is most trying upon the nerves and patience of any who may be watching. I must admit that I do not find the performance of these players pleasing to the eye, even though the figures they produce may leave little to be desired.

It is not my intention to deny by what I have written that there has been no improvement among golfers themselves in the past thirty years. Indeed, I should regard it as very sad if this were the case. Men have learned to run faster and to jump higher and farther. It would be strange if they had not also learned to play better golf. Every generation learns from those that have gone before, and so progress is made.

There are certainly more people playing golf today. More youngsters are playing the game, and the very substantial nature of tournament prizes causes the professional side of the game to have considerable attraction as a means of gaining financial security. The "winter circuit" of the 1920's has become a year-round tour offering a tournament for important money every week of the year.

Naturally, with the possibilities of reward so much greater, the amount of effort that can be inspired is proportionately greater. To improve one's play and rate of performance in tournaments can now be made a full-time occupation and study. Most of the competitors of today are full-time players, whereas in my day most of the winter-circuit boys were working club professionals in the summer season. The touring pro of today can get more tournament experience and seasoning in one year of active play than used to be possible in a decade.

So while I think it is true that the best of the old-timers could play all the shots as well as anyone around today, I think it cannot be denied that the top few in any tournament of today will make fewer mistakes than their counterparts of the earlier days. This may be attributed partly to the fact that the game of golf today, because of improved equipment and grounds, is a more precise game than it ever was before, but also because the modern player has attained a more complete control over his own physical shot-making machinery. He has also, through increased experience, learned a lot more about the management of himself and his game in tournament play.

In golf, you know you can't rely on the old adage that there is safety in numbers. Indeed, it works the other way. In a close finish, if there are only two or three players a couple of shots away, you may hope that all three may be off a bit that day. But when you have a dozen or so on your heels, you know that some of them will stick with you to the finish.

Presenting Metropolitan Golf Writers Gold Tee Award to Francis Ouimet in New York, January 1960. I had just received from Vice President Richard M. Nixon the special trophy on the table commemorating the 30th anniversary of the Grand Slam.

CHAPTER *18*

The Stymie—Let's Have It Back!

o In comparing the golf of today with that of former times, other factors to be considered as affecting conditions of play are the rules.

I have always been thankful that the ruling bodies on both sides of the Atlantic have resisted changes in the rules. Throughout the years there have been plenty of suggestions, and even agitations, for changes. But few have been made. Clarifications, yes, but few real changes.

One alteration of importance affecting scoring has taken place in the formerly rigid requirement that in stroke play, play once begun must be continued, regardless of weather. At Winged Foot in 1929 we played one round, the second, when every hole was in running water. We played a qualifying round for the Amateur at Brookline in 1922 when several of the greens were inundated. Nowadays there is a considerably greater readiness to postpone play.

Perhaps the convenience of spectators is of more importance now. But I think the main reason has been supplied by the realization of the great danger from exposure to lightning on the golf course. No one should quarrel with this. The one place where I think a real mistake was made came with the elimination of the stymie—and because I am still hopeful that this very important feature of match play may be restored to the game, I shall set out my argument in some detail.

It has been appalling to me to find that there are golfers of today who do not even know the meaning of "stymie." Twenty years ago I should never have dreamed that it would ever be necessary to explain that a stymie results in match play when one ball on the putting green interposes some of, or all, its mass between the other ball and the hole.

Yet there is not one appearance of the word "stymie" in the rule book of today, and Rule 35-2 makes certain that no stymie will appear in actual play.

The present rule has evolved from several attempts in the same direction. For a while, the offending ball could only be removed by the concession of the remaining putt; but now a player may insist upon its removal if he "considers that it might interfere with his play."

Obviously the objection to the stymie originated in the conception that each player must be permitted to play his own game free of any influence by his opponent. Why this should be an essential when the contest is man-to-man and head-to-head, I have never been able to see. The other charge that the stymie is unfair can have gained acceptance only because the victims and their sympathizers have felt justified in agonizing over the tragedies, whereas the beneficiaries have been restrained by generosity to a fallen opponent or shame because of a tainted triumph.

To be sure, bad luck can be a factor in the stymie. A typical case where this is true runs like this. A plays a shot to the green three feet from the hole. *B* plays the like, thirty feet away; *B* putts and stymies A. Thus A is prevented from winning the hole. That is bad luck for A. It is also not the typical stymie situation.

Two very typical stymie situations are in my mind. The first, occurred on the nineteenth hole at St. Andrews in the British Amateur of 1930. Cyril Tolley and I are playing the first extra hole of an exciting match in which the strain upon both players and a large gallery has been terrific.

After two good drives I play the odd, a better-than-fair shot ten feet from the hole; Cyril plays a definitely slack second, off the green on the left. The chip is tricky, but again Cyril's shot is not good, seven feet short. I putt carefully, leaving my ball two inches from the hole, directly in Cyril's line, completely blocking the hole.

One might say that it was a lucky win. Yet I had played the hole better all the way, after the tee shot. The question is, "How much better must a man play a hole in order to be entitled to win it?"

Two aspects of the stymie (under the rules in force at the time I played) must be understood. If the balls lie so that the space between them is less than six inches, the nearer one may be lifted. Thus if a player's first putt should leave his ball less than six inches from the hole, he cannot be stymied. Also, within a radius of two feet, a competent player can make, almost every time, any stymie that may be laid him. It is not likely, therefore, that anyone will ever lose a hole by reason of a stymie, unless he has left himself in a vulnerable position.

The other illustrative stymie situation occurred on the thirty-fourth hole of the final match of the 1936 Amateur Championship at Garden City. Jack McLean, of the British Walker Cup Team, was playing Johnny Fischer of our team. Coming to this hole one up, McLean appeared almost certain to be the first British player to win our championship since Harold Hilton in 1911.

McLean's second shot to this thirty-fourth hole had stopped less than ten feet past the hole. Fischer had been in the rough off the tee, been short of the green with his second, and had chipped not too well, so that in three his ball lay short of the hole and only a very little nearer than McLean's.

I was standing with Grantland Rice in the gallery behind the green. I think we both appreciated the possibilities in the situation. Obviously, it was a time for conservative play by McLean. The wise play here was to sneak his ball down as close as possible to the hole, leaving Fischer the job of holing his putt to avoid being two down with two to play. A good putt here would make a punishing stymie impossible.

I was horrified to see McLean going boldly for the putt on that keen green. The ball overran by more than a yard—and Fischer stymied him.

Still trying to win the hole, McLean attempted to pitch from the dangerous distance. I just knew he was going to knock Fischer's ball in for the win that would have squared the match. Fortunately McLean made overly certain that this would not happen, but he had to hole a four-footer to save a half. I have never experienced so many chills and thrills in so short a time.

This hole cost McLean the championship. They halved the thirty-fifth in beautiful birdie fours, but Fischer holed a great putt to win the thirty-sixth, and won out at the first extra hole.

The stymie had been the decisive factor, but the blame lay squarely upon McLean. Whether it was the fault of his judgment or his putting touch, he had invited his own destruction.

Without the possibility of the stymie, the situation on that thirty-fourth green would have been completely routine. With the stymie always in the picture, suspense and excitement were present from the moment the players walked onto the green.

With the stymie in the game, match-play golf becomes an exciting duel in which the player must always be on guard against a sudden, often demoralizing thrust. More than anything else, it points up the value of always being the closer to the hole on the shot to the green and after the first putt. The player who can maintain the upper hand in the play up to the hole rarely suffers from a stymie.

In my observation, the stymie has more often been the means of enforcing a decision in favor of the deserving player, rather than the contrary. I think it merits a respected place in the game. I know a return to it would greatly enhance the interest and excitement of match-play golf for player and spectator alike.

The easiest kind of stymie. This shot only becomes difficult as the opponent's ball moves closer to the hole, or your own lies farther away.

CHAPTER *19*

Augusta—An Idea Is Born

Not long ago Clifford Roberts and I had been discussing some matters related to the Masters Tournament in Augusta. Suddenly he said, "Bob, we've really got a bear by the tail with this thing. Do you suppose we would ever have started it if we had known where it was going to take us?" "Frankly, I do not know," I replied.

Although I do not believe that in 1930 either Cliff or I would have been deterred by any clairvoyant knowledge we might have had of the present stature of the Masters Tournament, I do believe quite sincerely that our ambitions would have been effectively restrained had we known of the travail we were to have with the club during the early years.

The Augusta National Golf Club itself was born of very modest aspirations to begin with. Cliff had been coming to Augusta for some years as a reasonably regular winter visitor. He and I were close friends of Walton H. Marshall of the Vanderbilt Hotel in New York City, who also operated the Bon Air Vanderbilt in Augusta during the winter season. We were also patrons of both Marshall hotels.

Living in Atlanta only a short distance away, I had come to Augusta often over a period of years for friendly golf and an occasional charity match. As I have recounted earlier, I also played in the Southeastern Open Tournament over the country club and Forest Hills courses in Augusta during the early part of 1930. I had always been impressed by the fact that, especially during the winter season, golf courses around Augusta were considerably better conditioned than courses near Atlanta, and since at that time we were doomed to coarse Bermuda grass for putting greens in the summer, it was in winter golf that our best hope lay.

In any event, when Cliff came to Atlanta during the late fall of 1930 to suggest to me that I join him in organizing a club and building a golf course near Augusta, I found myself in a very receptive frame of mind.

The attractive aspects of the proposal were somewhat as follows:

Augusta was well known to me as a resort area and a pleasant setting for golf during the winter months. Cliff and I had a number of friends among the permanent and winter residents there who could be counted on to form a nucleus around which to build our club. I felt that the financing of such a project would be infinitely more likely to succeed in Augusta than in Atlanta.

Secondly, I was acutely aware of the fact that my native Southland, especially my own neighborhood, had very few, if any, golf courses of championship quality. The prospect of myself building a course according to the high standards of excellence which I would set, based on what I considered to be a very wide experience in the game, was most intriguing. I truly regarded it as an opportunity to make a contribution to golf in my own section of the country, as well as to give expression to my own very definite ideas about golf-course design.

Thirdly, the piece of ground available, as described by Cliff and as later confirmed by me in a personal visit, seemed ideally suited to the purpose Cliff was suggesting. In brief, the dream was completely enthralling, especially at a time when I was, I suppose, flushed with success and already deeply involved in enough golfing projects to preclude, at least for many years, my taking any serious interest in other activities.

As the name implies, the new club was set up on a national basis. We planned to have only a small group of local members upon whom we could rely for help in the day-to-day administration of the club's affairs. Our aim was to develop a golf course and a retreat of such nature, and of such excellence, that men of some means and devoted to the game of golf might find the club worthwhile as an extra luxury where they might visit and play with kindred spirits from other parts of the nation. This policy has never been changed, and I am happy to be able to say that the club apparently has adequately fulfilled this mission.

In this view, of course, the all-important thing was to be the golf course. I shall never forget my first visit to the property which is now the Augusta National. The long lane of magnolias through which we approached was beautiful. The old manor house with its cupola and walls of masonry two feet thick was charming. The rare trees and shrubs of the old nursery were enchanting. But when I walked out on the grass terrace under the big trees behind the house and looked down over the property, the experience was unforgettable. It seemed that this land had been lying here for years just waiting for someone to lay a golf course upon it. Indeed, it even looked as though it were already a golf course, and I am sure that one standing today where I stood on this first visit, on the terrace overlooking the practice putting green, sees the property almost exactly as I saw it then. The grass of the fairways and greens is greener, of course, and some of the pines are a bit larger, but the broad expanse of the main body of the property lay at my feet then just as it does now.

I still like to sit on this terrace, and can do so for hours at a time, enjoying the beauty of this panorama.

With this sort of land, of a soft, gentle, rather than spectacular beauty, it was especially appropriate that we chose Dr. Alister MacKenzie to design our course. For it was essential to our requirements that we build a course within the capacity of the average golfer to enjoy. This did not mean that the design should be insipid, for our players were expected to be sophisticated. They would demand interesting, lively golf, but would not long endure a course which kept them constantly straining for distance and playing out of sand.

There was much conversation at the time to the effect that MacKenzie and I expected to reproduce in their entirety holes of famous courses around the world where I had played in competitions. This was, at best, a bit naïve, because to do such a thing, we would have had literally to alter the face of the earth. It was to be expected, of course, that the new layout would be strongly influenced by holes which either MacKenzie or I had admired, but it was only possible that we should have certain features of these holes in mind and attempt to adapt them to the terrain with which we were working.

I think MacKenzie and I managed to work as a completely sympathetic team. Of course, there was never any question that he was the architect and I his advisor and consultant. No man learns to design a golf course simply by playing golf, no matter how well. But it happened that both of us were extravagant admirers of the Old Course at St. Andrews and we both desired as much as possible to simulate seaside conditions insofar as the differences in turf and terrain would allow.

MacKenzie was very fond of expressing his creed as a golf-course architect by saying that he tried to build courses for the "most enjoyment for the greatest number." This happened to coincide completely with my own view. It had seemed to me that too many courses I had seen had been constructed with an eye to difficulty alone, and that in the effort to construct an exacting course which would thwart the expert, the average golfer who paid the bills was entirely overlooked. Too often, the worth of a layout seemed to be measured by how successfully it had withstood the efforts of professionals to better its par or to lower its record.

The first purpose of any golf course should be to give pleasure, and that to the greatest possible number of players, without respect to their capabilities. As far as possible, there should be presented to each golfer an interesting problem which will test him without being so impossibly difficult that he will have little chance of success. There must be something to do, but that something must always be within the realm of reasonable accomplishment.

From the standpoint of the inexpert player, there is nothing so disheartening as the appearance of a carry which is beyond his best effort and which offers no alternative route. In such a situation, there is nothing for the golfer to do, for he is given no opportunity to overcome his deficiency in length by either accuracy or judgment.

With respect to the employment of hazards off the tee and through the green, the doctor and I agreed that two things were essential. First, there must be a way around for those unwilling to attempt the carry; and second, there must be a definite reward awaiting the man who makes it. Without the alternative route the situation is unfair. Without the reward it is meaningless.

There are two ways of widening the gap between a good tee shot and a bad one. One is to inflict a severe and immediate punishment on a bad shot, to place its perpetrator in a bunker or in some other trouble which will demand the sacrifice of a stroke in recovering. The other is to reward the good shot by making the second shot simpler in proportion to the excellence of the first. The reward may be of any nature, but it is more commonly one of four—a better view of the green, an easier angle from which to attack a slope, an open approach past guarding hazards, or even a better run to the tee shot itself. But the elimination of purely punitive hazards provides an opportunity for the player to retrieve his situation by an exceptional second shot.

A course which is constructed with these principles in view must be interesting, because it will offer problems which a man may attempt, according to his ability. It will never become hopeless for the duffer, nor fail to concern and interest the expert. And it will be found, like old St. Andrews, to become more delightful the more it is studied and played.

We try very hard in Augusta to avoid placing meaningless bunkers on the course. Some of the natural hazards are severe, but usually so for the ambitious player. Possibly the dearth of bunkers on the course is a feature most commented upon by visitors. Yet there are some which perhaps could be dispensed with, except that they are in use to protect players from more dire consequences. Occasionally a bunker may be used to stop a ball from running into a hazard of a more serious nature.

I have already said that 1931 was a very bad year in which to start a new golf club. The depression got worse instead of better. The early years of the club were not easy from an operating standpoint.

The golf course, on the other hand, gave every indication of fulfilling our ambitions for it in a most gratifying way. We very soon became convinced of the soundness of the basic conceptions upon which the course had been built. Most important of all to me was confirmation of my hope that during the spring months a combination of Bermuda base and Italian-rye surface could provide as good putting as was to be found anywhere. For the first time I became aware that championship golf could be played in the South.

Somewhere during the second year of the existence of the golf course in its completed form, and from somewhere within the hard core of faithful who had accepted responsibility for the direction of the club, there came the suggestion that we try to get the National Open Championship for our club. We had many conversations on the subject among ourselves, and with officials of the United States Golf Association.

The idea was regarded among all of us as not entirely without merit, but in the end, enough objections were found to cause us all to agree that the project was not feasible, the most important opposing reason being that the championship would have to be played during the early spring instead of, as customarily, during the month of June or the first half of July.

These conversations were really the beginnings of the Masters Tournament, because from them Clifford Roberts came up with the idea that we might stage a tournament of our own. In this way we might just as well demonstrate the virtues of the kind of golf course we had created and, at the same time, bring to Augusta and the adjoining section an annual golfing event which would give our people the opportunity to see the world's best players in action on a first-class golf course.

It was Cliff also who persuaded me that the tournament could be set apart from the rest of those springing up as fixtures on the winter circuit, by casting me in the role of host and building the tournament around this as my one appearance in competition. I must confess that the prospect of annually entertaining my old playmates and the later arrivals in the upper crust of competitive golf was quite attractive.

From the very beginning we planned the tournament on an invitational basis. As president of the club, it was to be my privilege to invite a limited number of men whom I considered likely to grace the tournament because of their past accomplishments in the game, their present stature, their promise, or even upon my own feeling of friendship for them.

We have ever since retained the invitational character of the tournament, but it took no time at all for us to discover that on the original basis, I and others in the club's official family had let ourselves in for a considerable amount of embarrassment so long as we should construct the invitation list on any such free and easy basis. Our club's facilities, which are still not spacious, were at that time stringent indeed. It was an utter impossibility to include everyone whom I might wish to invite for any reason, and still keep the field down to manageable numbers. It became obvious that the only possible solution was the one which we followed, namely to adopt a definite set of qualifications which a player must meet in order to be considered for an invitation. And obviously, too, this set of qualifications, after its adoption for any one tournament, had to be so rigid that even I was not able to deviate from it.

The first tournament was called the Augusta National Invitation Tournament, but, even before its playing, Cliff had begun to think and talk of it as the Masters. I have occasionally forgotten this fact, but having had my memory refreshed, I remember very well that I resisted for a time the application of this name to our tournament. When Cliff suggested it, I vetoed it on the basis that it was a title entirely too presumptuous for us to apply to a tournament of our creation. I am not so certain that our ends have not been served best by this reluctance. I think the tournament is now quite well entitled to be called the Masters, because it has continued to assemble those who are entitled to be called masters of the game; and although we must admit that the name was born of a touch of immodesty on the part of Cliff, yet it has only attached itself to the tournament because of the approval and adoption of the name by the newspaper boys who have followed it.

Even though some of my playing experiences in the tournament have not been altogether rewarding, at this point I have no hesitancy in saying that the Masters Tournament has provided one of the most truly wonderful aspects of my life with the associations and excitement it has brought and with the satisfactions we have felt in the development of the tournament and the golf course.

Although the strain of open championships had always punished me severely, the practice rounds for these events played with the pros had always provided the most enjoyable golf I had ever had. I held the notion, therefore, that I could have this same enjoyment in Augusta, not only in the practice rounds, but during the tournament itself, since I was convinced that I should never again feel the strain and responsibility to the same degree that I had when I was competing seriously.

I had continued to play reasonably well in friendly golf since my retirement, and I entertained no doubt of my ability still to do reasonably well, even though playing in one tournament a year. After all, for a great many of the years when I had been winning championships, I had only played in two tournaments a year. I could even produce arguments to the effect that it was an advantage to be able to point for one tournament without having to play in one every week.

I think things might very well have worked out this way, for a while at least, had the Augusta tournament been played on any ordinary golf course. It seems a bit ironic I know, but I do believe that the course I had helped to create was exactly the kind of course to make most difficult these once-a-year appearances, especially after an absence of four years from competition.

It was one thing to drive and play iron shots as well as before, but quite another to reacquire the delicate touch and confidence around the green which was so necessary on this course. None of the informal golf I had played around Atlanta, or even at the Augusta National, had been played on greens anything like those at Augusta in tournament condition. I soon found there was a great deal of difference.

I remember quite well starting that first round in the first tournament playing with Paul Runyan. Periodically during my active golfing years I had had trouble with a calloused place on the side of the middle finger of my right hand. As the callus would grow, it would split, and I had to keep it wrapped in tape. I noticed as I wrapped this finger before going to the tee that my hands were trembling a bit, and I felt the familiar unpleasant, vacant sensation in my stomach. This was neither worrisome nor surprising. I had become accustomed to these feelings and had learned actually to welcome them, because they usually meant that I was to play good golf.

I did all right for the first three holes, even though a couple of putts overran the hole a bit more than I should have liked. As I hit the first tee shot, I was delighted when I felt the ball on the center of the club face and saw its flight down the fairway. Evidently the strain was working on the long game just the way it used to.

The first hole was good enough, the second putt being less than six inches. But on the next green, I had a warning. I knew that I had not been swinging my putter, and I knew that I must swing it. Further, I knew that to get back the old sweeping stroke I must make my backswing plenty long. The putt was some twenty-five feet. I swung the putter back, but I gave it a jerk as I hit the ball and it went about two yards past the hole. I holed the next, but again I felt the jerk. I think I knew then what was coming.

Nevertheless, the first three holes were taken in par, and on the fourth, which is now the thirteenth, a par five, I played a very nice, fading brassie shot from a hillside lie to the vicinity of the hole and got down in two putts for a birdie four. One under par for the first four holes was a very acceptable start.

But stepping onto the fifth tee, I was aware that the nervousness was still with me and may even have been increasing all the while. This was definitely not normal, because in the past it would have disappeared within a hole or two. I think the uncertainty I felt about my putting was the one thing that kept me from settling down. I realized that on that particular course if I could not become comfortable on the greens, I had no chance to work out a score. It is possible to overcome bad driving or weak iron play by chipping and putting, but a missed putt is a lost stroke and there is no place to get it back.

Anyway, as I stepped up to hit the tee shot from the fifth tee, a motion-picture camera started whirring, and I stepped away from the ball. Ordinarily again, this would have been only a momentary distraction, but now I could not take hold of myself as I had done before. I hit the tee shot before I had completely settled down and pushed it into the woods on the right.

At that very instant I realized that this return to competition was not going to be too much fun. I realized, too, that I simply had not the desire nor the willingness to take the punishment necessary to compete in that kind of company. I think I realized, too, that whatever part I might have in the Masters Tournament from then on would not be as a serious contender.

After the great finish of the 1954 Masters, in which Snead and Hogan tied for first place, with Billy Joe Patton, the amateur, only one stroke behind. Left to right: Patton, Hogan, myself, Snead.

CHAPTER ***20***

The Course

o Our over-all aim at the Augusta National has been to provide a golf course of considerable natural beauty, relatively easy for the average golfer to play, and at the same time testing for the expert player striving to better par figures. We hope to make bogies easy if frankly sought, pars readily obtainable by standard good play, and birdies, except on the par fives, dearly bought. Obviously, with a course as wide-open as needed to accommodate the average golfer, we can only tighten it up by increasing the difficulty of play around the hole. This we attempt to do during the tournament by placing the flags in more difficult and exacting positions and by increasing the speed of the greens. Additionally, we try to maintain our greens of such a firmness that they will only hold a well-played shot, and not a ball that has been hit without the backspin reasonably to be expected, considering the length of the shot.

Generally speaking, the greens at Augusta are quite large, rolling, and with carefully contrived undulations, the effect of which is magnified as the speed is increased. We are quite willing to have low scores made during the tournament. It is not our intention to rig the golf course so as to make it tricky. It is our feeling that there is something wrong with a golf course which will not yield a score in the sixties to a player who has played well enough to deserve it.

On the other hand, we do not believe that birdies should be made too easily. We think that to play two good shots to a par four hole and then to hole a ten-foot putt on a dead-level green is not enough. If the player is to beat par, we should like to ask him to hit a truly fine second shot right up against the flag or to hole a putt of more than a little difficulty. We therefore place the holes on tournament days in such locations on the greens as to require a really fine shot in order to get close. With the greens fast and undulating, the putts from medium distances are difficult and the player who leaves his ball on the outer reaches has a real problem to get down in par figures.

The contours of the greens at Augusta have been very carefully designed. We try to provide on each green at least four areas which we describe as "pin locations." This does not mean that the pin is always placed in one very definite spot within these areas, but each area provides an opportunity for cutting the hole in a spot where the contours are very gentle for a radius of four or five feet all around.

The selection of the pin area and the exact location of the hole is decided on the morning of play by a committee appointed for the purpose. The decision will be affected by the condition of the putting surface itself, the state of the weather to be expected, and the holding qualities of the ground. Naturally, the job of placing the holes on tournament days is one which calls for a considerable knowledge of the game and good judgment. I am sure that the players involved would be interested, too, that the committee be composed of individuals of benign and charitable natures. The placement of the flags is one of the most controversial matters in any golf tournament, because it can so drastically affect the difficulty of the play.

Even though it is too much to expect that persons deciding on pin locations in the very early morning should be able to foresee weather conditions to prevail during the actual play, it is nevertheless important that they have in mind what conditions are likely to confront the players. They should also take into account the playing condition of the fairway from which shots to a particular green are to be played.

I think it is also most rewarding for spectators, in watching the play, to be aware of the effect of variables in wind and lie of the ball. If a player is to be asked to play a quickly-stopping shot to a closely guarded green, he has every right to expect that his ball will have a very good chance of finding a clean lie, where it will be accessible to the gripping effect of his club. If the fairway in question, or the fairways in general, are not in good condition, the holes should never be cut too close to guarding bunkers.

Although a following wind tends to rob the ball of backspin and so makes more difficult the problem of stopping a pitch in much the same way as a lush lie, I do not believe that it offers the same argument in favor of leniency in the placing of the holes. After all, the wind is a circumstance of play wholly outside the control of those running the tournament and, unlike a bad lie, it is not subject to the vagaries of chance. Since, within reasonable limits, it is the same for all players, the difficulty of the problem to be presented may very properly be decided by the committee.

If one were to set out to make a golf course as difficult as possible, he would place the holes forward, with the wind behind, and at the back of the greens with the wind against. It must be in the light of this basic principle that the committee's decision for each particular hole will be made.

It may not be readily apparent at this point why a far-back location increases the difficulty when playing against the wind. An opposing wind is a great comfort to the player when the flag is located immediately behind a bunker guarding the front of the green. The ball can then be played boldly over the bunker with assurance that it will not finish too far past the hole. But if the pin be moved to the back of the green, and trouble lurks behind, the player must be bold indeed and extraordinarily accurate in his judgment of distance in order to bang his ball right up to the flag. Players of less confidence and skill will be continually leaving themselves far short and with a great deal of putting to do. Several greens at the Augusta National, with shelf-like areas along the back and an abrupt fall-off or bunker in the rear, are well suited to emphasize this problem.

It has been said, and I hope it is true, that the Augusta National has exerted influence in the designing or remodeling of several hundred golf courses in the country. I hope this is true, because I sincerely believe that the general concepts which have influenced the construction and later modifications of our course have been quite sound from the standpoint of making the game more enjoyable for the people who support it. I believe our members could be counted upon to testify unanimously to this effect. As for the other side of the coin, I feel quite certain that the contestants in the Masters Tournament would attest very nearly as unanimously that the course provides a real competitive test. It is a fact that hardly ever has any player done exceptionally well in Augusta who has not had a quite respectable record in tournaments played elsewhere.

I believe it is true that with modern equipment and modern players, we cannot make a golf course more difficult or more testing for the expert simply by adding length. The players of today are about as accurate with medium or long irons as with their pitching clubs. The only way to stir them up is by the introduction of subtleties around the greens.

The finishes of the Masters Tournament have almost always been dramatic and exciting. It is my conviction that this has been the case because of the make-or-break quality of the second nine. This nine, with its abundant water hazards, each creating a perilous situation, can provide excruciating torture for the front runner trying to hang on. Yet it can yield a very low score to the player making a closing rush. It has been played in thirty during the tournament and in the medium forties by players still in contention at the time.

I hope the following description will communicate a fair appreciation of the important playing features and characteristics of the golf course.

Note: Throughout this and all my other writings on the game, I have used the word "bunker" in what I have understood to be the traditional golfing sense, meaning a pit in which the soil has been exposed and the area covered with sand. I regard the term "sand trap" as an unacceptable Americanization. Its use annoys me almost as much as hearing a golf club called a "stick." Earthworks, mounds, and the like, without sand, are not bunkers.

CHAPTER 21

Playing the Masters

Drawings by George W. Cobb, Golf Course Architect

Hole No. 1, 400 yards, par 4 This hole can be played straight away from tee to green, although the fairway does expand on the right as it approaches the green. Ordinarily, the fairway bunker on the right presents no problem for the tournament player. With a heavy wind against, however, as often happens, a half-hit tee shot may catch this bunker.

At the same time, a drive down the right side of the fairway is only important when the wind is behind and the hole is cut immediately behind the bunker at the left front of the green. Under these circumstances, the drive down the right side makes it possible for the player to play more nearly for the pin with his second shot.

The player who drives down the left side must play his second either over the bunker or into slopes which tend to direct his ball off the right side of the green.

A sort of shelf across the back of the green offers several interesting pin locations, especially when the wind is against. With the flag far back, the player thinks twice before he goes boldly for the pin and often leaves himself a very difficult approach putt from the lower level.

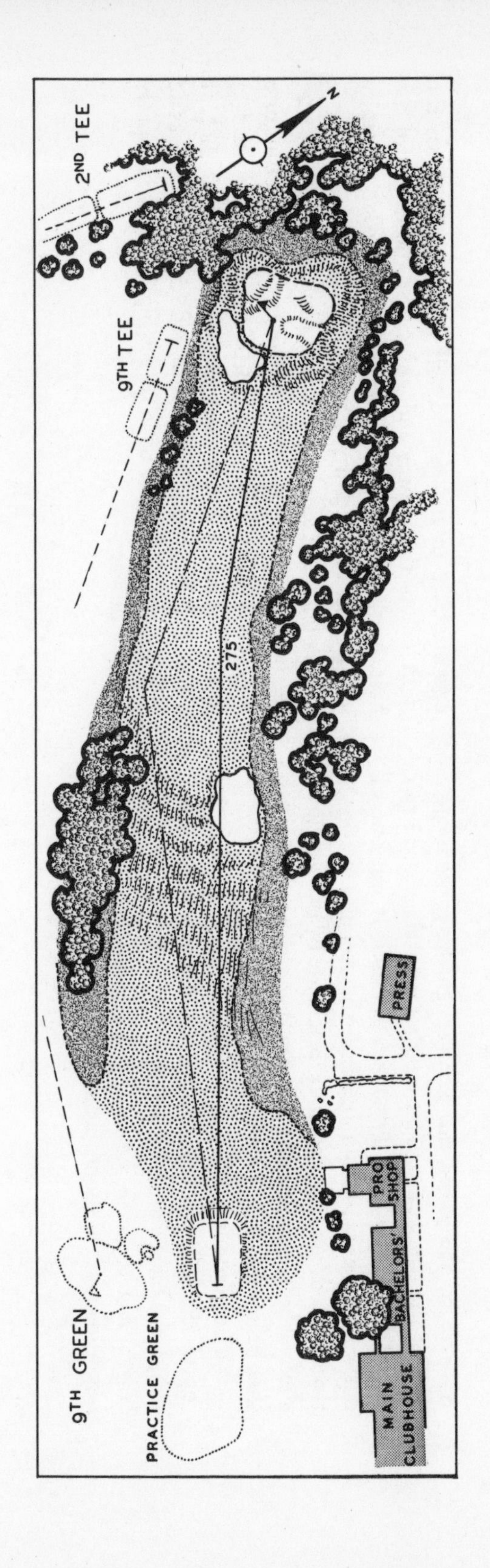
N
2ND TEE
9TH TEE
275
PRESS
PRO SHOP
BACHELORS'
MAIN CLUBHOUSE
9TH GREEN
PRACTICE GREEN

Hole No. 2, 555 yards, par 5 Although this is the longest hole of the course, a well-hit tee shot will take a good run down the fairway as it slopes over the hill. It was one of our guiding principles in building the Augusta National that even our par fives should be reachable by two excellent shots. The possibility of using the down slope off the tee shot brings this long hole into this category.

The contours of the fairway and the mounds at the top of the hill were constructed for the very purpose of aiding the player to make use of the slope in order to gain length. But to do so, he must drive accurately across the big bunker. If he should wander slightly to the right, the opposite face of the mound will turn his ball down the right side of the fairway and so increase the length of the hole. A drive too close to the corner is likely to kick abruptly into a most unpleasant place.

After a fine tee shot, a second played over or just past the bunker at the right front of the green may finish quite near the hole if it is placed on that side. With the flag located behind the left-hand bunker, the second shot, if played for the green, should be aimed for the center of the putting surface, in the hope of getting down in two putts for a birdie four.

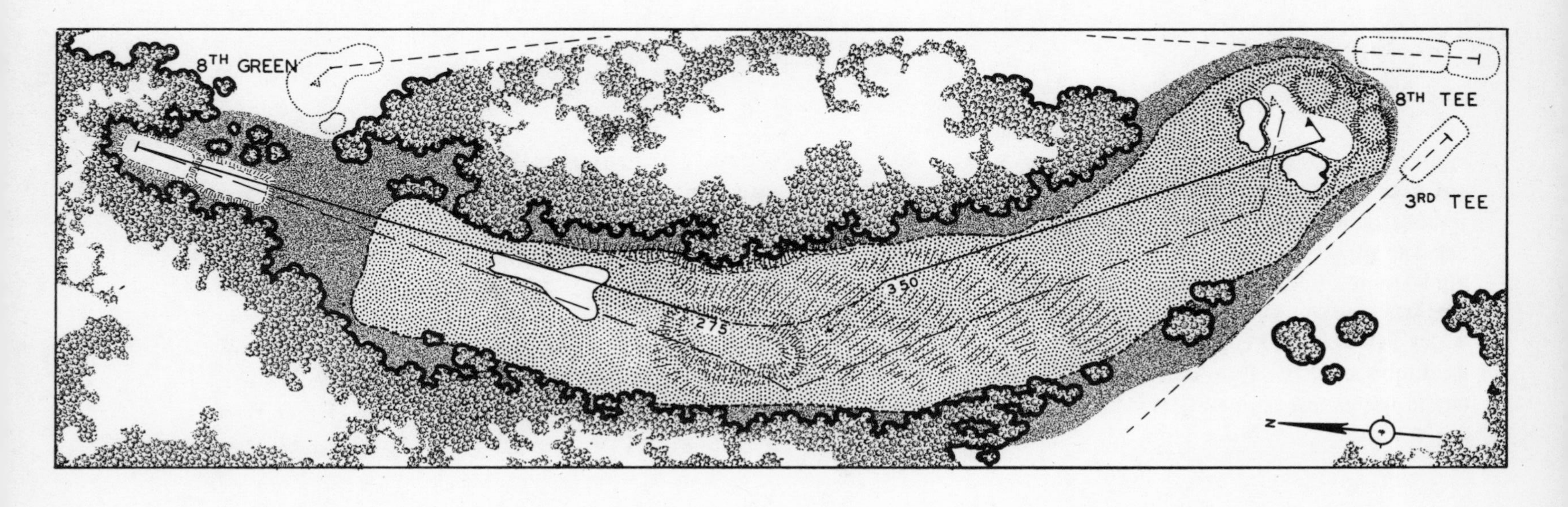
8TH GREEN
8TH TEE
3RD TEE
350
275
N

Hole No. 3, 355 yards, par 4 The aim here should be slightly right of the center of the fairway onto the high ground which gives good visibility of the green and also provides the best angle of approach to any flag location. A tee shot pulled to the left side of the fairway is very likely to follow the run of the ground into the big bunker.

The green on the left is very shallow; on the right side, it is very deep but slopes away from the player so that it is not easy to be certain of the exact location of the flag.

The main problem presented by the second shot, which is normally played with a wedge or eight iron, is to gauge the distance precisely. With the pin on the left a second shot played either short or over leaves a very difficult pitch to be made which almost always results in the loss of one stroke, often two. With the wind behind, the wise player will play for the center or left-center of the green, hoping to get down in two putts for a par four.

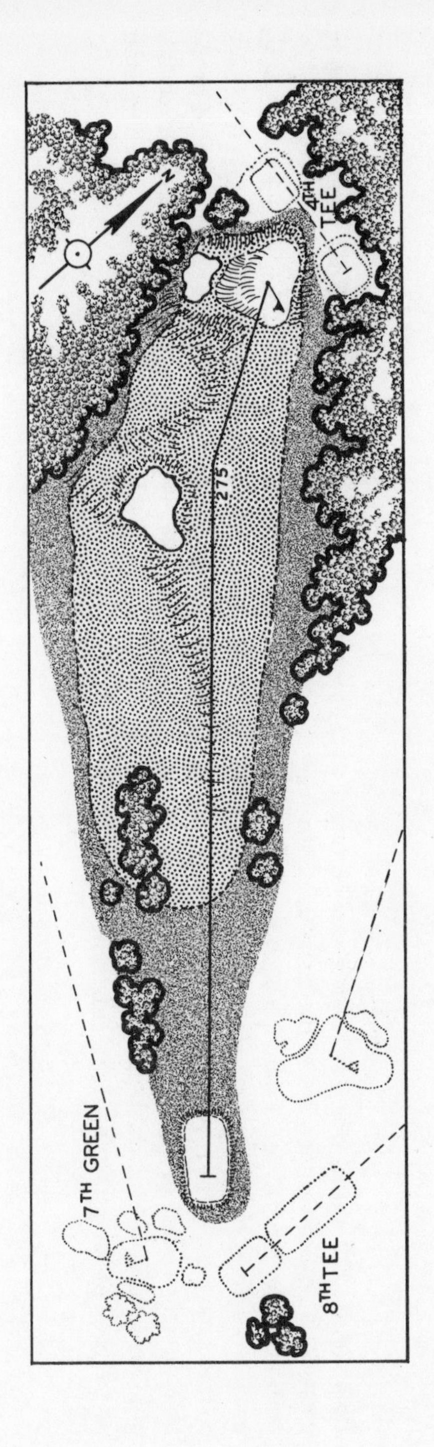
N
4TH TEE
275
7TH GREEN
8TH TEE

Hole No. 4, 220 yards, par 3 This hole can be varied a great deal, depending upon use of the back tee or the rear portion of the forward tee. From the back tee the shot is usually a strong iron or even a four or three wood. At tournament time there is very often a heavy wind on this hole directly against or quartering off the right. With the pin immediately behind the bunker or on the high ground at the back of the green, a precise judgment of distance is required to avoid either a long, difficult approach putt or an exacting chip.

The green is so large that a shot played to the outer reaches more often than not will result in a bogie. The back tee is somewhat elevated so that the shot is exposed to the violence of any wind which may be blowing. On certain days the wind will place many players in the left-hand bunker or beyond.

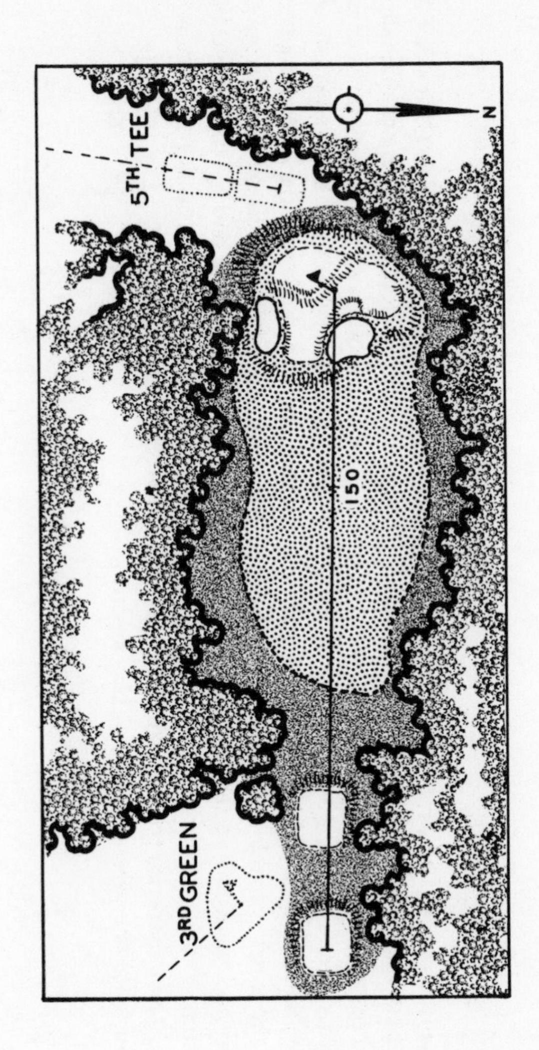
5TH TEE
N
150
3RD GREEN

Hole No. 5, 450 yards, par 4 The proper line here is as closely as possible past the bunker on the left side of the fairway. It is not necessary to carry this bunker in order to direct the drive into a groove in the fairway on top of the hill. But it is a very comforting safety factor to have sufficient length for the carry should the shot be pulled slightly. The bunker and the woods to the left of it usually represent dire disaster.

Players lacking the confidence to play along the dangerous line sometimes become overcautious and play down the right side of the fairway. From this side the second shot becomes much longer and far more difficult.

On this hole, with the greens surfaces in proper condition, the second shot must be dropped short and allowed to run up. The bunker in back of the green was placed there not for penalty, but as an effort to minimize the loss from an overplayed second. Without the bunker such a shot would run far down the slope and cause the recovery to be much more difficult.

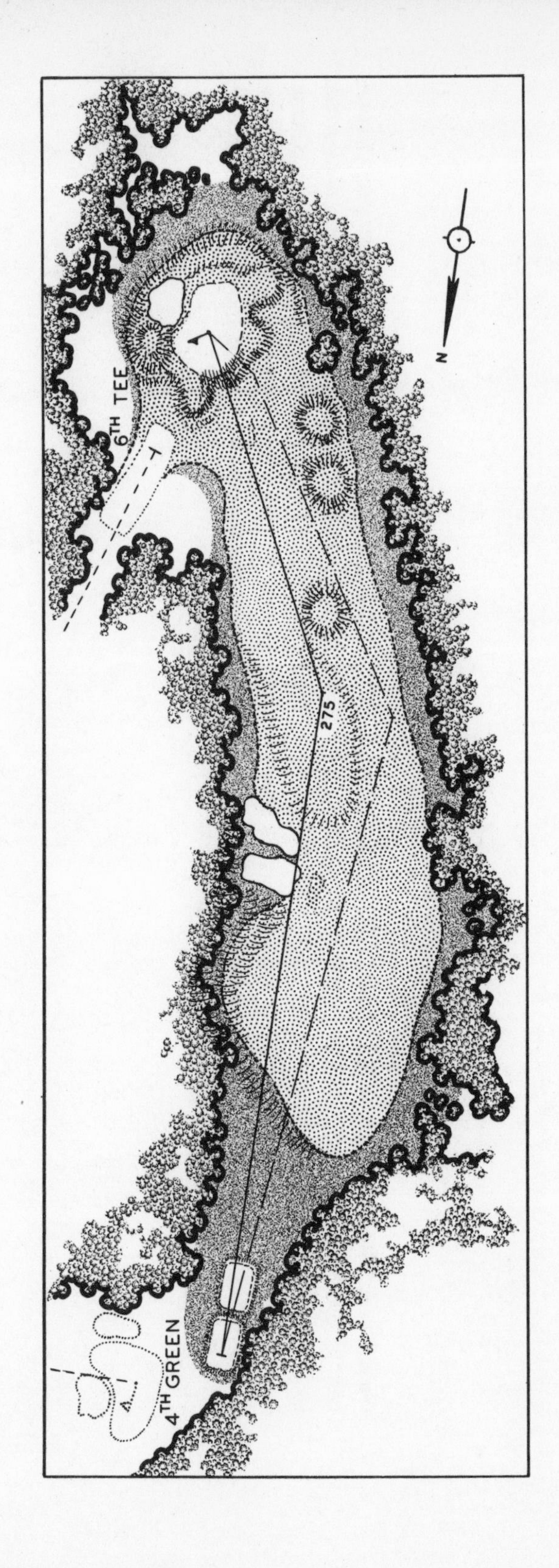
6TH TEE
N
275
4TH GREEN

***Hole No. 6,* 190 yards, par 3** The really difficult pin area here is formed by the plateau at the right back corner. To land upon and hold this plateau, the shot must be very accurately struck. With the ball left either short of this area or to the left, the first putt is extremely difficult.

The front of the green immediately behind the bunker is the easiest location. Back of this, the side slope is severe. This is one of the easiest holes on the course, but the setting of the big green is very lovely when viewed from the elevated tee. This area comprising the sixth hole and the spectacular sixteenth is one of the most popular spectator spots.

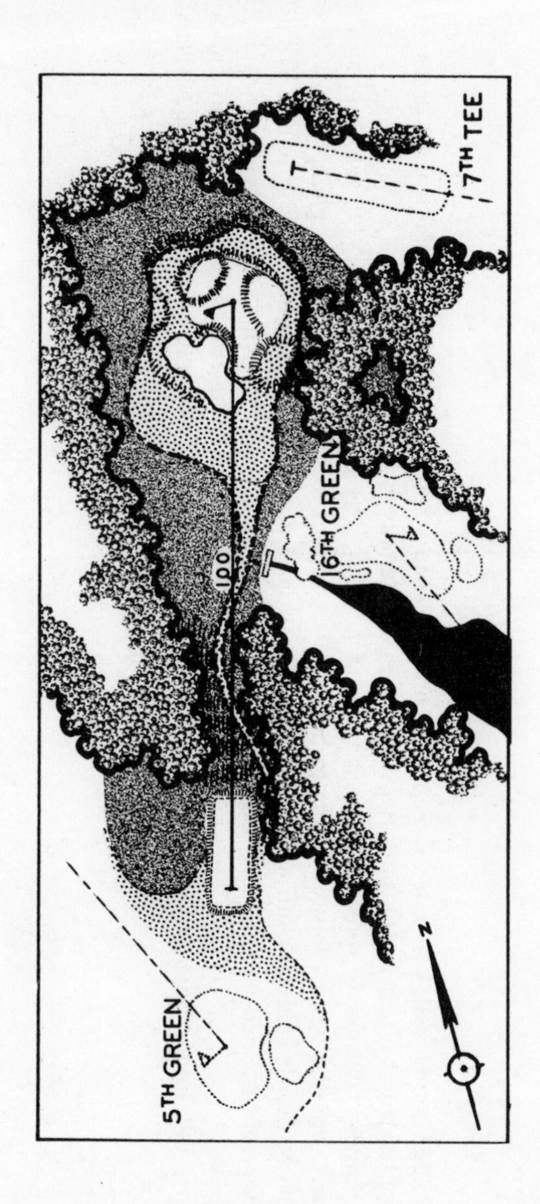
7TH TEE
16TH GREEN
100
5TH GREEN
N

Hole No. 7, 365 yards, par 4 The tee shot on this hole becomes tighter year by year as the pine trees on either side of the fairway continue to spread. Length is not at a premium here, but the narrow fairway seems to have an added impact because it suddenly confronts the player when he has become accustomed to the broad expanses of the preceding holes.

Actually, the second shot *is* somewhat easier if it can be struck firmly so that the needed backspin may be obtained.

The green is quite wide, but also very shallow. The second shot is normally a steep pitch, often with a wedge, and precise judgment of range is required. We are aware of our responsibility for keeping this fairway in the best possible condition so that the players will uniformly encounter good lies from which they may be expected to produce controlled shots.

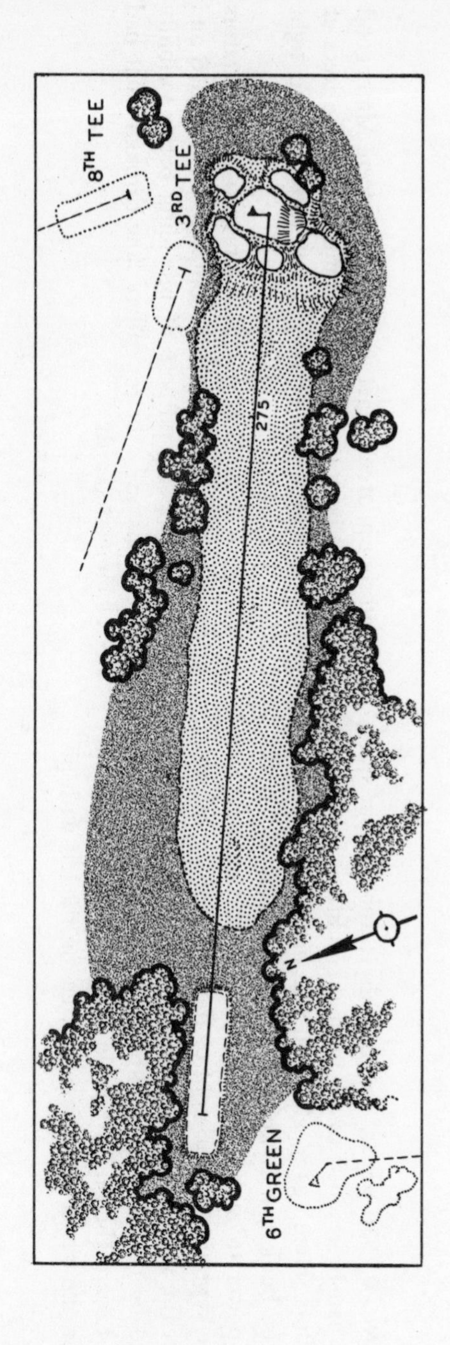
8TH TEE
3RD TEE
275
N
6TH GREEN

Hole No. 8, 530 yards, par 5 This is another par five which can be reached under normal conditions with two fine shots. Here again, although the line is not directly over the bunker, it is well to hit the tee shot with sufficient power to make the carry. It is important that the ball be kept a bit to the right of the center of the fairway so that the second shot may be played through the saddle formed by the mounds at the top of the hill and so directly toward the green. Should he play left to avoid the bunker, the player must skirt the trees on the left with his second shot in order to get very near the green. Many good rounds have been spoiled by encounters with the trees at this point and a second played out safely to the right leaves a very difficult approach.

It is an indication of our interest in our spectators in Augusta that this green was completely redesigned and rebuilt for the sole purpose of providing better visibility for spectators and a better gallery flow through what had been a congested area.

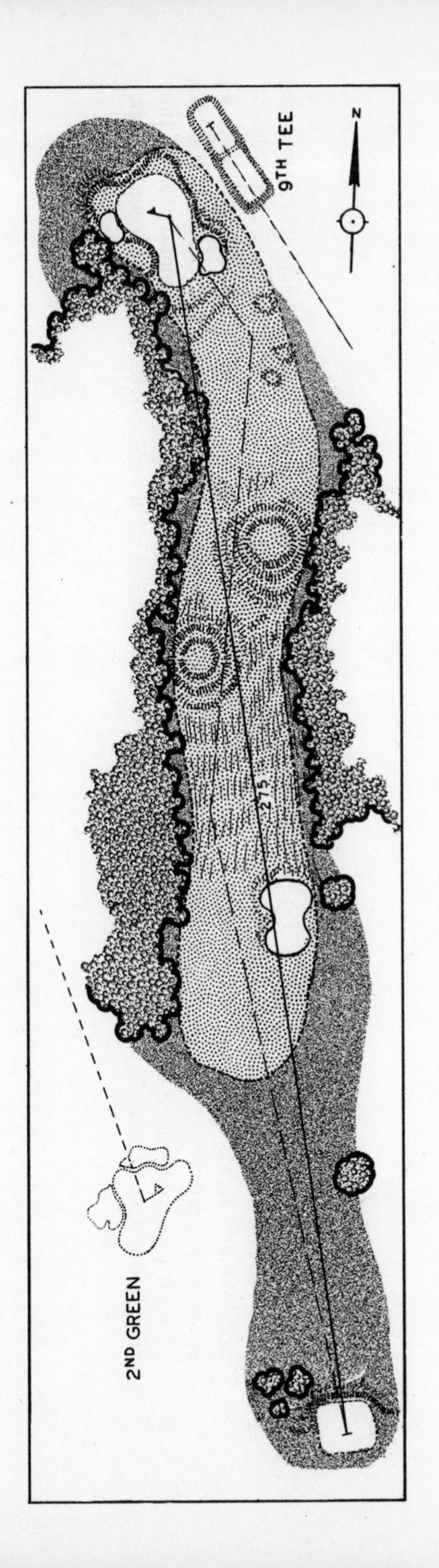
9TH TEE
N
275
2ND GREEN

Hole No. 9, 420 yards, par 4 This is a slight dogleg to the left which invites the player to skirt the trees on the left side. Actually, this is a delusion, because it is only with a strong wind against that this line has any advantage. The player is thus called upon to make use of local knowledge and good judgment and to resist the temptation to play close to the corner simply because the dogleg is presented.

Under normal conditions, a long drive straight down the middle will give the best result since it will reach a reasonably flat area and provide an open shot for at least half the green. The hole opens up more and more as the drive is played to the right, but the distance becomes longer.

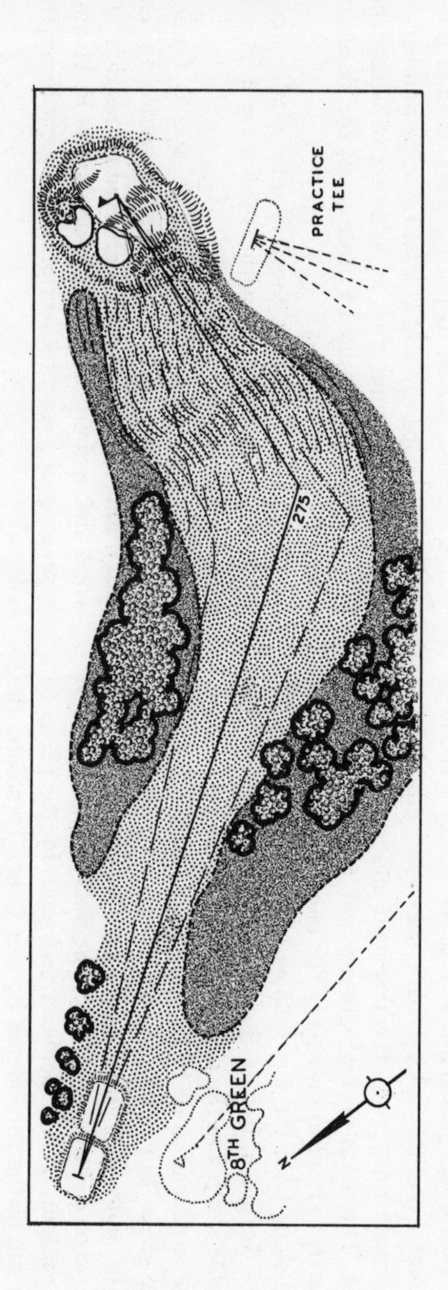
PRACTICE TEE
275
8TH GREEN

Hole No. 10, 470 yards, par 4 This, to my mind, is one of the most beautiful holes I have ever seen, especially at tournament time when the dogwood and redbud are in bloom. The tee is on high ground and, I might add, immediately in front of my cabin. The fairway goes down in a broad slope from the tee, following on the left a straight line to the green; but on the right, fanning out to a considerable width. On the right side, the fairway continues in the same general slope to the bottom of the hill just short of the green. But on the left at about 230 yards from the tee, the slope runs off abruptly into a valley of fairway some 30 or 40 yards wide. Since the hole is of good length for a par four, it is decidedly advantageous for the player to make use of the run offered by this slope. Therefore, the line of play is down the left side as closely as one may dare.

A tee shot played to the right which does not avail itself of the slope will add at least two club numbers to the length of the second shot, in addition to which the approach to the green must be made across the slopes, rather than directly into them.

A good drive down the left side usually makes it possible to play the second with a medium iron, sometimes even less if the wind be behind.

The green nestles on a hillside and is framed by some giant pines which give the impression of Gothic spires, and the wooded areas all around are rich in dogwood and redbud. When the dogwood is in bloom, the impression of a recent snowstorm adds great beauty to the hole.

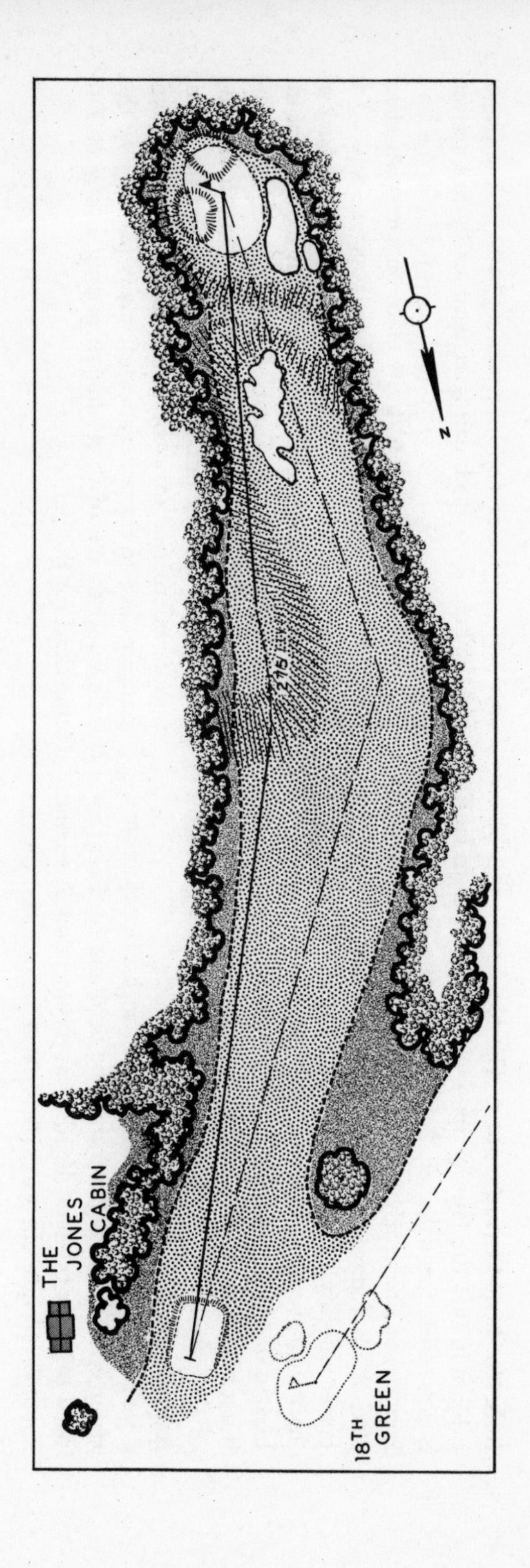
THE
JONES
CABIN
N
18TH
GREEN

Hole No. 11, 445 yards, par 4 The tee shot to this hole is blind in that the fairway upon which the ball is to land is not visible from the tee. Nevertheless, the limits of the fairway are sufficiently well-defined by the trees on either side. A drive down the left side of the fairway provides better visibility of the forward portions of the green, but slightly to the right of center is better should the pin be located on the promontory of the green extending into the water hazard on the left. The pin location on this projection of the green is often reserved for the final round of the tournament.

The second shot is usually played with a three iron or a stronger club, and a player must be bold and confident indeed to go for the pin when it is in this location. A second shot played into the water here must be dropped on the near bank, with water still intervening between the player and the hole. Too much daring here can easily cost a seven or an eight.

With the pin located at any place on the green other than the left-hand projection, the hole appears simple. Yet it has a puzzling difficulty. Should the pin be at the back of the green, the player tends to let up on his second shot for fear of the severe penalty involved in overplaying. Often he leaves himself an approach putt of more length than he would like. With the pin on the forward area of the green, a shot underplayed may bound to the left and come dangerously close to the water. A great many players play this hole safely to the right, relying on getting a long putt or chip dead for the par.

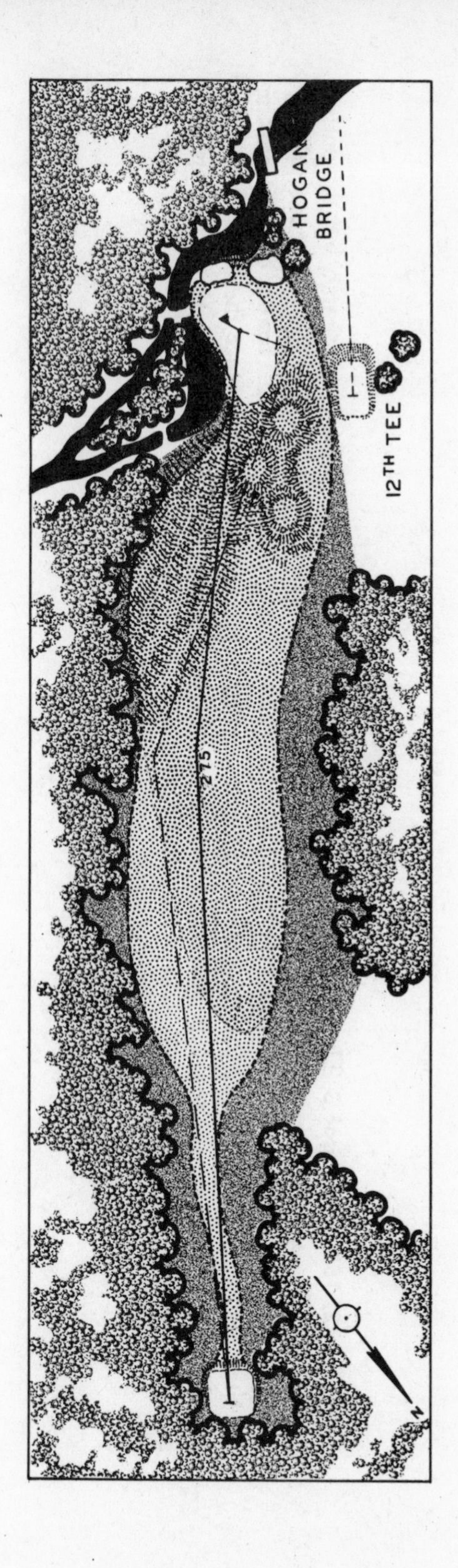
HOGAN BRIDGE
12TH TEE
215
N

Hole No. 12, 155 yards, par 3 The championship location for the pin here is in the shallow area of the green on the right. Here the distance must be gauged very accurately and the wind sweeping down Rae's Creek is often deceptive to the player standing on the tee. The inclination here is to be well up, or to favor the left side where the green is wider. To play safely to the left is simple, but the putting problem which results is not easy. Pin locations on the left side of the green can be made, testing only by pushing them far forward or far back. Once the tee shot has been played into the creek, the short pitch to the shallow green is terrifying indeed.

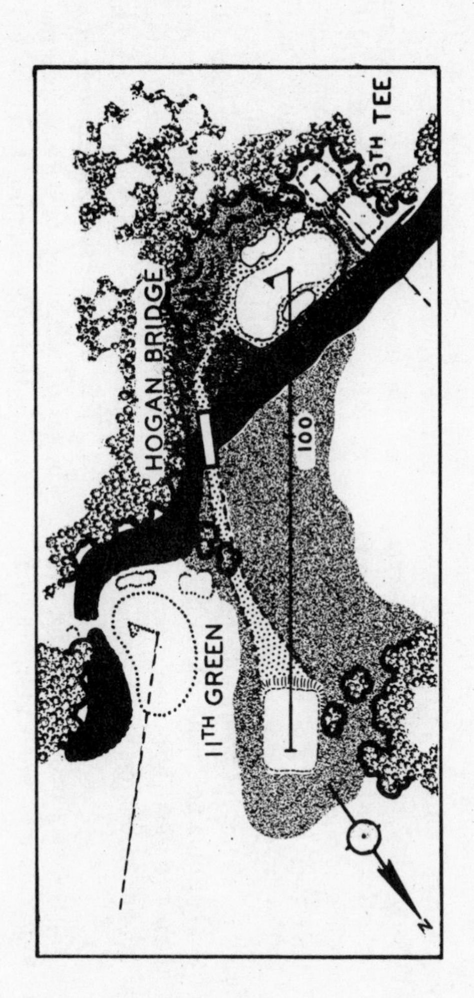
HOGAN BRIDGE
11TH GREEN
13TH TEE
100
N

Hole No. 13, 475 yards, par 5 Number ten at 470 yards is a par four because of the favorable slope of the ground offered to the tee shot. We call thirteen a par five because under certain conditions of wind and ground, few players will risk trying for the green with a second shot. In my opinion this thirteenth hole is one of the finest holes for competitive play I have ever seen. The player is first tempted to dare the creek on his tee shot by playing in close to the corner, because if he attains his position he has not only shortened the hole, but obtained a more level lie for his second shot. Driving out to the right not only increases the length of the second, but encounters an annoying side-hill lie.

Whatever position may be reached with the tee shot, the second shot as well entails a momentous decision whether or not to try for the green. With the pin far back on the right, under normal weather conditions, this is a very good eagle hole, because the contours of the green tend to run the second shot close. The chief danger is that the ball will follow the creek.

The most difficult pin locations are along the creek in the forward part of the green. A player who dares the creek on either his first or second shot may very easily encounter a six or seven at this hole. Yet the reward of successful, bold play is most enticing.

Several tournaments have been obviously won and lost on holes twelve and thirteen. Others, upon careful analysis, will be seen to have been won or lost here, even though the decision may not have been obvious at the time.

This hole is a splendid example of what can be done by taking advantage of natural features. The splashes of sand in the woods behind the green and the azalea along the left side were placed there in order to add beauty to the natural setting.

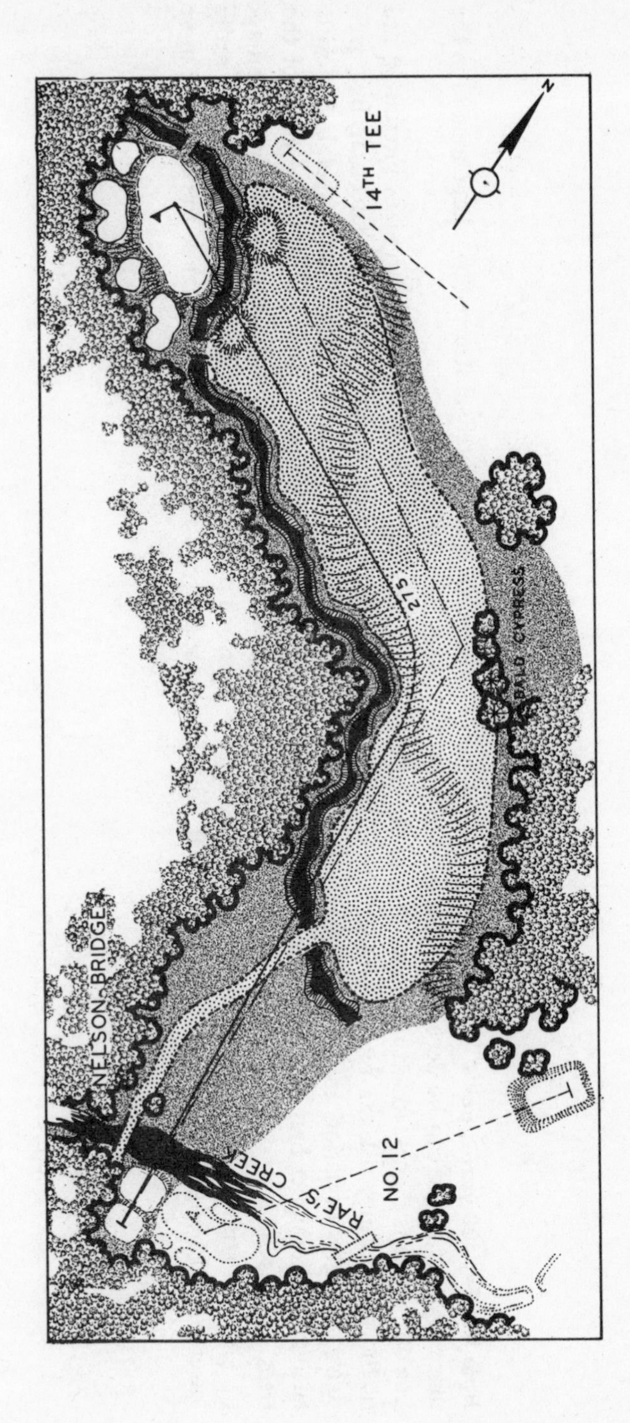
14TH TEE
275
NELSON BRIDGE
RAE'S CREEK
NO. 12

Hole No. 14, 420 yards, par 4 This is another hole whose innocent appearance can be deceiving. The most popular line off the tee is slightly to left of center, to gain the crest of the hill and not risk the run-off of the fairway to the right. A slight deviation to the left of this line often encounters the upper branches of the small group of pine trees on this side.

A drive straying off to the right leaves the player on lower ground from which his ability to see the left side of the green is completely obstructed by a large mound in the middle of the fairway.

The green is quite large and with many interesting and difficult contours. A mound in back protects against over-running the left side of the green, but no such buffer exists on the right. The putting surface along the front of the green spills over the contours into the fairway. But an approach putt from this area is exceedingly difficult. A really good second shot leaving the ball close to the hole is most comforting.

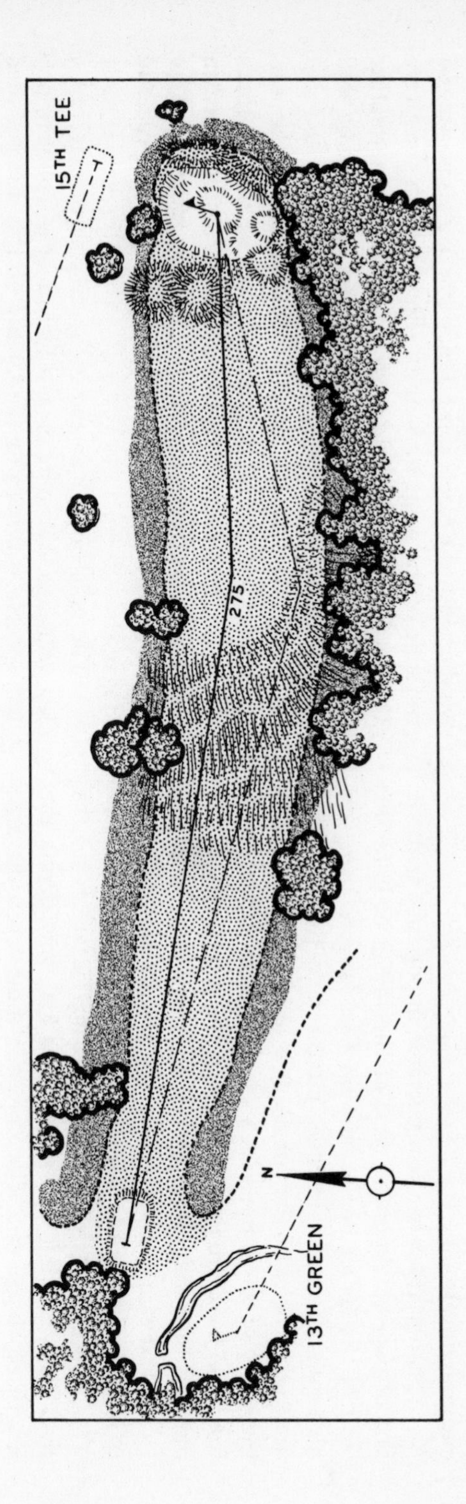
15TH TEE
275
N
13TH GREEN

Hole No. 15, 520 yards, par 5 The fairway of this hole is quite wide. The short rough on the left is far removed from the line of play and there is no demarcation on the right between the fairway of the fifteenth and that of the seventeenth. The tee shot may be hit almost anywhere without encountering trouble.

It is nevertheless of considerable importance that the line of play be along the crest of the hill, a little to the right of the center of the fairway. This fairway, being on high ground, usually provides more run to the ball than most other holes of the course. It is also more exposed to the effect of any wind which may be present. Two tees, front and back, are provided so that the length may be adjusted within wide limits according to playing conditions.

The design of the green causes it to be most receptive to a second shot played from the right-center of the fairway. The greater depth of the putting surface is on the right side. The left side is quite shallow, considering the length of the second shot, and the most severe hazards lie on this side. A ball played over the green on this side may very well run down into the pond at the sixteenth hole. More often than not, it is the better part of wisdom to play the second for the main body of the green, even though the hole may be cut on the left side.

When Gene Sarazen holed his second shot with a three wood for his famous double eagle, the hole was cut near the back of the green. Gene's ball landed on the tongue of the green in front and rolled directly into the cup.

Under almost any conceivable conditions the second shot to this hole suggests precarious possibilities. With the wind against, the player must decide whether his power and the state of the game warrant an effort to reach the green. With a following wind he may have to consider whether he will be able to hold the green, even though it be well within reach.

Billy Joe Patton's magnificent bid to be the first amateur to win the Masters ended when he tried to reach this green from the rough on the left. The ball finished in the pond. The resulting six was one too many. Had he played safely for a five, he would have tied with Snead and Hogan.

The only bunker on the hole was placed there just a few years ago, not so much as a feature of play, but to protect spectators occupying the mound on this side provided as one of our special vantage points. Without the bunker, players uncertain of their ability to reach the green were using this area as a sort of haven for the second shot. Now they either play directly for the green or, quite frankly and safely, short of the pond.

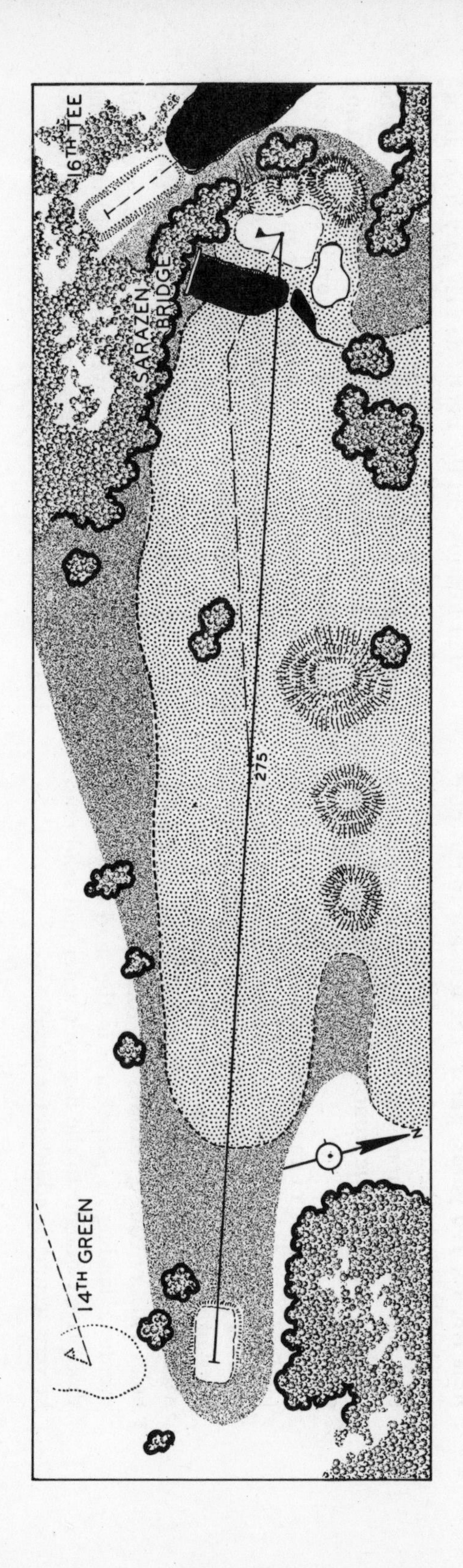
16TH TEE
SARAZEN BRIDGE
275
N
14TH GREEN

Hole No. 16, 190 yards, par 3 The tee shot to this hole will be played by the tournament players with a number two, three, or four iron, depending upon the wind. The pond extends from the front of the tee very nearly to the edge of the green.

The contours of the green are such that several pin locations can be found along the left side close to the bunkers and the pond. This is also the low side, so that a tee shot played for the middle of the putting surface, but with a slight draw, can be made to curl down toward the hole. This, of course, involves risk that the draw may be overdone, landing its perpetrator in the sand or water. A shot played straight to the flag over water and sand must be very accurately adjusted for length.

Pin locations on the right side may vary from an acceptable one in the V-shaped front of the green through a crown about halfway back, from which the ball may be expected to fall off to the left, back to a gently gathering area at the rear. This latter area will provide a good opportunity for a birdie to a player who has hit an accurate tee shot. With the pin on this side, the threats come from the bunkers on the right and the run-off of the green toward the left.

Apart from the visible hazards on this hole, the player who leaves his ball on the forward area of the green with the pin near the back can have quite a problem getting down in two putts. Three putts on this green sealed Hogan's defeat by Snead in the 1954 play-off.

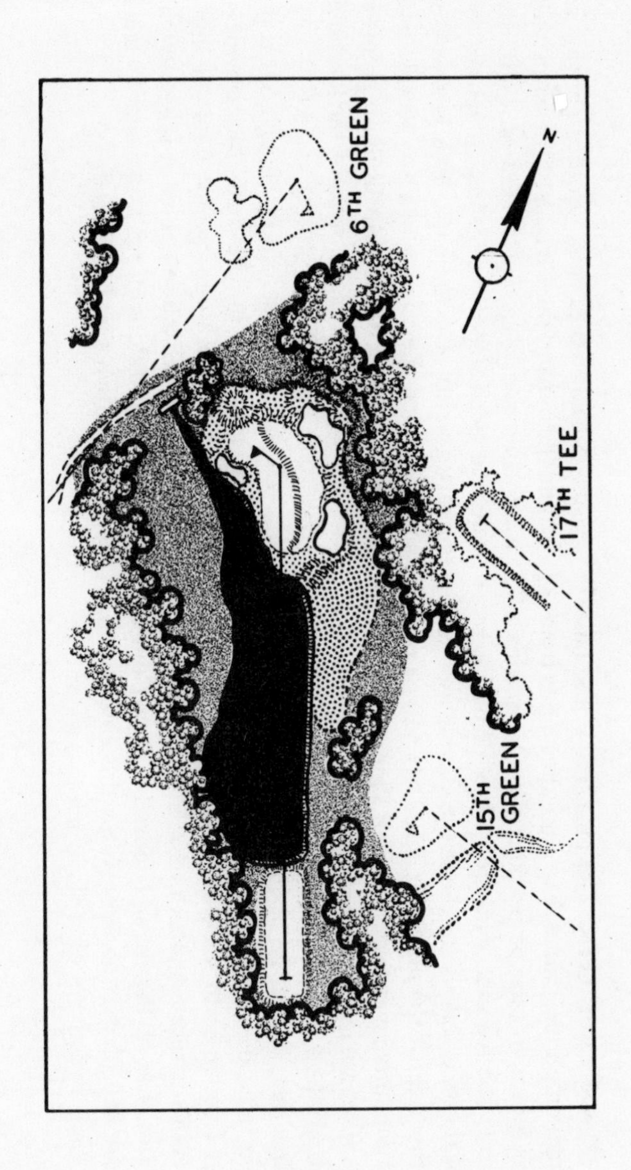
6TH GREEN
17TH TEE
15TH GREEN
N

Hole No. 17, 400 yards, par 4 The pine tree in the fairway, although only a little more than a hundred yards from the tee, has grown to such proportions that it provides a real menace to the tee shot. The proper line of play is to the right of this tree, but also to the left of the big mounds and two other trees at the top of the hill. Depending upon the wind, a fine drive may leave a second shot of anything from a good five iron or easy number four to a short pitch. To become involved with the mounds on the right may impose difficulties of either lie or visibility, or both.

On the left side the green slopes gently, but quite perceptibly, from front to back. With a following wind, therefore, even the shortest pitch over the bunker and the slopes off the base of the mound must be played quite accurately. A ball played too strongly to this side of the green may take a good run off a slope at the back and so leave a difficult return chip. On the right side immediately behind the bunker, there is a nice little basin which provides a most inviting place for the pin on quiet days. On this side, the green slopes very definitely upward toward a sort of plateau area near the back. This is a very difficult pin location when the wind is against, because a shot played boldly to get near the hole is likely to go over the green, down a considerable slope, whereas the less bold shot must leave some very difficult putting to do.

The hole looks innocuous enough, yet it provided the decisive moments in the 1956 tournament when Jack Burke, in a stretch run against Ken Venturi and Cary Middlecoff, scored a birdie three at the hole, while Venturi took five and Middlecoff six. Burke won by one stroke over Venturi and two over Middlecoff.

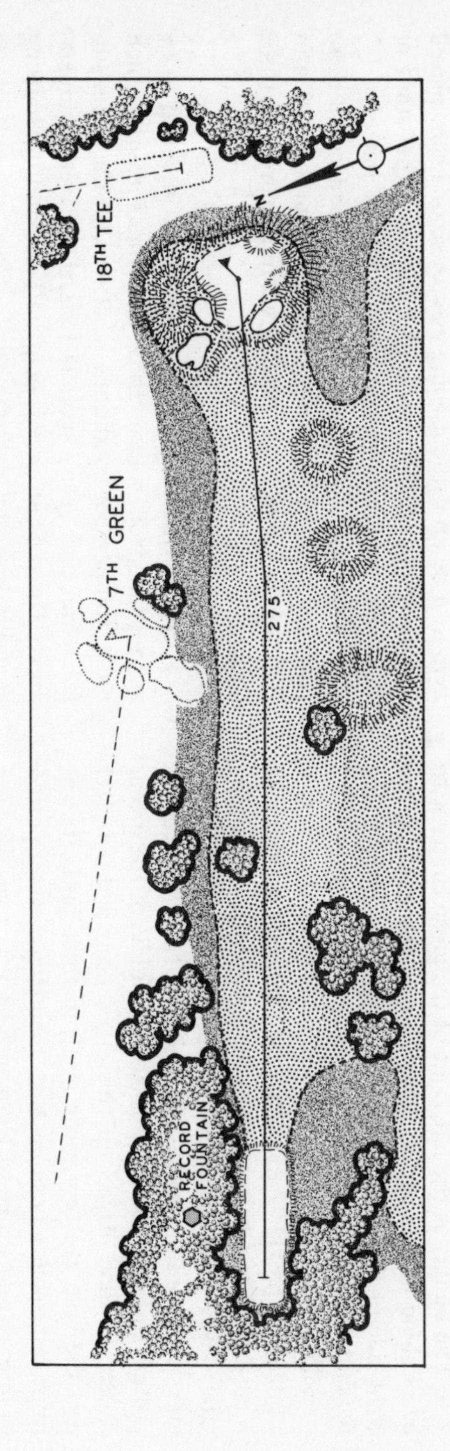
18TH TEE
7TH GREEN
275
RECORD FOUNTAIN
N

Hole No. 18, 420 yards, par 4 This hole is a slight dogleg to the right, the bend in the fairway coming at the top of a hill which can just about be carried by a fine tee shot.

The bunker at the left front of the green causes it to be of some importance to drive close to the trees up the right side of the fairway, or even, if possible, to bend the tee shot a bit around the corner.

The front area of this green is nicely molded to receive a pitch and provide a good putt for a birdie when the hole is cut here. Yet a ball driven to the left side of the fairway safely away from the trees must be pitched quite closely over the guarding bunker. Behind this friendly area the putting surface slopes upward to the middle of the green. A second shot played up this slope even a dozen feet past the hole can very easily result in three putts. It was from just such a position that Ben Hogan three-putted to lose by one stroke to Herman Keiser in 1946. In 1958 both Doug Ford and Fred Hawkins tried and missed similar putts to tie Arnold Palmer.

This eighteenth green is quite long. The rear one-quarter of the putting surface embraces a plateau area which is often used as a pin location. The great difficulty here is to be up without going over. A second shot played into the slope in the middle of the green either stops or rolls back, so that the ensuing putt is difficult indeed.

In the 1957 tournament Doug Ford avoided all these putting difficulties by holing a full blast from the bunker in front of the green to give him a winning margin of three strokes.

Overall, the Augusta National is not intended to be a punishing golf course. It is, however, a course which under tournament conditions (that is, with the green surfaces firm and keen) severely tests the player's temperament. The difficult greens demand fierce and unremitting concentration and determination. When the golf course is wet and the wind quiet, it is easy. We always hope it will not be that way during the first week in April.

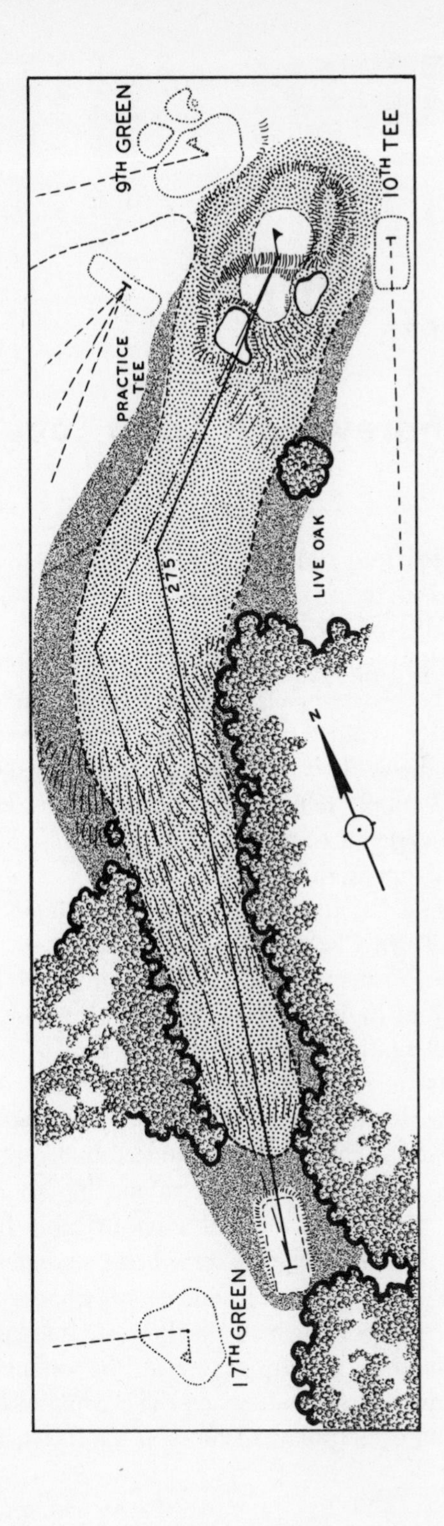
9TH GREEN
PRACTICE TEE
10TH TEE
275
LIVE OAK
N
17TH GREEN

CHAPTER 22

St. Andrews—A Short Love Story

O I have often read and heard it said that a man's life may pass through his mind in the space of a few seconds. I am now prepared to believe that this is entirely possible.

When I first learned that the World Amateur Golf Team Championship was to be played in October 1958 at St. Andrews, Scotland, I determined that I would take advantage of this very good excuse to go back to St. Andrews. This, even before I was named Captain of the American team. I simply felt that this might be my last opportunity to revisit the city and golf course that I love so well, and that I should by no means let this opportunity pass.

Shortly before I was to leave, namely on September 9, I received a cable from the Town Clerk of St. Andrews asking if I would be willing to accept the Freedom of the City while there. I had no earthly idea what was meant by Freedom of the City. I assumed it was something like the presentation in this country of the key to a city, which is largely an excuse to have the visitor's, and incidentally the Mayor's, picture printed in the afternoon newspaper. But whatever the nature of the ceremony was to be, I was happy indeed to accept any gesture of hospitality which might be extended to me by St. Andrews.

Immediately, however, I received a return cable from the Town Clerk telling me that arrangements were being undertaken and that I would be advised of the program in due course. Shortly after this, I received a copy of the speech which the Provost, the equivalent of the Mayor, of St. Andrews was to deliver at the ceremony.

Our party arrived in St. Andrews on the evening of Friday, October 3. On the morning of Saturday, October 4, the Town Clerk called to make an appointment for me to meet with himself and the Provost to discuss plans for the presentation. This we did that afternoon. And in a discussion of some hour and a half, I began to get an inkling of what was meant by Freedom of the City. It seemed that the only American to have been accorded such an honor by the city of St. Andrews had been Dr. Benjamin Franklin, and that the list of the six or eight persons who had been similarly honored contained the names of some great figures in literary and political circles. It was by no means a thing to be taken lightly, a fact that was further emphasized by the very earnest request of the Town Clerk that I give him my speech in writing in advance. I must confess that at this point the matter was assuming alarming proportions.

I have never had any reason to take pride in my ability as a speaker. I remember being appalled upon learning from newsreels that in 1930 I made almost exactly the same acceptance speech four times, if allowance is made for the different names attached to persons, places, and trophies. I don't like to make speeches because, I suppose, I know that I don't do very well at it. I did determine, though, that I would not disappoint these people if I could possibly avoid doing so. And therefore I did try several times to write out something which I thought might do as a response to the Provost.

Between this meeting on Saturday and the Freedom Ceremony, which was scheduled to take place on Thursday evening, October 9, the Provost, the Town Clerk, and I had two other meetings, and on Thursday afternoon we met at the Younger Graduation Hall for a rehearsal. Again the Town Clerk asked me for my speech, and I had to apologize, saying that I had tried to write something, but that I had not been able to produce anything that I felt would be suitable, my experience having always been that nothing appropriate can be written without the help of having the feel of the actual situation. I tried to speak as though I had no doubt that the proper words would come to my mind, but this only to reassure the Clerk. In my heart I felt the gnawing fear that I might get up before the audience and draw a complete blank. Although I was not satisfied at all with what I had written, I determined that I would stuff some notes into my pocket, just in case of dire emergency.

The hall in which the ceremony was to take place was a very beautiful auditorium, seating some 1700 people, with a very adequate elevated stage. The seats were on two levels, with a sizable balcony. The Provost, handsomely gowned in his crimson robe with wide ermine collar and adorned with the magnificent chain of his office, was to enter first, followed by me, then the principal dignitaries of the town, the Co-Presidents of the World Golf Association, and my family, represented by my wife, Mary, my son, Bob, III, and my younger daughter, Mary Ellen. Our older daughter, Clara, had had to remain at home to care for her two children.

Tickets had been provided for members of the World Cup teams and delegates from the various countries. The remainder of the tickets, I was told, had been exhausted to townspeople in less than two hours. And the Provost told me that the crowd could have easily been two or three times as large, had space been available. When we left the hall after the ceremony, there were many hundreds of people waiting outside in the streets.

The ceremony began with great dignity, by the Provost requesting the Reverend Rankin to pronounce a prayer. This was followed by the reading of the citation by the Town Clerk, who had donned the white wig of his office. And then the Provost spoke. I shall set down his speech in full, because it was not only most affecting to me, but I considered it to be an example of rare good taste at the same time. Here it is:

> Ladies and gentlemen, we are met here today to confer the Freedom of the City and the Royal Borough of St. Andrews on Mr. Robert Tyre Jones, Jr., of Atlanta, Georgia.
>
> Among its many other claims to renown, St. Andrews has for long been recognized as the metropolis of the golfing world—and the presence of golfers from all parts of the globe at this time to take part in a great new international competition for the Eisenhower Trophy is further confirmation of this fact. Mr. Jones is recognized as the most distinguished golfer of this age—one might well say of all time. Thus it is appropriate that just such a place and just such a personality should be linked together at just such a time as this.
>
> But the conferring of the freedom of a city, although it may have a certain formal symbolism of this kind, can never be a merely formal matter—and it can rarely have been less so than on this occasion. As representatives of the community of St. Andrews, we wish to honor Mr. Jones because we feel drawn to him by ties of affection and personal regard of a particularly cordial nature, and because we know that he him-

self has declared his own enduring affection for this place and for its people.

Like many cordial and enduring partnerships, it was not, I think, a case of love at first sight. Probably few St. Andreans paid much attention to the visit of a relatively unknown young American golfer for the British Open Championship of 1921, and I believe that for his part, the first impression that Mr. Jones formed of the Old Course was something less than favorable, and there—with any other person and any other place—the matter might well have rested. But back he came in 1927 to master the intricacies of golf at St. Andrews as they had never been mastered before, even by our own giants of the Nineteenth Century, and to win his way, not only to the Open Championship, but to the hearts of St. Andrews' people from that day to this.

Even now, more than thirty years later, it is possible to recapture the thrill of that occasion in Mr. Bernard Darwin's incomparable prose.

As he says—and remember that he is writing of the days before crowd control, when great multitudes surged over the Old Course in pursuit of their favorites—"Many vivid pictures remain in my mind's eye from this day, but there is one in particular. Bobby lay just short of the home green in the hollow called The Valley of Sin. He ran his long putt up dead, and the crowd stormed up the slope and waited breathless for a moment at the crest. He popped his ball in, and the next instant there was to be seen no green and no Bobby—nothing but a black and seething mass from which there ultimately emerged the victor bourne on enthusiastic shoulders and holding his famous putter, Calamity Jane, over his head in a frantic effort to preserve it."

Three years later, in 1930, when he won both the Open and the Amateur Championships of Britain and America alike—a feat never accomplished before or since—it was here that Mr. Jones attained what he himself probably regarded as the most perilous and desirable among these four contests for an American—the British Amateur Championship—a win that was acclaimed in St. Andrews almost as the triumph of a favorite son.

Nothing could ever surpass the achievement of that memorable year—the climax of seven years scarcely less memorable, in every one of which he had won a major award. Let me detail them: the American Open in 1923 and the Amateur in 1924 and 1925; the American and the British Opens in 1926; the American Amateur and the British Open in 1927; the American Amateur again in 1928; and the Open again in 1929; finally all four in 1930. And so at the height of his attainments and still at the height of his powers, Mr. Jones retired from major competitive events—to reign forever after in our hearts, as Mr. Darwin suggests, as the champion of champions to the end of his days.

And so we feel that when we welcome back Mr. Jones to St. Andrews, we welcome an old and dearly loved friend—as we welcomed him on his last visit in 1936 when he played around the Old Course attended, one might well imagine, by practically the entire population of the town.

We welcome him for his own sake; we welcome him also as an ambassador in the cause of international understanding and good will which the competition of this week is designed to promote. We welcome him moreover not only as a distinguished golfer but as a man of outstanding character, courage, and accomplishment well worthy to adorn the Roll of our Honorary Burgesses. And that an American should once again be entered in that roll may well be thought timely, for it is just one year short of two hundred years ago, in October 1759, that our predecessors welcomed Dr. Benjamin Franklin of Philadelphia and accorded him the privileges of a Burgess and Guild Brother of the city of St. Andrews.

What these privileges now are in any tangible sense, even the Town Clerk hesitates to suggest—though Mr. Jones may be interested to know that any that are ever mentioned relate specifically to the links—to cart shells, to take divots, and to dry one's washing upon the first and last fairways of the Old Course.

These are homely terms—and perhaps in an American as well as British sense—but they may help us to convey to our new Honorary Burgess just what we mean by this Freedom Ceremony—that he is free to feel at home in St. Andrews as truly as in his own first home of Atlanta. One of our own number, officially now, as he has been so long unofficially.

The "Freedom" ceremony in Younger Graduation Hall, St. Andrews. My wife Mary is the lady farthest to the right. My daughter Mary Ellen is immediately behind me. Bob III is fourth from the left. The motto on the arms of the town is "Dum Spiro Spero" which might do very well for a golfer. It means "While I breathe, I hope."

The Provost and I had been seated each in a high-backed armchair in front of a table on either side of the lectern where the microphones were located. At this point he placed the scroll read by the Town Clerk in a beautiful silver casket adorned with the seal of the city of St. Andrews, which he presented to me. I rose to receive the casket, placed it on the table in front of me, and at the Provost's request, resumed my seat to sign the Burgess' Roll. It was then that the Provost applied the touch that did so much to reassure me.

Since we had become fast friends by that time, he stepped back with a broad smile and a delightful twinkle in his eye, and said, "Now, Bob, the ordeal is yours."

Within the few seconds it took me to make my way to the lectern along the table so thoughtfully provided, I found out how a man's life, or a great part of it, can flash through his mind in an instant. I knew in that instant that I had no need for the notes in my pocket. I knew that I would have no difficulty finding things to say to the people of St. Andrews. I was happy that the members of the international teams and the delegates were there; but after all, they were to me merely sympathetic witnesses. This reunion was mine with the people of St. Andrews, and it was to them that I intended to speak.

I began by thanking the Provost for the kindly manner in which he had treated my early mistakes, and then I asked my audience to remember that at the time of my first appearance on the Old Course, I had reached the ripe, mature age of nineteen years. One thing I had learned about the Old Course was that she was not likely to be kind to young, inexperienced golfers.

I told them of how I had started in that Open Championship of 1921 with two fair rounds, a total of something like 151. When someone among the players tittered, I hastened to state that that was for two rounds, not one. Since very few of the players in the tournament had been able to break eighty in either one of the first two rounds, it was not difficult for them to agree that this was not too bad.

But then, I told them, the wind was really blowing on the morning of the third round. I had battled it as best I could to the turn in forty-six, had started home with a six at ten, and had put my tee shot into the Hill Bunker at the eleventh. Here, I wanted to correct a bit of their history recited in a guidebook I had read. I had not played two shots in the bunker and then knocked my ball over the green into the Eden River. My ball had come out of the bunker only in my pocket, and it was my score card that found its way into the river.

I spoke of how the Old Course had come to have a real personality for me. Even in the beginning, I think I was never angry at the course, only puzzled and a bit bewildered. I think it was not long before I began to see her as a wise old lady, whimsically tolerant of my impatience, but all the while ready to reveal to me the secrets of her complex being, if I would only take the trouble to study and to learn. I did not try to develop this area of my thought, because it seemed too fanciful. But I did say that I thought the Old Lady had been satisfied with the early chastisement she had given me, and pointed out that she never again permitted me to lose a match or a contest. The more I studied the Old Course, the more I loved it, and the more I loved it, the more I studied it—so that I came to feel that it was for me the most favorable meeting ground possible for an important contest. I felt that my knowledge of the course enabled me to play it with patience and restraint until she might exact her inevitable toll from my adversary, who might treat her with less respect and understanding.

"But," I said, "my thoughts are not of championships and trophies as I stand here tonight. You people possess a sensitivity which causes you to be able to extend cordiality and express friendliness in the most ingenious way."

I was thinking, of course, of the scene at the final green when I won the Open Championship in 1927, the scene mentioned by the Provost. I was thinking of the murmur of warmth and approval that went through the crowd when I asked if I might leave the Open Championship trophy for the year of my possession with the Royal and Ancient Golf Club, of which I had the honor to be a member. I remembered, too, how after I had won the Amateur Championship of 1930, these people had made a lane through which I might pass from the side door of the Royal and Ancient Club to my hotel across the street, and how they called to me with "Good boy, Bobby," "Come again," "Well done," etc.

I was not quite equal to talking of those things, but I did speak of my next visit, when I went there in 1936 to play what I had expected to be a very casual round. My wife and I had set out with Kate and Grantland Rice to attend the Olympic Games in Berlin. On the boat going over we had met Nell and Bob Woodruff with some friends of theirs who were bound for the same destination. It developed that the Woodruff party had planned to go up to Gleneagles in Scotland for a few days of golf, and they persuaded us to go along with them.

On our last evening at Gleneagles, some little while after dinner we were talking about means of returning to Southampton to take the boat for Germany. During the conversation I had said that I could not bring myself to get this close to St. Andrews without going over for a game. After some conversation it was decided that we should go over to St. Andrews the next day and return to London from there. My intention was that we should drive over for lunch and play a round in the afternoon.

The trip over and the luncheon were as expected. I had busied myself around the hotel while one of our party went over to make arrangements for starting times and caddies. I suspected nothing until I arrived at the first tee to find at least two thousand people there waiting for me.

I had not been playing very much golf and had not really expected to play any on this trip. I had brought my golf clubs along because of an ingrained habit. What golf I had played had been very bad, and I was certainly not pleased with the prospect of exhibiting my game in its present state, especially to the people of St. Andrews.

I have seriously and sincerely wondered to this day if there might have been some magic inspiration derived from finding myself back on the Old Course and in that wonderful golfing atmosphere I loved so well. Whatever the cause, and very much to my astonishment, I played as well that afternoon as I ever played in my life, at least for ten holes.

Instead of the informal game I had expected, it had again been decided without my knowledge that because of the crowd, I should play with two professionals, Willie Auchterlonie, the club professional, and Gordon Lockhart from Gleneagles. We started out in this fashion, but as the crowd continued to grow, Gordon withdrew after a couple of holes and Willie and I continued together.

I shall never forget that round. It was not anything like a serious golf match, but it was a wonderful experience. There was a sort of holiday mood in the crowd. It seemed, or they made it appear at least, that they were just glad to see me back, and however I chose to play golf was all right with them, only they wanted to see it.

I have ever been thankful that for at least part of what was to be my last golfing at St. Andrews I was permitted to play so well. I holed a good putt for a three at the second hole, was through the green with my second at the long fifth, and chipped back for a four, played a run-up in true St. Andrews fashion through the swale in front of the sixth green, and holed a two-yard putt for another three, holed one of about three yards for a two at eight, and so finished the first nine in thirty-two.

On the eighth tee I was paid the most sincere compliment I can ever remember. It was one of those things one does not talk about. I have never mentioned it before, and did not mention it at the Freedom Ceremony. But since this may be my last utterance on the subject of golf, I must put it down here.

The eighth hole of St. Andrews is a short hole and the pin this day was tucked in behind a small mound to the right of the usual pathway leading to the front of the green. Having the honor, I had played a soft shot with a number four iron, which had faded neatly around the mound and finished some eight or nine feet from the hole. As I stepped back for Willie to play his shot and to slip my club back in my bag, my caddie, a pleasant-looking young man of about twenty years of age, said to me under his breath, "My, but you're a wonder, sir." I could only smile and pat him on the shoulder. I do not know his name nor where he is, but I hope he will now understand what pleasure he gave me.

Four at the tenth was normal, but the eleventh put an end to my dreams. The hole that day was cut where I had never seen it before —on a flat area at the very back of the green and directly behind Strath Bunker. The ground was firm and the wind following and slightly off the right. Never in a tournament would I have played directly for the flag. But this was quite evidently an unusual day, and I must say that at this point I was beginning to think that I could do no wrong. The five-iron shot directly on the flag was a bit too strong, and finished in a small pot bunker in the bank of the Eden directly behind the hole.

The ball was lying cleanly. The bunker was shallow, and it was the kind of shot which held no terrors for me. But I tried to flick it up by the hole, left it still in the bunker, flicked again up four feet from the hole, and missed the putt. That five broke the charm. I three-putted two or three greens from there in, and finally holed a ten-foot putt for a three at the last hole to finish in seventy-two.

I am happy to say that no one seemed to care about the forty coming home, and the thirty-two out was good enough for me. I spent thirty or forty minutes in the vestibule of the R & A Club House signing autographs for the crowd, mostly women and children. It had been one of the great days of my life.

I talked some of this day, not, I am thankful to say, at the length I have here. And you may be sure I did not mention the caddie on the eighth tee. But then I wanted to tell the people of St. Andrews of something else they had done for me in their peculiarly entrancing way.

A short while after the British Amateur Championship of 1930, without any warning or preliminary, I received at my home in Atlanta a package containing a wood box some eighteen inches high and of a cross section six inches on a side. Upon opening it I found the most perfect, gem-like miniature of the British Amateur trophy. It was a perfect reproduction in every respect, down to the last detail of lettering, and displaying the names of all winners of the championship up to date. The one thing not reproduced from the original was the following inscription engraved upon one of the plates on the base, "To Robert Tyre Jones, Jr., a golfer matchless in skill and chivalrous in spirit, from some fellow members of the Royal and Ancient Golf Club." Was there ever a more adroit flattery, and could there be anything more inspiring to try to deserve? I described the cup and told of my immense pride in it—that up to now it had been my most highly prized possession. After a slight pause I had to admit that I could not trust myself to repeat the inscription. "And now," I said, "you have done this for me," indicating the handsome silver casket containing the citation.

Then it occurred to me to speak of my interpretation of the words "friend" and "friendship," which are among the most important in our language, and yet are so often loosely used. Friends are a man's priceless treasures, and a life rich in friendship is full indeed.

"When I say, with due regard for the meaning of the word, that I am your friend, I have pledged to you the ultimate in loyalty and devotion. In some respects friendship may even transcend love, for in true friendship there is no place for jealousy. When, without more, I say that you are my friends, it is possible that I may be imposing upon you a greater burden that you are willing to assume. But when you have made me aware on many occasions that you have a kindly feeling toward me, and when you have honored me by every means at your command, then when I call you my friend, I am at once affirming my high regard and affection for you and declaring my complete faith in you and trust in the sincerity of your expressions. And so, my fellow citizens of St. Andrews, it is with this appreciation of the full sense of the word that I salute you as my friends."

Then thinking of the World Cup competition and its purpose, I went on to say, "It seems to me, too, that it is entirely in keeping with the extreme good taste I have come to expect of this city that you should have chosen to sound this keynote of friendship at this particular moment during this first World Amateur Team Competition for the Eisenhower Trophy. For the fostering of friendship and understanding on an international scale is also the keynote of this event. We shall all be trying our very best to win in the golf competition because our high respect for our fellow competitors and for the game of golf demands that we do so. But all of us have come here with the hope that attachments will be formed here and reports will emanate from here which will provide an impetus toward a growing friendship among nations of the world. I am not so naïve as to expect that a golf tournament may accomplish miracles, but I do hope that we may sow some seeds here which may germinate later on into influences toward peace in the world."

Turning then to the Provost, I said, "Bob, I am afraid I have talked too long, but I think I may best express my emotions if you will permit me to paraphrase your own closing remarks by saying to the people of St. Andrews that I consider they have now officially given me the right to feel as much at home in St. Andrews as I have for so long presumed to do on my own. I am grateful indeed for this honor."

Then we all stood and sang "God Save the Queen." One of my fellow Burgesses, a lovely lady, Mrs. McNaughton, presented a corsage of roses to my wife; my son assisted me down the stairs, and the Provost and I rode out of the hall in my electric buggy, which had been backed down in front of the stage, and in front, too, of the flag of the State of Georgia which my hosts had somehow acquired.

I am not the least bit ashamed to admit that I had been deeply moved by the ceremony—as much by the awareness of the depth and sincerity of my affection for these people as by their expressions to me. It is a wonderful experience to go about a town where people wave at you from doorways and windows, where strangers smile and greet you by name, often your first name, and where a simple and direct courtesy is the outstanding characteristic.

But I did not weep or cry, as I later read in some reports coming to my own country. I had to stop several times in my speaking in order to avoid a show of excessive emotion, and I did have to avoid saying a few things I had not the composure to utter. I prefer to think that Herb Wind was more accurate, even if overly generous, when he wrote in *Sports Illustrated*, "Bobby spoke for ten minutes, beautifully and movingly. . . . He said near the end of his talk, 'I could take out of my life everything except my experiences at St. Andrews and I'd still have a rich, full life.' He left the stage and got into his electric golf cart. As he directed it down the center aisle to leave, the whole hall spontaneously burst into the old Scottish song "Will Ye No' Come Back Again?" So honestly heartfelt was this reunion for Bobby Jones and the people of St. Andrews (and for everyone) that it was ten minutes before many who attended were able to speak again with a tranquil voice."

I had reached precisely this point in my narrative of St. Andrews when Mary, completely unaware of my thoughts, handed me a newspaper cutting of years before that she had just found among some things of her mother's. It was a column by Grantland Rice begun, as was for so long his habit, with a piece of verse:

Past Glories

Dream if you will of the fame that once made you one of
the upper set.

The lacquered chest behind me contains my important (to me) trophies —all medals. The middle cup on top is the miniature of the British Amateur Trophy sent by some friends at St. Andrews.

But only remember they rarely remember as quickly as they forget.

Too many have rushed to the heights you surrendered that only the mob can see.

So please don't expect you can ever collect for the fellow you used to be.

You had your day, and you had your glory, but time sets a dizzy pace.

They fill the gap in a blasting hurry the second you quit the race.

Take it out in dreams if there is nothing better, for the old cheers loud and free;

But please don't expect you can ever collect for the winner that used to be.

Grant was right, of course, if the game and the competition should mean only championships and medals. But golf has been much more than that for me.

Quite honestly, I have no longing for the "old cheers, loud and free." I had my day long ago and I am quite content now to applaud with the other spectators. But the wonderful thing about golf is that it holds forever the interest of all who play it; and so I find myself today a member of a sort of fraternity of those who walked the fairways with me, with numbers considerably augmented by the many who have come since.

It is possible, I know, that I assigned to that return to St. Andrews a greater significance than the people themselves intended. But it just happens to be a part of my devotion to golf that I extend an equal devotion to those who treat the game with love and respect. I think I have never played a tournament round from which I did not come with a feeling of warmth and heightened regard for my opponent or playing companion.

The championships have been very much worth the effort they cost, but more important by far have been the expanding interests they brought and the avenues to friendships with individuals and groups of people they opened for me.

That these rewards should endure so long makes it easy to see why for me golf will always be the greatest game.